Electronically Yours

Electronically Yours

Vol. I: My Autobiography

Martyn Ware

CONSTABLE

CONSTABLE

First published in Great Britain in 2022 by Constable

3 5 7 9 10 8 6 4 2

Copyright © Martyn Ware, 2022

All images from the author's personal collection unless otherwise stated.

A CIP catalogue record for this book
is available from the British Library.

ISBN: 978-0-34913-515-1 (hardback)
ISBN: 978-0-34913-514-4 (trade paperback)

Typeset in Bembo by Hewer Text UK Ltd, Edinburgh
Printed and bound in Great Britain by Clays Ltd, Elcograf, S.p.A.

Papers used by Constable are from well-managed
forests and other responsible sources.

Constable
An imprint of
Little, Brown Book Group
Carmelite House
50 Victoria Embankment
London EC4Y 0DZ

An Hachette UK Company

www.hachette.co.uk

www.littlebrown.co.uk

To my Mum and Dad, Kitty and Jack
for all your love and sacrifices.

To my sisters Maureen and Janet –
thanks for my childhood musical inspiration.

To my brother Steve (1948–2020) –
my hero and my role model. Rest in Peace.

But most of all to Landsley, Elena and Gabriel.

I do it all for you.

Contents

Take a deep breath . . . calm down . . . OK, what on earth am I doing here? A nervous, underqualified, musically self-taught young lad from a very poor, working-class steelworker's family, bluffing my way in the very frightening, very dangerous but exciting music business – no manager, no business experience, but still hoping to make it big one day . . . and this is definitely as big as it gets . . .

Well, be careful what you wish for. My head is exploding. On the one hand, Tina, international superstar with decades of experience on TV shows, live and in the studio. On the other, a rookie producer with very limited TV experience, singing backing vocals live on TV for the first time ever, for anyone.

It's 1983, and we're sitting in the cramped dressing room at the nation's hottest music TV show – *The Tube*. It is twenty minutes before transmission time, and Glenn and I have just polished off two pints of lager each in a futile effort to stifle the mounting panic of appearing live on national television with one of rock's greatest living legends, Tina Turner. The single I produced for her – a cover version of Al Green's 'Let's Stay Together' – is starting to break out, and this TV appearance is to be the booster rocket to send sales into the stratosphere. As we are changing into our Burton suits, with our trousers around our ankles, in walks Tina unannounced with her two backing singers/dancers, Ann Behringer and LeJeune

Richardson. We quickly make ourselves decent, zipping up our flies, as Tina makes an announcement in her mezzo growl . . .

'Hi boys, we've had an idea for the show . . .'

This isn't helping our nerves at all.

'Er . . . OK, Tina, what is it?' I stutteringly reply.

'Ann is blonde, so Ann, you should stand with Glenn. LeJeune, you will stand with Martyn.'

'Sounds good to me,' I reply.

'Then, when the middle eight arrives, we need to spice it up for the cameras,' Tina mysteriously teases . . .

Hmm, I think, *what does she mean?*

'Ann and LeJeune will kneel down at your feet and run their hands up and down your legs and bodies.' Tina seems quite insistent. Pretty standard procedure in the world of Las Vegas showtime, it would appear.

Terrified, I look at Glenn (whose mind I can read) and immediately retort, 'I don't think that's a very good idea, Tina. We might get a little, um, overexcited.' This is the most delicate way I can put our concerns. The potential for mortal embarrassment in full world view is just too big a risk to take. There is an uneasy pause, then . . .

Tina laughs and very kindly withdraws the offer, thank the Lord, but we are both still concerned that Ann and LeJeune might do it anyway just out of a sense of mischief . . .

On stage, they don't – but the fear that some other showgirl moves are going to be put on us just make us even more nervous (which you can clearly witness on YouTube). Also, I am used to having a keyboard as a prop: what the hell do you do with your hands while you're singing? They feel like cartoon appendages, flapping around – do I dance? Does LeJeune want to dance with me? A million thoughts go through my exploding mind. Two Sheffield electro-soul boys in suits awkwardly juxtaposed with

Tina and her dancers dressed in *Flintstones* outfits. Are we cool? Or are they cool and we're too straight? God knows.

As Tina introduces us on stage, she refers to us as her 'producers'. That sounds very flattering and grown-up, but inside my head it's a different story ... I am having an out-of-body experience, floating above the stage, looking at my awkwardness. How did I get here? Am I worthy of such attention? I don't feel like a pop star, I feel like an imposter ... Shut the fuck up, Martyn, and be grateful, for God's sake.

Well, we managed to get through the song without too much embarrassment, even though I missed my first cue and LeJeune, who was part of the original Ikettes, gave me a look that said, *Jesus, who is this jerk?* We relaxed a little into the song as it rapidly became obvious that Tina was the only person on stage that the audience was interested in. She was magnetic and magnificent. As the song thankfully ended and the riotous applause started, we even took a linked-arm bow. Of course, I panicked and gave Tina a peck on the cheek, which seemed to surprise her. (God, what was I thinking?) But then it was over. The relief was immense and the feedback was overwhelmingly positive. The biggest public test of our careers had been a triumph.

What's more we had a major worldwide hit on our hands. The performance had worked its magic. The single shot up the charts around the world, and in the US the record was becoming a hit in the clubs and on the radio. Amazingly, 'Let's Stay Together' soon became the biggest-selling maxi-single in US Billboard chart history. Tina's career had officially been relaunched, and my career as an internationally in-demand producer seemed to be guaranteed. I had no idea where this ship was going, but I was definitely the captain, full of youthful confidence and optimism, except for the occasional wobble. Anything seemed possible (or even probable).

This was 1983, the year of Band Aid, and Heaven 17 and my production identity British Electric Foundation – BEF – were both blossoming. Bob Last (who originally signed my previous band The Human League to Fast Records and then got us a deal with Virgin Records) had been managing Heaven 17 since The Human League split in 1981, but left us to our own devices while continuing to manage the new version of the original band. Ian Craig Marsh had left BEF after the first *Music of Quality and Distinction* album a year ago (still no idea why), so I was running my production career solo, which was a major leap of faith for me.

I had come to this point on pure chutzpah and intuition. I was lucky enough to have a supportive group of friends and, of course, my family around me, but I was now getting into deeper and deeper water and had literally no idea how this would pan out. How far was I prepared to go to capitalise on this astounding turn of events? What if it meant abandoning my secure and familiar life in London, cocooned by love and familiarity? Could I hack it? Up to this point, I had always followed the principle of grabbing every emerging opportunity without hesitation, but I suspected that soon I would be inundated with offers of work, and I would have to choose carefully. I've never been a strategic thinker, just a hard-working 'doer' with an appetite for risk. To this day, I have never made a business or life plan, just relied on gut instinct. Did I need a manager with experience of the big boys' world of the international music business? I'd already heard stories about the nefarious sharks stateside, and the thought of being out of my depth secretly terrified me. In a nutshell, could I deal with all this alone?

Ah, fuck it, let's have a go ... What could possibly go wrong?

Many, many times over the forty years of my professional musical career, I've been asked to consider writing my autobiography. Many, many times I've thought it through and decided I'm not interesting enough. What is it with me? Is it my upbringing in a poor household in post-war Sheffield? Is it my default suspicion that one day someone will discover that I've been blagging it all along? Or perhaps I like the mystery associated with keeping my personal details private and separate to the art project that seems to encapsulate my creative/professional life? Are there too many skeletons in the cupboard? Did I lock and board up the cupboard for a good reason?

In a particularly lucid moment recently, I posted a tweet pretentiously stating that 'we are all gods in our own mythological universes'. I like this, and what's more I believe it's true. We all have our own version of something like the Marvel Cinematic Universe, featuring truths, half-truths and downright fictions about our lives, our friends, lovers, acquaintances and enemies. We all have our own heroes and villains, some real, some imaginary. Sometimes I feel like a minor deity in a workaday universe, overwhelmed by the other characters/gods and their authority, but occasionally I rise up the hierarchy to the top table, and I feel a certain (probably unjustifiable) power of command over my own destiny. This happens rarely, but nowadays a bit more frequently as I finally get close to something approaching maturity. That's why, at last, I've decided I have enough of an idea of who I am (and was) to write this autobiography.

I want this book to feel as intimate and conversational as possible, while avoiding being too self-indulgent or smug. Quite a challenge for a post-war Sheffielder, always in fear of bragging too much in case people say, 'Ooo the fook duz ee think ee iz?' or 'Eeez changed since ee moved down ter that London.'

Well, finally, I can honestly say that I don't give a fuck what anyone thinks any more. I'm proud about what I've achieved in my professional life (and I have few regrets in my personal life), and if

I don't write this autobiography now, I probably never will. At the time of writing, we're all in the middle of a coronavirus lockdown, so I'll almost certainly never have this much undistracted free time ever again and, more to the point, this process is keeping me sane.

I started by organising the timeline of significant events on a spreadsheet with the help of my daughter Elena. After two weeks, this had expanded to a printout filling most of the wall of my study. It became apparent that to try to cram my life into one book was going to mean some severe restriction on the ramblings I had planned, so I've made the decision to write this in two volumes. I liked the similarity with the artistic conceit used on the first British Electric Foundation album, *Music of Quality and Distinction Volume 1* – of course, at the time, I had no idea there would ever be a volume two, but it seemed ironically confident. I feel the same way about this first volume.

And why the title *Electronically Yours*? I designed the artwork for the front cover of our first Human League single 'Being Boiled' and, at the time, I liked the idea of using a strapline or slogan that would 'humanise' the product. I was already bored with the 'electronic music is so cold and emotionless' brigade, so this phrase was part two-fingers up to them, and part an attempt to subtly imply that we could create a 'human' connection using technology, hence the name The Human League.

In this volume, I'll be covering my austere-but-loving upbringing in various council houses in Sheffield, my development through a state grammar school (which was a wannabe public school) and all the teenage fun, torment and embarrassing first steps into adulthood and transgression. At that unique moment in time, Sheffield was a fertile breeding ground for a flavoursome version of creativity and free-spirited investigation but with a bolshy, ironic wink. I was introduced to Meatwhistle, a council-funded arts/performance youth-club project which changed my life. It's where I met Glenn and Ian, my future bandmates, and a combination of white-hot experimentation and love of electronic music would lead to the creation of The Human League, British Electric Foundation (BEF) and Heaven 17 – and beyond . . . This in turn led to an unexpectedly fruitful production career working with some of the world's greatest singers. For those of you less familiar with my musical history, here is a little more detail . . .

After my initial crazy experiments with proto-groups with my best mates – mainly just for one performance each – with names like Musical Vomit, Underpants, Dick Velcro and the Astronettes, The Dead Daughters and VDK and The Studs, the fact that Ian Craig Marsh and myself had somehow managed to get half-decent, relatively well-paid jobs as computer operators meant that we could afford to contemplate buying synthesisers on the never-never. So that's what we did. Suddenly we had the means to create what was in our fevered imaginations, and when we sacked Adi Newton and recruited a new lead singer, my best friend from school Phil Oakey, The Human League was born. Our first record-ing was a strange but interesting song called 'Being Boiled' (reviewed in *New Musical Express* by Johnny Rotten in two words – 'fucking hippies'). This was released on an independent label called Fast Records, which immediately caught the attention of the legendary John Peel, the primary influencer of the cool kid's national musical taste. Big word-of-mouth sales followed, and sure enough, the major labels (and some minors) came knocking – EMI, Virgin, Fiction, Island and a few others, but our sights were set on the hottest, hippest label of the moment – Virgin Records. We were excited and overwhelmed by the idea of such national inter-est, but we were unprepared for the pace of our careers taking off. We were being carried along on the tsunami wave which would later be known as New Wave. I'll reveal my hopes and fears, my astonishment at the variety of stuff I shoehorned myself into, and the overarching realisation that everybody is bluffing their way to success, and that I could do it too. But looking back, some of it was not bullshit at all. Some of it was, of course. The journey so far has been a rollercoaster ride of epic proportions; hold tight and join me ...

I'm approaching this book as a kind of 'travel writer of my interior thoughtscape'. If it seems a little overly obsessed with my music career, that's because it is my life – a life that I'm eternally grateful for. As many of my musician friends ironically say, 'One day I'll wake up and I'll have to do a proper job.' I've rejoiced in my passion being my 'proper job' for over forty years, and that is something I'll never take for granted. Imagine that – making music and helping others make theirs ... I should be paying them.

So, let's start this journey ...

1956–70: Growing Up in Sheffield

'When I was very young I realised ...'

During the research and preparation I did before starting to write this book, I realised I had only a sketchy knowledge of my family's provenance. It's not that it doesn't interest me, it's just that all my life I've spent *doing* stuff, not really considering the effect or consequences, regarding the past as irrelevant to my hunger to reach some indefinable future. Also, there's a kind of built-in self-effacement in Sheffield folk, as though merely acknowledging that you may have an interesting family 'isn't for the likes of us'. It's not really got anything to do with cap-doffing to the classes above (well, I hope not), but it's more about an unspoken acceptance that there's nothing particularly interesting about an average, poor-ish, working-class family – a bit of a chip-on-the-shoulder, I suppose, but not uncommon in our world.

Well, in the process of getting my ducks in a row, I became kind of curious, so I foolishly asked my somewhat obsessive wife Landsley to help me trace a few interesting characters from my family tree (she'd recently started the process as part of the necessary research to prove my Irish heritage to enable me to get an Irish passport in the wake of all the ludicrous Brexit bullshit – she's Irish, by the way). A ramble through a few generations of my lineage on my mother's side – the Edleys – revealed a mixture of steelworkers, tailors, soldiers and farmers, mainly from Sheffield, Essex, Birmingham and the US, whereas Dad's line is an assortment of steelworkers, soldiers, labourers, shoemakers and domestic staff, born in a wide range of areas from Sheffield to Somerset and Belfast, Bath, Waterford and even India.

Then I asked Landsley if she could dig a little more to find some funny or curious earlier ancestors. 'Maybe you could go back as far as, oh I don't know, the 1700s?' I casually threw in. This was probably a mistake, as it became a two-week-long continuous series of astonished exclamations and news bulletins delivered with increasing regularity, often in the middle of the night, as she delved deeper and deeper into my bloodline. She burst into the bedroom one night and whispered in my ear, 'Charlemagne,' which completely freaked me out.

Here is a minuscule fraction of the incredible and insane detail that she has revealed . . . the characters discovered make TV's *Who Do You Think You Are?* look like a badly researched piece of boring tat . . .

So . . . I command you to kneel and pay homage to some of my ancestors. We'll start working backwards from the 1600s . . .

- Andrew Warner (tenth great-grandfather, 1595–1648) – Plymouth puritan, one of the earliest settlers in America.
- Robert le Strange, Lord of Wrockwardine (twenty-second great-grandfather, 1267–1324) – knight!
- Ralph d'Aubigny (twenty-fifth great-grandfather, 1134–91) – Crusader killed at the Battle of Acre.
- Princess de Bourgogne d'Ardennes (thirty-second great-grandmother, born 872) – that explains my love of their pâté . . .
- Ragnhildr Hrólfsdóttir (thirty-fifth great-grandmother, 825–92) – in *Orkney Saga* legend, the warrior-mother of Rollo.

- Rothaide de Bobbio (no really, I'm not making these names up; thirty-eighth great-grandmother, 820–58) – Italian noblewoman.
- Eystein Ivarsson Glumra 'the Noisy' (my favourite name, possibly ever; thirty-sixth great-grandfather, 810–70) – Viking warrior.
- Bernard, Prince of Denmark (thirty-first great-grandfather, 880–955) – prince!

One particularly bizarre discovery was my eighth great-grandfather John Carrington. For unknown reasons, he was charged with witchcraft at a court held on 20 February 1651 in Connecticut. He was the first man to be convicted and executed for witchcraft in New England.

The indictment read:

Thou art indicted by the name of John Carrington of Wethersfield, carpenter, that not having the fear of God before thine eyes thou hast entertained familiarity with Satan, the great enemy of God and Mankind; and by his help has done works above the course of nature, according to the laws of God and the established laws of this commonwealth thou deservest to Dye.

Cool provenance, don't you agree?

Now we're getting to the good stuff . . . you'll love these:

- Saint Itta de Nivelles (forty-fourth great-grandmother, 592–652) – I'm descended from a SAINT, motherfucker.
- Charles 'Martel' (forty-first great-grandfather, 676–741) from Liege, Mayor of the Palace, effectively ruled as king of Francia (France), and grandfather of Charlemagne, Emperor of the Romans! What a dude . . .

- Kari 'Wind' Fornjotsson (forty-fifth great-grandfather, 189–240) – King of Kvenland, wherever that is or was . . .
- Gaius Julius Severus (sixty-fifth great-grandfather, 25–80) – tribune of Legio VI Ferrata, Rome.
- Adobogiona (sixty-eighth great-grandmother, 90–50 bce) – Celtic princess!

And finally . . .

- Attalus (seventy-second great-grandfather, 269–197 bce) – King of Pergamon, Izmir, Turkey.
- Ptolemy (seventy-seventh great-uncle, 376–334 bce) – Alexander the Great's right-hand man!

Impressive stuff, eh? Or just plain nuts. Something to chat about over a pint, at least. Thanks again to my crazy wife . . . love you . . . but I'm not really sure what to think. I had no idea I was the progeny of kings, princes, saints and witches, and nor did anyone else. I was just a working-class lad from an industrial town in the north. And that's what most journalists wanted to talk about . . .

'Is there something in the water up there?'

If I had a pound for every time a journalist had asked this question, I'd be a . . . well, at least £50 richer. Sheffield is an unusual city, often called 'Britain's biggest village' because of its friendly inhabitants. It has a population of around 550,000, and it was a massive northern industrial powerhouse before the term had been appropriated by politicians, and a centre of steel and cutlery production since, believe it or not, the fourteenth century. It was world famous for the steel products created there (I still look at cutlery for the 'Made in Sheffield' mark wherever I visit in the world). Then the

1970s arrived, and a combination of factors including the 1973 oil crisis and ultimately the rise of Margaret Thatcher made sure the main steel employers in town lost a total of around sixty thousand jobs that decade. It was a massive shock to the people of Sheffield.

But growing up in Sheffield wasn't all bad news. My memories were almost all happy ones from my childhood, despite our privations. We simply knew no different. My parents Jack and Kitty were from solid working-class, trade-union roots. My mum was a seamstress and then full-time mother, and my dad was a proud toolmaker who worked at Joseph Thompson's on Townhead Street in Sheffield city centre for almost fifty years, retiring early through ill health, partly caused by smoking eighty Capstan Full Strength unfiltered fags a day for most of his life. He did relent eventually, at the age of eighty, by moving to filter-tipped, but after a few weeks he started breaking the tips off. The perpetually circulating, ground steel dust in the air in his awful, dangerous factory space didn't help either. He once took me to his workplace when he deemed me old enough – I was about twelve – and I will never forget the hell-like conditions he had to endure every day of his working life. I couldn't wait to get out at the end of the visit, and I strongly believe (although he never admitted it) that he took me there to ensure that I never, ever made the same mistake as he did.

In the Second World War he was also an air-raid warden, a job that he was proud of, but he never talked about the details. He ARP'd at night, fitting this around working full-time during the day. Sheffield was heavily bombed in the war (due to armaments manufacturing), so part of his job was not only warning of a forthcoming air-raid and getting people into their shelters, but also sounding the all-clear and searching the destroyed buildings and rubble for survivors. I was told later by some of my extended family that this was not the insignificant job that my dad played down, but a highly dangerous and even traumatic one, having to cope regularly with finding buried victims of the air-raids. There were also rumblings that he was admitted to Whiteley Woods mental hospital in Sheffield after the war, possibly with PTSD.

He did confess to me later that his main ambition in life was to get a job in an office, as he proudly told me he had passed a series of exams to receive a 'merit certificate'. This was apparently quite something in the 1930s but, as fate would have it, the only jobs available during the Great Depression in Sheffield were either steelworker or toolmaker – and toolmaker was deemed to be the more technically challenging, so the smarter kids were placed in those roles. His fate was sealed from that moment – he never escaped to the promised land of paperwork and typewriters. This was one of his life's biggest regrets.

He would work fifty hours a week plus overtime in grim conditions, so the only time we had to spend together was Sundays, when he loved to take me to the local park, buy me a Vimto (what a luxury) or even a bottle of Coca-Cola (now *that* was a treat). I treasured those Sundays. Dad would give us a small amount of money to go and fetch him and the family some chocolate on Sunday afternoon – Mars Bars were a favourite, and Bounty – we'd bring a couple of bars back, and he'd carefully divide them into slices, like the precious commodities we were convinced they were at the time.

One Sunday (I must have been six years old) we were returning from the shop – myself and my sister Janet, who is ten years older than me – when I carelessly ran into the main road without looking and was instantly hit by a Ford Prefect car. As I lay on the ground dazed, the driver picked me up, horrified, and shouted at Janet, 'Where do you live?' She replied, 'Just down the road on Hope Street.' They rushed me home and my main memories were two things – one was that I could feel warm liquid running down my leg, and I was terrified it was blood – fortunately the shock had cause me to wee, but it was scarily embarrassing. The other thought was, *Have I broken anything?* I cried and begged the distraught driver, 'I don't want to go to hospital – pleeeaaase.'

Once we were home, our family doctor was summoned (we had no telephone, so had to borrow a neighbour's) and he arrived post-haste. After a quick examination by my weeping mother, solemn dad and the doctor himself, it seemed that I was only bruised. As I was explaining how happy I was not to be carted off in an ambulance, the driver interjected, 'Bloody good job I had the brakes repaired yesterday, or your lad might have been a goner.' I still haven't been admitted to hospital since then. Life is risky enough thanks . . .

In those days, children spent 90 per cent of their time with their mother, and it's fair to say I absolutely loved my mum Kitty – she was the domestic rock of the family, cooking, cleaning, shopping, cuddling, bathing (we had no bathroom, only an outside toilet and a tin bath) – and in return, she adored me (and all my siblings). As I was growing up, my parents would argue a lot, nearly always about money, of which there was little. I listened at the top of the stairs to one of their arguments, where she threatened to walk out on my dad – as a six-year-old, I thought it was really going to happen, so I became clingier and clingier to her until I confessed I'd heard the argument. 'Don't be silly, I'd never leave you,' she cooed, but I'm convinced it made me insecure in my relationships for decades to come. No doubt, it had a big effect on me. Yep, my family's lack of money was always a real and present problem, although at the time my parents never used to complain, except to each other.

There were hardly any cars on our street, so football on the cobbles (yes, at that time, all the side streets were cobbled) was a big part of our lives, especially on Sunday afternoons in the summer when the entire street would take part in a thirty-a-side game with kids, dads, mums, brothers, aunts, dogs, sisters, grandmas, uncles, brothers, cats, grandads and toddlers all taking part. It was a kind of working-class version of the Eton wall game, but much gentler and more fun. Those were among the happiest times of my early years.

It was not uncommon for the family's cash to run out midweek (no savings, of course), and Mum had to apologise for a less-than-gourmet vegetable soup, or just chips and fish fingers. But for the most part, her cooking was fantastic (if basic). Favourites included meat and potato pie (drowned in the ultimate Sheffield condiment, Henderson's Relish – a Worcestershire sauce a bit like Lea & Perrins but sweeter), corned beef hash (an Oxo-cube-based thin but tasty stew with veg), slow-braised brisket of beef with veg (one of the cheapest cuts, very trendy now of course). Friday was fish-and-chips day (always cod), Saturday was always tuna sandwiches for tea, and Sunday was either a roast beef dinner, or, if we were splashing out, roast chicken (still a treat in those days – chicken was relatively expensive).

Dad's weekly treat was several pints of Ward's best bitter on Saturday night at St Philip's Working Men's Club on Weston Street. This place was the heart and soul of his and fellow workers' funtime – usually featuring an incredibly loud cover-version rock group ('Smoke on the Water' was a particular favourite), a tombola, a drummer and organist almost always called something like Frank and Ernest, an MC ('Give order please, thank-you please . . .') vainly trying to get the attention of the raucous crowd who had been partially deafened by the aforementioned rock group's ear-splitting rendition of 'Yellow River' or some such current hit – you just knew they'd rather be playing Black Sabbath or Wishbone Ash. Understated it was not.

Our council house at 33 Hope Street had four rooms – two bedrooms, a kitchen and a front room with a small, rented TV and a sofa. My sisters Maureen and Janet slept in the smaller bedroom; Mum, Dad, my brother Steve and I all slept in one cramped bedroom. This also had a potty under the bed (no one went to the outside toilet at night, especially in winter), so our bedroom constantly reeked of piss. I just thought this was normal. The rooms downstairs, however, were completely covered with nicotine stains, and therefore stank even more. We must have gone to school stinking of fags, but as it was omnipresent at home, we just assumed everyone's house was suffused with the same aroma. Of course, there was also no central heating – the house was warmed only by a coal fire/cooking range in the kitchen and, if Dad had worked some overtime that week, a fire in the front room. The bedrooms were absolutely freezing in winter, so water bottles were necessary to avoid hypothermia. But it was our home ...

One of my earliest memories of hot summer evenings in Hope Street was lying in bed with the windows open, listening to the distant sound of the drop forges travelling down the valleys from Attercliffe ... kaboom, kaboom ... it sounded like a giant's heartbeat, which was so reassuring that it lulled me to sleep. Maybe my love of this 'musique concrète' led to my predilection for found sound and industrial noise in my future career. All I know is that the sounds and smells of industry were everywhere in the centre of Sheffield. I never gave it a second thought at the time, I assumed all cities sounded like that.

At home, we only had six books, all subject-based volumes of *Encyclopaedia Britannica* – 'Science', 'History', 'Geography', 'Physics', 'Biology' and 'The Commonwealth'. My parents must have gone into hock to buy these on the never-never, and indeed almost all of our clothes were bought on credit. Every Whitsuntide we would get a brand-new set of clothes, and the tradition was to go around all the neighbours' houses, knocking and pleading when the door opened, 'Do you like my new clothes?' at which point they would give you what they could afford, a working-class tradition showing financial solidarity in a really cute and society-gluing way.

'Playing out' was our main recreation, but this depended on there being no rain at all. One of my strongest memories from that time was begging my mum to let me play football outside. She would always reply, 'If them [roof] slates are wet, then you're not going out.' I would stare longingly out of the window, willing the sun to come out or the wind to dry up the slates so I could play with my mates, mainly because there was bugger all to do indoors. As I reached seven or eight years old, I became more friendly with the girls in our street, and less interested in wandering off with the 'gang' – I've always been a bit of an outsider, and I still don't like that gang mentality. Although I'm not sure how that fits with my love of football, but anyway . . . If I was stuck inside, I would have to resort to our six books. I must have read these all cover to cover at least ten times each. My favourites were 'Biology' and 'Physics', and the one I most struggled with was 'The Commonwealth' (I still do).

My parents died in the late 1990s. Mum died first of breast cancer, Dad followed within a year of being diagnosed with lung cancer – I remember him saying near the end as I held his hand, 'Martyn, I'm goooin' oooem ["I'm going home" in a thick Sheffield accent] . . . I want to see Kit.' Of course I said, 'Don't be daft, Dad, you've got loads to live for,' but he really didn't, and he died within a week. I was heartbroken, and for the first time I felt I understood what it meant to be an orphan. My father's pride and joy was the gold Omega watch he received for fifty years' service at work, which was worth a lot of money in those days, and it was certainly the most expensive thing he ever possessed. Even then, later he would say in an embittered way, 'Fifty bloody years, and all I got was a bloody watch.' His main gripe was that he received very little superannuation (workplace pension) because he had to retire three years early due to ill health. The union fought his case, but he only received around £1000 instead of the £10,000 or more he would have received had he retired at sixty. This resentment troubled him until the end of his days. When he died, the only thing I wanted were the six *Encyclopaedia Britannica* books which were my constant childhood companions, and a beautiful, engraved carriage clock I had bought them for their sixtieth wedding anniversary. My mother never had any money of her own to leave, but we were always loved and looked after well, and never went without food or clothing. I miss them so much – I am very grateful to have had them in my life. I think about them almost every day. They were the kindest, most gentle and stoic people, which I now appreciate is a rare thing.

I was an accident: the result of an August bank holiday drunken moment, I suspect. I was born on 19 May 1956, six weeks premature at the Jessop Hospital in Sheffield. My father was fifty and my mother was forty-four, unusually old parents for that time, but it seems that I was treasured by all my family, especially my two sisters Maureen and Janet, who were twenty and ten when I was born. I was their new toy, and, of course, I became my brother Stephen's football pal. He was eight when I was born. Ah, football . . . Sheffield Wednesday were (and still are) our family's love. In the absence of any God-fearing interest in religion, it was very much like the kind of quasi-religious devotion present in Liverpool's football obsession and culture. My dad always used to say there were two football teams in Sheffield: Sheffield Wednesday (the Owls) and Sheffield Wednesday reserves. He'd scowl at the mere mention of Sheffield

United (the Blades) – in fact, all talk of SUFC was banned in his company. He even wouldn't eat streaky bacon as it had matched SUFC's strip of red and white stripes. My grandfather Richard lived nearby, and we would visit him every Sunday – he'd give me a big, beardy, bristly, smoky kiss and a handful of Murray mints (which I never liked but I couldn't break it to him). Longevity seems to run in my father's side of the family – my grandfather was born around the time of the forming of SWFC in 1867, so all generations of the Ware family were solid Wednesdayites since the start. The alternative was never an option.

My first-ever home game was by far the best game I've ever seen in the flesh ... 31 August 1968, Sheffield Wednesday 5 Manchester United 4. Wednesday were 2–4 down and came back to win against all odds in front of a crowd of 54,000. I was on the Spion Kop with my sister's then-boyfriend Jeff (they're still married now). United's team featured a panoply of superstars – Best, Law, Stiles, Charlton, Stepney, Kidd, Morgan ... a young lad called Jack Whitham scored a hat-trick for the Owls that day – I was bewitched, and I was doomed ...

Wednesday will always be an important part of my life (I still have two season tickets even though I live in London). I helped to start the original SWFC Supporters Trust, now known as Wednesdayite, and if I were a lot richer, I would have loved to have been involved at board level with the club. I've also released two singles for the club under the pseudonym of The Hillsboro' Crew, the first of which was co-written by Ian Reddington – 1986's 'Steel City (Move On Up)', written for the FA Cup semi-final game against Everton, which of course we lost. Kudos to Virgin Records for letting us release it, though, especially as they managed to manufacture a fake news story in the *Daily Mirror* proudly stating that it had sold half a million copies on the week of release – more like 5000, and all in Sheffield – don't believe the hype, kids!

Then there was the Official 1993 Sheffield Wednesday Cup Single, 'If It's Wednesday It Must Be Wembley', this time by The Hillsborough Crew (subtle difference) – in anticipation of winning at least one of the two major cups in 1993. The title was inspired by the 1969 cult comedy film *If It's Tuesday, This Must Be Belgium*. Our record featured an audacious vinyl picture-disc of the whole SWFC squad in traditional centre-of-the-pitch three-row pose but wearing Ray-Bans à la *The Blues Brothers*, and with Ian and me in the centre of the photo dressed as goalkeepers (no Ray-Bans). My biggest thrill associated with this was a contract signed with the SWFC players' pool (an ad hoc joint venture organised by the players to 'pool' all commercial gains from the cup runs). The organiser was my hero Chris Waddle, who had just been voted Football Writer's Player of the Year and was having the most incredible season. As is par for the course for the life of a Wednesdayite, we lost both cup finals in the most painful way possible – typically the FA Cup was thrown away in the last minute of extra time (Chris Woods, take a bow) in a tightly fought replay. We used to paraphrase the famous saying, 'you draw some you lose some'.

These vinyl records neatly exemplify my life of joy and suffering as a Wednesdayite, the pain of which appears to be on course to continue until the day of my demise and on through the generations via my son Gabriel, whom I indoctrinated at an early age. His first home game at the age of six was a 0–5 loss to Norwich, which proved to be an eerily prescient pre-echo of our future misery. Recently Gabe said to me, 'Do you realise, Dad, that I've never ever seen us win anything?' *Plus ça change*, as they say (but not in Sheffield). However – 'Up The Owls', 'Wednesday 'Til I Die', 'We're All Wednesday Aren't We?', etc., etc., repeat till fade ...

We shall undercome ...

One day in 1969, my dad called me into the front room, and in hushed tones he said, 'Martyn, I want you to have this, my father gave it to me, now I'm passing it on to you.' He handed me a scruffy-looking hardback book, covered in aged brown paper. On the cover there was the handwritten title, *The Romance of the Wednesday* by Richard Sparling – the definitive history of Sheffield Wednesday FC from 1867 to 1926. This, I found out later, was informally called 'The Wednesdayites' Bible' by the faithful. I was so touched – he had so few private possessions, and he could see that I loved Wednesday as much as he and his father did. This really meant a lot to him, and to me. I shall pass this book on to my son Gabriel and so on and so on – cultural history is so important.

As I grew up in a love-filled but very financially challenged environment, I became curious about the world around me, which in our confined two-up two-down house largely meant our Dansette record player and stacks of vinyl. These were bought by Maureen and Janet, who were both massive pop fans in the sixties, and I literally spent hours and hours playing and replaying the increasingly crackly singles (and occasional LP), stacking up to six of them on the spindle to watch the magic of the automatic drop of each single in turn. Imagine no mixtapes, no recording off the radio, nothing except the same playlist in a different order time after time . . . but I loved it, it was my favourite toy.

A little later, I was given for my birthday a treasured transistor radio, which in timeless clichéd-but-nevertheless-true fashion, I used to sneak into my bed and listen to. This was incredibly exciting and I would avidly consume all the latest music and even the DJ patter (Emperor Rosko, Kid Jensen, etc.) from the semi-forbidden and daring 'pirate' station Radio Luxembourg. This was the engine driving my personal taste in music and therefore my growing sense of identity (as opposed to aping my sister's tastes). Music completely defined who I was at that time. Radio Luxembourg played all the best Motown and pop classics from that golden age, and I have particularly strong memories of 'Good Vibrations' by The Beach Boys, 'Reflections' by The Supremes, 'Bernadette' by The Four Tops, 'Green Tambourine' by The Lemon Pipers,' You Keep Me Hangin' On' by The Supremes (again), 'Patches' by Clarence Carter, Sandie Shaw (who I later worked with), the incomparable Dusty Springfield, Gene Pitney, etc., etc., etc. . . . all drifting and filtering in and out of audibility, riding on the charismatic and mysterious oscillations at the end of the medium wave band – Fabulous 208 . . . I became deeply emotionally connected to the stories of the songs and the soundscapes (well, as much as my childish mind could comprehend), and I'm sure this gave me an unusual perspective on my professional songwriting later.

I was also very enamoured of my sister's collection of soundtrack albums including *West Side Story*, *South Pacific*, *The Sound of Music*, together with a large collection of Anthony Newley albums and singles ('Idol on Parade' springs to mind), and, unfortunately, Cliff Richard. In fact *Summer Holiday* was the first film I saw in the cinema, closely followed by *Those Magnificent Men in Their Flying Machines*. I was utterly mesmerised by the sheer glamour and scale of the big screen at the Odeon – it's hard to imagine a world with only two TV channels in black and white, and then suddenly to be thrust into a beautiful alien universe of colour. I'm still head over heels in love with big-screen cinema. Let's hope it survives the digital age.

Every year, people at my dad's workplace would save up for the big night out at Christmas – the pantomime at the Lyceum Theatre. Magical colours, shouty camp men dressed as women, mysterious transitions, women dressed as boys, live music, free sweeties thrown into the audience, living in mortal fear of being dragged from our seats to be humiliated on stage – it's all reminiscent of one of our

Heaven 17 concerts. I think it's safe to say that pantomime was responsible for my love of theatre.

To be honest, I felt my life at home was as rich and interesting as I could imagine. I suppose ignorance is bliss, but genuinely we seemed to be happy with our lot in life. I suspect that my mum and dad hid the worst effects of our privations in their typically selfless and stoic manner. Later, when I reached adulthood, I could never understand the constant moaning about people's family situations; arguments, grudges, resentments and all that seem to be part of a normal family's life. I can only praise my remarkable parents and siblings for giving all of us the most emotionally secure and loving upbringing in some of the most difficult circumstances imaginable.

1966–70: First Loves

'With concentration, my size increased ...'

I was bullied at school. Nothing unusual about that, but to be bullied multiple times by several different and unconnected groups of people makes me feel there may have been a pattern. I was a quiet, shy and studious kid who really didn't care for gangs or boys' stuff, and when I wasn't playing football with my friends, I was much happier hanging with the girls in our street. I found them fascinating ... what made them tick? Why did they smell so nice compared to boys? Why did they talk incessantly and make up kissing games and gabble about emotions? None of my male friends ever talked about such stuff. I was a gentle, sensitive boy who had been nurtured in a loving way by my parents and in particular my older sisters and my mother, and I just felt I was totally normal. I was wrong.

The bullying started in the final year of junior school, when we had moved to Burngreave, a rough part of Sheffield with an even rougher school called Pye Bank Junior School. I was the new kid in class, and in those days they used to seat you in the classroom according to your ranking in various tests, a bit like a living league table. As I was very good at mathematics and science in particular, I was soon ranked number one in the class, sat next to my first 'love', Judith, who was number two. We quickly became close, and

I dreaded every test that would come along in case my ranking dropped and we could no longer sit together. This fortunately never happened, as the rest of our class were mainly disengaged dummies who tried their hardest to disrupt any attempt at learning. No wonder they hated me – and they were all boys. Regularly I would be confronted in the playground, asked for pocket money, and when I refused punched, kicked, Chinese-burned, taunted ... you know, the usual 'we'll get you after school' stuff. I lived in nervous anticipation of breaks and after-school walks home. This continued until a new family called the Sanettis (name changed) moved into our block of council flats, on the floor directly above us. I know they sound like something out of *The Sopranos*, but in reality they were a poor Italian family of six, with twin boys who joined my class at school. They had absolutely no intention of taking part in any sensible way in class, and made it their mission to disrupt everything, usually to the point of temporary exclusion. Fortunately they attended intermittently, but when they did it was chaos. One day, they followed me home from school, taunting me in broken English. My pace quickened in an attempt to lose them, but as I finally reached home and thought I was safe, one of the twins pinned me against the concrete wall inside the stairway of the flats, away from public view.

'Give me your money,' a Sanetti twin snarled.

'I don't have any,' I pleaded pathetically.

Then they both attacked me without warning, punching me in the stomach and then, as I was lying on the floor, kicking me in the face. This was no Chinese burn. They ran off, upstairs to their apartment, but not before warning me not to tell anyone. This was going to be a challenge, as I was in an obviously beaten-up state with a rapidly developing black eye and severe bruising on my body. In a state of shock, I tried to compose myself before entering my house.

'What has happened to you, love?' my horrified mother gasped. I must have looked quite a disturbing sight.

'Err . . . I fell down the stairs and banged my head, Mum.'

'Tell us what really happened, darling.'

I burst into tears and told her the whole story – not just this violent act, but the months of torture I'd been suffering.

'Right – I'm calling the coppers,' growled Kitty.

My mum was a gentle sort, and her compassion was legendary, but nobody messed with her son. I begged her not to as I feared this would lead to more beatings, but she was right, this had to stop, and the only way was to stand up to the bullies. She called my dad at work (we still didn't have a phone, so this was only for emergencies), and he came home early to deal with the crisis. Both my mum and dad strode up the stairs to the Sanettis' apartment and read them the riot act. Of course, the twins denied it, and their parents refused to believe it at first, so they brought me to the front door and showed them my battered face. I was never bullied from that day onwards by the Sanettis, and the police threatened to take the twins to court. A few months later, they were thrown out of their flat for rent arrears and we never saw them again.

There were various other examples of bullying throughout my early teenage years, but this was much more standard stuff, none of which I gave in to. One thing I'd learned from the Sanetti incidents was that giving in created more and more threat, not less, so best to be brave and face up to your tormentors.

But why did I attract bullies? I wasn't rich or big-headed, I was always friendly to people, I didn't make myself a target in any way, I was popular as I was pretty good at football . . . to this day I don't really understand why. Except . . . there are many abused and disturbed children from dysfunctional families who are restaging their own conflicts in an attempt to gain control of their own lives. I had a happy upbringing, and this vibe must have wound up kids who had little love (or worse, suffered abuse) at home. Maybe it was also because I was regarded as a teacher's pet as I was always top of the class, partly motivated by my desire to keep my seat next to Judith.

My crush on Judith had been encouraged by the music teacher, who started a handbell-ringing group and asked me if I'd like to join the all-girl ensemble. *Great*, I thought, *more time with Judith, more time with girls – hold on, I'll be picked on for this, more bullying, I suppose – ah well, let's do it anyway* ... Although I'd played recorder and sang with the school choir at my previous school, this required some discipline and rudimentary music-score reading, but anything to be with my secretly beloved Judith. One particular practice featured sixteen bells and four players including myself, which was quite challenging. I overheard Judith and the other two girls discussing the size of the bells that each had. 'But Judith has the biggest bells,' I interjected. This caused enormous hilarity, as it transpired that they were discussing the size of their newly arriving breasts. I was mortified.

As we arrived back at school for the final term, I couldn't wait to get to my favourite desk to see Judith. 'We're going to rearrange the desks a little for this term,' the teacher announced. 'Judith has left the school with her family to move to Nottingham.'

Oh noooooo ... cruel fate. For the first time in my life, I was truly heartbroken. I would never meet another girl like her, oh woe is me, etc. This proved not to be the case, but nevertheless it feels like the end of the world when you're eleven years old. I'm sure this cameo has been played out since the beginning of time.

I took my eleven-plus examination and passed with flying colours, getting as close as dammit to top marks, and my parents Jack and Kitty were absolutely thrilled. Our preferred school was King Edward VII Grammar School in Broomhill, designed and built by the Sheffield architect William Flockton in 1838, a *very* posh-looking and massive Palladian-style neo-classical building, built on the site of an original charter school from 1604. It was by far the most prestigious and successful state secondary school in the Sheffield region, particularly noted for preparing students for Oxford and Cambridge admissions. Of course, all this was pie in the sky for our family line, who had never sent a child to any university, let alone Oxford or Cambridge. The plain truth was that even with free student grants and housing rent support (can you imagine?), there was no way our family could subsidise the student life. In reality, it was expected that sons and daughters of poor working-class families should enter the world of full-time work as soon as possible to help support the family's economic survival. The possibility of university entry wasn't ever discussed, no matter how intelligent or ambitious we were – true social mobility was a rare thing in the seventies in Sheffield. Always bubbling under the surface was the 'not for the likes of us' mantra, despite all the surface bolshiness.

Apart from Phil Oakey and myself, famous alumni from the school include Bruce Dickinson (Iron Maiden), Graham Fellows (Jilted John and John Shuttleworth), Joe Elliott (Def Leppard), Paul Heaton (Beautiful South and Housemartins), Julia Bradbury, Emily Maitlis, Toddla T and Elizabeth Henstridge. The school itself was a fusty, musty tradition-bound wannabe-public school, with 'fags' (years one and two were humiliatingly required to wear short trousers and caps), Flashman-style prefects (that elitist blue lapel edging) and masters who were required to wear black gowns (very *Harry Potter*). Everything was designed to entrain the students into an established hierarchy of conventionality.

Unfortunately, many of the teachers (called 'masters') had long since lost their enthusiasm for their respective subjects, passing on their disaffection to their students by way of sarcastic indifference, intermittently punctuated by acts of random violence involving thrown wooden blackboard erasers and chalk, and occasional beatings for no apparent reason. Subjects that I am now obsessed with, history, geography and physics, were taught in such a dry and passionless way that they almost destroyed my love of learning forever. Thank God they didn't.

One particular subject, history, vexed me. There were two masters who both appeared to loathe their chosen subject and were clearly marking time in preparation for their forthcoming retirement. Textbooks that had been passed down for probably twenty or so years were reclad in brown paper at the start of each year, facts fossilised, no discussion possible. Totally one-way traffic, with hardly any attempt at discussion or analysis. Simply cramming. Amazingly, the subjects for history being taught then are more or less the same as now – the Tudors, William the Conqueror, the Romans, the Victorians, the World Wars and, most importantly, the British Empire. Jeezus, no wonder the UK is in the state it's in: British exceptionalism bred into every boy and girl, with an unhealthy dose of xenophobia. It was only when I left school and started absorbing knowledge voraciously that I realised how fucked up this all was, and that there were many perspectives from different cultures which, if we'd been encouraged to consider at the time, would have helped create a much more rounded view of the world. I know now this was never the intention of the British secondary school system: indoctrination was the name of the game. (Have we moved on since then? – discuss.)

However, the silver lining of my education was this: it was the start of my lifelong passion for learning and later teaching and sharing knowledge, which is to me a precious commodity, but which had been withheld deliberately by my supposed top-ranking educational establishment.

The only lessons I really enjoyed were Music Appreciation, with the ageing but avuncular Mr Barnes, who also ran the school choir and orchestra. In his lessons, the pupils were encouraged to bring in their own music to play to the class. This led to some bizarre and hilarious choices, ranging from my first album, *Pretties For You* by Alice Cooper, to Indian folk songs, dense prog-rock, posh kids' opera, even spoken word (John Betjeman) – one of the class jokers brought in the first Frank Zappa/Mothers of Invention album, *Freak Out!*, which had some naughty words in it, causing teenage transgressive tittering at the back of the class. But Mr Barnes was nothing if not open-minded, and I fondly remember him as a genuinely positive influence on my burgeoningly eclectic musical tastes.

One of the happiest days of my life was the final day of school at the end of year two. As I took my usual bus from King Ted's to my home in Burngreave, I finally realised that I would never have to wear short trousers or, more to the point, my hated cap ever again. As I was sitting with my friends on the top deck of the number 82 bus in town, and we drove towards Lady's Bridge over the filthy River Don, I symbolically threw my cap into the river with a flourish. Good riddance. My first act of protest, and it wouldn't be the last.

Years three and four (today's years nine and ten) were pretty uneventful – more football on the 'close' (the green area in front of the school) and more revising for the forthcoming O levels. But most interestingly, there was a growing pubescent interest in girls and sexuality. Masturbation was a hot topic – there was a race to understand: A) What an orgasm was. B) What was this strange liquid emanating from our private parts? Was it normal? Why did it feel so good? C) What did this have to do with girls? It's hard to comprehend how little was generally known by boys at that time in a single-sex school – sketchy sex education classes had more in common with dissecting lab rats than any form of sexual/psycho-logical understanding. There were no textbooks about all this, and no internet to sneakily refer to, and the teachers seemed unwilling to discuss the subject for fear of humiliation, so it was left up to our own resourcefulness. We would pool some of our dinner money, and the one of our group who looked the oldest would embarrass-ingly sneak a copy of *Parade* from the top shelf at a newsagent's. *Parade* was the cheapest and frankly most 'readers' wives' version of porn that was available – home snaps of blousy housewives posing on chintz sofas (the sophistication of *Playboy* and *Penthouse* were to come later). A single copy of *Parade* exchanged hands daily for weeks. Yes, I know, disgusting, but there was nowhere else to go in the feverish and demented world of the pubescent imagination.

This new interest in the opposite sex reached a peak one summer's evening, when a group of three of my schoolmates and myself were loitering after school near a friend's house. Still in uniform, we were messing about playing football when we noticed a group of four girls watching us and giggling. They were 'skinbirds', a not particu-larly attractive female version of the skinhead trend, but curiously attractive to horny young boys. Dressed in long Abercrombie coats, hair shorn to a number-two cut, Doc Martens boots, Sta-Prest slacks – these girls were from the local secondary modern school, and definitely from the wrong side of the tracks.

'What yer doin'?' one of the cocky girls imaginatively opened with.

Shocked that they'd even talk to us, I plucked up the courage to respond. 'Nothing much,' I replied, faking insouciance.

'Fancy coming to our 'ouse, it's only round the corner – we've got some cider and me mum and dad are out all night.'

We looked at each other – was this a wind-up? None of us had ever had a girlfriend at this point, and we were terrified but didn't want to admit it. My mate Alan and his sidekick Chris quickly mumbled, 'Err – no thanks, I've got to get home for supper.' This left Dave (lanky and spotty), Chris 2 (short and young-looking) and me (best of a bad bunch). I nervously whispered to them, 'This could be fun,' but they clearly didn't agree, and slunk away.

'That just leaves me then,' I said, stating the obvious.

'OK, you'll do,' said the prettiest of the shorn teenagers. What did she mean?

Within ten minutes, I was inside their house; within twenty (after the required glass of Woodpecker cider) the most forward of the four girls (I never asked their names) had ushered me upstairs to the bedroom. This was definitely getting out of hand, but then again, this was like an erotic dream – too good to be true. As we lay on the bed, there was much inept fumbling and petting, but just as it seemed we might be going much further than intended (condoms were a thing of legend), she left the bedroom . . . what? She then ushered in a second girl for more shenanigans – this was torture of the most exquisite kind . . . you really couldn't make it up. In fact, all I could think was that nobody would believe any of it at school tomorrow. The third and fourth girls took their turns – by this time I was ready to explode.

And then, with very little warning, the first girl announced that I'd have to leave. I got the impression that this was possibly a regular occurrence, and that I was just one of a long line of experimental sexual subjects. But however odd it was, I was quite proud of myself for at least taking the risk. I strode into the class the following day beset with questions from my cowardly cohort – and by the end of the day, my reputation as the self-proclaimed year-four Casanova had been sealed . . . at least in my imagination.

1970–4: The Phil Years

'Dada Dada Duchamp Vortex ...'

The fourth form at King Edward VII School in Sheffield wasn't exactly full of characters. Many of the kids from well-off families were proud to proclaim that they already knew what they wanted to do when they finished school – you know the stuff, twelve O levels, four good-grade A levels, Oxbridge exams and then straight into Daddy's accountancy or lawyer's practice, or to be a doctor or dentist, or banker, etc. Nothing could have been further from my thoughts – I had literally no idea what to do or which direction to follow. My parents had no experience of the professional world, or contacts, or anything really to help: all they knew is that they wanted me to have a 'proper' job, with a steady potential for 'making my way in life'. This sounded awful to me, but I had no other ideas to fill the vacuum so, like so many bright working-class kids, it appeared I had no option but to go with the flow.

In early 1971, I was preparing to take my O levels (I'm proud to say I passed eleven, without really revising much). The classes were beyond dull, the teachers were disengaged and bored, and this was reflected by the lack of motivation of the pupils, who mainly regarded the whole thing as a barely necessary charade. Then, on yet another nondescript day of pointless revision and boredom, a new pupil was introduced to our class ...

'Pay attention!' our form master 'Kicker' Cook shouted. (His favourite disciplinary trick was to bring unruly students out before the class and kick them hard up their arse. Nice.) 'We have a new student joining the school today, and he has the misfortune to be joining you lot – he's called Philip Oakey, and his father is Chief Postmaster for Sheffield.'

What kind of posh twat was he going to be? The poor lad looked mortified and embarrassed, but unbowed. My first impressions of Phil were that he was tall and good-looking, with curtained, draped hair framing his face. He looked as though he shouldn't be wearing a blazer and grey serge trousers, and certainly not a tie. There was something about him, a magnetic quality, which later proved to be a shrewd assessment. I sensed that he was a bit of an outsider, which appealed to me, so I made a point of making friends as soon as I could.

He seemed very open and friendly, but his manner was strangely blunt with an unidentifiable accent – was it Midlands or north? He told me that he was born in Solihull, but that he'd moved several times as his father was regularly transferred to better posts in different cities, and that his dad's previous placement was in Leicester. *That would account for the mysterious accent then*, I thought.

We quickly became very close friends – although I had already had some good friends in the school, Phil seemed to offer so much more. Although he was my age, he seemed to exude a worldliness and mystique that I'd never encountered before, and our relationship developed rapidly into a big brother, smaller brother mode – this was merged with my admiration for his dark, attractive looks (it's never a bad thing to be a wingman to a better-looking friend), and the inexplicable feeling that I could learn a great deal from him. To say we were close is a massive understatement. The truth is we were inseparable.

It was clear that Phil was a very friendly, social creature who was keen to establish a coterie of friends. The first weekend after we met in class, he invited me to his house – a semi-detached, quite luxurious home in a leafy suburb called Fulwood – and, when I arrived, his parents were nowhere to be seen. In fact, during the nine years I knew Phil, I don't recollect meeting his father at all, and his mother perhaps twice. Phil seemed to have the house to himself most of the time, which, of course, was a dream come true for teenagers. In contrast, I had grown up in a series of tiny council houses and flats where my family were constantly on top of me. This was all new and exciting to me, and our little get-togethers soon developed into full-scale, full-on raves with twenty to thirty excitable adolescents, all craving fun and the freedom to experiment with music, drugs and sex.

Across the road from our all-male school, there was an all-female school, the imaginatively named Girls' High School. This was a hotbed of dating possibilities, as the girls could watch the boys playing football on the 'close' in front of the school. They would giggle and flirt from a distance, and the boys would occasionally acknowledge their admiration. We were all trying awkwardly to give the impression of being too cool to care, but were really too scared and full of hormones, to the extent that sometimes it felt like we would burst. I was an OK football player, and I tried to get Phil involved, but he clearly had never kicked a ball in his life, so we had no option but to take a more direct route.

Soon enough, we plucked up the courage to approach some of the girls who had been watching (or ogling?) us. I was very shy and inexperienced, but Phil, who I could tell the girls were cooing over, had no problem asking a group of the most attractive young ladies to a house party at the hippest venue in town, Phil's, on the following Saturday night. I was astonished and excited by this – I'd never been to a house party where there was no parental supervision, and the fact they'd all immediately and enthusiastically said yes was unimaginable.

The big day arrived, and the usual 'bring a bottle' instruction was issued. We were sixteen with a bullet, not at all ready for the avalanche of experiences that were about to hit us. Phil welcomed the guests who started arriving around 8 p.m. – some of the most beautifully (and some would say inappropriately) dressed girls were dropped off nervously by their parents, clutching bottles of Woodpecker cider or some cheap wine. Heaven only knows what the parents suspected was going to happen to their precious, naive progeny. Remember, no mobile phones, so all pickups later had to be prearranged – also no photos or later evidence of impropriety.

I had been going out with a girl from the High School called Sarah (name changed) for a few weeks, a pretty blonde who was also a horse-riding instructress, and I was (temporarily, although it felt like forever at the time) madly in love with her. We'd kissed and messed around a little, but I was still a virgin, and so was she, and neither of us had any opportunity to be private long enough to move up to the next level. Maybe this could be my big chance! The house was certainly big enough – four bedrooms, very chintzy, the opposite of my poky council flat, where there was never, ever going to be any privacy. Maybe tonight could be the night ... it really could.

Soon the house was full of rampant, drunk, loud teenagers, dancing to Bowie's *The Man Who Sold the World*, which was playing on Phil's newly acquired eight-track cartridge player (particularly exciting as it could play continuously forever on a loop). Some of the more edgy types (including me and Phil) were in the back garden rolling and smoking spliffs with some of the naughtier girls, and the overall atmosphere of paganism was already getting excitingly out of hand. Then, as T. Rex's *Electric Warrior* blasted out, and the dancing and fumbling started to get more frantic, the scene looked more like an orgy than a house party. However, Sarah and I had more than just partying in mind, and I was getting more pissed by the minute, so popped the question.

'Maybe we should go somewhere quieter, upstairs perhaps?' I nervously and drunkenly slurred.

'Come with me,' she whispered. Before I knew it, she grabbed my hand and led me upstairs.

I could barely believe my luck. *What if this doesn't go to plan?* I panicked, but we were so charged with hormones and drink that it seemed we were being guided by an unseen hand, out of our control. We found a spare bedroom, placed a chest of drawers against the door and flopped on to the bed. *This is reckless,* I thought to myself, but it was too late to go back now . . . we were out of our clothes and under the covers, and I was fumbling around with my first ever condom, given to me by the more worldly Phil. God, I'd rehearsed this moment a hundred times, but everything felt awkward – concentrate, concentrate, concentrate . . . Sarah was uneasy too, but likewise super-excited. Then, without warning, we were actually doing it – wow – this wasn't what I was expecting *at all.* Sarah felt tense under me, and it all seemed very, well, clinical, matter-of-fact and yet exciting – is that even possible? I was also not prepared for this – it hurt, well, it did sting a little, which was off-putting and not very romantic at all.

Before we both knew it, the passionate clinch was over. The main feeling was one of relief that we were no longer virgins, but there were no choirs of heavenly angels and we were not glowing, just a little underwhelmed as in 'was that what all the fuss was about?' OK then – back to the party – it was almost as though it had never happened. We made up for it later, though, as over the coming months (excuse the pun) Sarah and I became obsessed with this new world of sensual experience ...

As the night wore on, parents arrived to the shocked realisation their precious babies were out of their ingenue heads. By the time we reached midnight, the party had thinned to the hardcore ten or so – there didn't seem to be any parental rescue for these poor souls. The lights went down, the remaining few paired up, the eight-track cartridge player repeatedly played *Hunky Dory* until dawn, and these blissed-out souls lost their virginity to the world of all-night parties ...

The summer of 1972 was a time of classic adolescent awakening. Sex was now an everyday part of our lives, as was dope, drinking and, for the first time, entire weekends away from home. It's hard to imagine, but up to that point I had never had a night away from home with or without my parents – we never could afford to stay in lodgings, even for a few days. The best we ever managed were daytrips to the seaside at Scarborough or Cleethorpes or Skegness – even Blackpool seemed unimaginably exotic to us, and the idea of staying in a guest house was the stuff of dreams. My newfound freedom was tantalisingly glamorous, and Phil and I took full advantage.

Phil had fallen in love with motorcycles, and he had bought a couple of old classics which he renovated (no idea where he was getting his money from, by the way – I just assumed this was what the son of posh parents did). The BSA ('Beezer') and the Norton Commando were his pride and joy, and I was thrilled when he asked if I'd like to ride pillion on a trip out into Derbyshire, which was only twenty minutes away. I'd never been on a motorbike of any description, and this 750cc Norton monster (top speed 115 mph) was a sensory overload of an initiation. As we swerved through the narrow roads and the lush summer countryside of the Peak District, I felt a freedom that was beyond any previous comprehension – exhilarating, startling, occasionally terrifying and even a little sexual. This was really living a better life than I could have imagined. What other delights waited in store? As it turned out, our lives were about to change forever.

Throughout our first year hanging out together, Phil and I had shared much, sometimes even girlfriends. The traffic of information, though, seemed to be mostly flowing in the direction of feeding my voracious mind: I was hungry for any and all new experiences and knowledge, I was reborn. Phil opened my mind to many exciting new cultural ideas, publications, art, genres of music and potential lifestyles – bear in mind we were only a few years after the hippie revolution and all the newly expressed freedoms that entailed. Among these pioneering gems of enlightenment, Phil turned me on to *Oz* (controversial counter-culture magazine, bursting with psychedelic and erotic imagery that blew my teenage mind), J. G. Ballard (*The Atrocity Exhibition* and *Crash*), Michael Moorcock (Elric of Melniboné and Jerry Cornelius), Harlan Ellison (*A Boy and His Dog* and 'I Have No Mouth and I Must Scream'), Anthony Burgess (*A Clockwork Orange*), Philip K. Dick (*Do Androids Dream of Electric Sheep?*) and a multitude of science-fiction and fantasy novels and authors. We also discovered a deep mutual love of American comics – mostly Marvel but some DC, and also *Mad Magazine*, which became a big influence on my life-long love of American humour.

Musically, Phil's taste and perhaps mentorship seeded my future eclecticism – an endless procession of progressive rock bands, led by the magnificent King Crimson and Van der Graaf Generator (later John Lydon would reveal Peter Hammill was a major influence on his singing style). Isao Tomita's *Snowflakes Are Dancing*,

Walter/Wendy Carlos, Annette Peacock's *I'm the One* and, most strangely, *Escalator Over the Hill* (which introduced me to avant-garde jazz), Can's *Tago Mago* and Krautrock in general – in fact, we would give just about anything a try. We even dabbled in cod-satanism, as exemplified by 'Come to the Sabbat' by Black Widow – 'Come to the Sabbat, Satan's there' – a ludicrous, post-hippie, over-dramatic rock dirge mainly featuring Hammond B3 organ and jazz flute, and satanic chants – what? Other illuminating songs included 'Attack of the Demon', 'Seduction' and 'Sacrifice', all great stuff for a teenage mind high on cider. We were so open-minded that I truly believe that my lifelong love and excitement of learning were hammered home during these heady, messing-around, hazy-summered, gorgeous days, months and years.

Meanwhile, another major event happened in my life – I had been dating a girl called Rebecca (name changed) for a few months, another lovely brunette with a kooky character from the Girls' High School. We were madly in love and lust, our teenage sexual appetites were prodigious. Amazingly we were allowed by her parents to spend private time together regularly in her bedroom. This proved to be a bad idea for obvious reasons, as our primal urges were much more powerful than our fear of getting caught. Inevitably, despite taking prophylactic precautions, one day our luck ran out, and over the following weeks I noticed that her breasts were getting larger and she was showing a more pouty belly (she was very skinny). I took regular visits to the central library to read everything I could about the symptoms of pregnancy, and I couldn't believe it was possible. We'd taken precautions, hadn't we?

Rebecca went to the doctor for a pregnancy test, and the worst was confirmed. Her parents were rightly appalled (she was only sixteen) and decided that she must terminate the pregnancy. This was a part of a grown-up world that I had had no intention of encountering so early in my life. I simply wasn't prepared for this brick wall of reality. I was forbidden from ever contacting her again and, for the first time in my life, I was truly heartbroken. Was this adult life to be shot through with misery like this? A few days later, I found the courage to tell my parents. There were many tears and I considered begging Rebecca to take me back. My parents were so, so kind and understanding, it made me realise just how fortunate I was to be part of such an empathetic and caring family. Up to that point, I thought all families were the same.

Phil's persona was gradually changing as he became more confident. Fitting for the times we were living in, he had a maverick attitude towards his clothing and hairstyles. One day, he turned up on his rumbling BSA clad in the most extraordinary jacket I'd ever seen. It looked like it was a carapace of insect scales in various textures of black fabrics, combined with ludicrously built-up shoulders. He truly looked like a film star, turning heads on the street. Who was this exotic creature? It transpires that he'd heard of an auction of theatre costumes and props at the Crucible Theatre, and that this was a costume from a recent production of *Macbeth* that was no longer required. It took some balls to wear this in public, but he definitely pulled it off, and I was really inspired by his 'I don't give a toss what anyone thinks' attitude.

Phil and I soon began to scour the sales in Sheffield department and chain stores for large-size ladies clothing and boots – a typical glam-nightclubbing outfit for me would consist of knee-length silver 6-inch heel, 2-inch platform zip-up boots, tight white loon pants tucked into the boots, a silver belt (sci-fi of course), a white T-shirt with a silver plastic knobbly bangle glued to the front (again, very *Doctor Who*), and the *pièce de résistance*, the pride of my wardrobe, my electric green fun-fur bolero jacket. The effect was completed with hair glitter (gritty and uncomfortable), eye shadow (usually iridescent blue/green) and sometimes a hint of lipstick. Now, you may think this would get me beaten up in early seventies Sheffield but neither Phil nor I was ever attacked for the way we dressed throughout the glam period – I think we were just regarded as eccentrics to be avoided. Beyond the occasional sotto-voce grunt of 'poof', the beer monsters just didn't know what to make of us.

As there was precious little to do in Sheffield culture-wise at that time, cinema was becoming a very important social and creative outlet for us, and the local fleapit (the Classic in Fitzalan Square) showed all-nighter five-film bills for a couple of quid. The entry fee included half-hourly offers of mountains of almost inedible grated cheese and raw onion sandwiches. At this age, we took anything we could get for free, but after the first round was partly consumed, even free food would sometimes prove to be a bridge too far. The most memorable night I had there was a while later with Glenn Gregory, Paul Bower and Ian Reddington watching an unmissable bill of Roger Corman's Hammer classics. If my memory serves me well, there were five films: *The Masque of the Red Death*, *The Tomb of Ligeia*, *The Pit and the Pendulum*, *The House of Usher* and *The Raven*. They were all gorgeously oversaturated, schlocky masterpieces and featured the Prince of Camp, Vincent Price, in each of the lead roles. What we discovered that evening was that Corman (never one for *not* skimping) had re-used *exactly the same footage* of a burning roof collapsing to rapidly conclude the wafer-thin storylines. By five in the morning and the final film, wired on cheese and raw onion sandwiches and Pro-Plus caffeine tablets, the partially conscious audience were gripped with anticipation to see if Corman had the gall to make it a nap hand of burning buildings, and when the shot finally arrived, ironic cheers rang through the auditorium.

The summer of 1972 was a time of awakening in many, many ways. The Students Union (SU) at the university was only open to students with an SU card. That wasn't going to stop us. A friend of ours had started a lucrative cottage industry forging SU cards for a fiver. Cheap beer, cheap music, fresher hippie girls – what's not to like? We were not really keen on students ('bloody timewasters'). It's a Sheffield thing, partly based on begrudgery that they had cheap beer and subsidised accommodation, but they certainly knew how to organise rock concerts. Like today, the union circuit was a great way for cool new bands to get a new audience without exposing themselves too early to the more critical general public. In June, Phil and I were hanging out in the cheap bars, checking out the cute student girls, pretty sure that our badly forged SU cards would be spotted at some point and we'd be chucked out, when I noticed a handwritten poster for a forthcoming gig – an all-day, free-entry, end-of-year celebration featuring an eclectic mix of new and more established bands. As we had little money, this felt like winning the pools. The two names that caught our attention were Gary Glitter (who at the time was a regular headliner on the student circuit) and the hottest ticket in town, a brand-new band called Roxy Music who at that time hadn't released any recordings, but were tipped by John Peel and *NME* among others.

The day arrived and, suitably well oiled, the afternoon started with Phil and me lounging on the bare refectory floor about ten yards from the stage – we dare not leave as the place was rammed, stinking of beer and patchouli oil, and we had no intention of losing our spot near the front. After a couple of very poor local acts, Kilburn and the High Roads (later Ian Dury and the

Blockheads) warmed up the stoned audience. We'd never heard of them, and I couldn't figure out if his limp and stick were props or not – his drawly, cockney delivery was disturbingly pub-rock, but his Richard III-style physical performance was mesmerising, prowling the stage, almost intimidating the semi-comatose rabble into funky, groovy, get-off-your-ass action, but not quite . . .

This was followed by another band causing a stir in the music press, Dire Straits. I thought, *What an appropriate name, fucking boring* – this noodling guitar-based rock was everything I thought needed to be thrown away as the last dying dregs of rock and roll. It's a good job I wasn't an A&R executive, and it wouldn't be the last time I'd be very, very wrong about an artist's prospects, as you'll see later.

They were followed by Hawkwind (pretty good lineup, hey?) who proceeded to blow the place apart with their sci-fi rendition of 'Silver Machine', while the semi-naked goddess of the space ritual Stacia mysteriously gyrated and caused a certain amount of sexual arousal among the smashed and horny audience – she was a grown woman and *naked*? Nope, never seen that before . . . At that time, Hawkwind were pretty much dominated by electronic washes and wild swoop-and-bleep solos which totally thrilled Phil and me. I wasn't as keen on the Status Quo-like guitar wall of sound, but hey . . .

The moment we'd been waiting for had finally arrived. Roxy Music took the stage to great excitement as they opened with 'Re-Make/Re-Model'. This literally changed the direction of my life. I had never seen or heard anything remotely like it. Ferry hammering away at his Rhodes (or was it a Wurlitzer?) and singing like a science-fiction version of Bob Dylan, looking like an Elvis tribute act, Andy Mackay in his green lamé top, scooped to the waist with a stand-up collar, looking like something out of *Flash*

Gordon – platform boots and tight pants ... Phil Manzanera had a beard and long hair, but had the coolest glasses *ever* – those fly glasses – if I could find them on eBay I could die happy. Paul Thompson looked like an extra from *The Flintstones* with his one-armed leopard-skin top, and looked a little out of place, like he'd been told he couldn't dress in denims and was uncomfortable that his mates might see him. But hands down, no question, the star of the show was Eno: mysterious, dangerous, sexually ambivalent and alien in his famous lamé top, crowned with giant iridescent bird feathers. He even had silver Lurex gloves, which hypnotically fiddled with the joystick on his magnificent VCS 3 synthesiser – what was he doing? I could do that, I idly thought. Despite Brian Ferry's desperate attempts to 'be the front man', there was no way that anyone could upstage Eno – I'm pretty sure that this was what led to the split – Eno wins every time, and, despite his charisma and talent, Ferry looked a little isolated and perhaps frustrated.

Mere words cannot express how exciting this performance was, definitely in my top three favourite concerts ever. Stunned, we became loyal fans and literally queued to buy the first album, which was released the following week. That record was worn out within a month – everything about it, the music, the artwork – it was all perfect and was *ours* – we owned this new world of shiny extroversion, this was the embodiment of the culture we were looking for. Just one thing – we need more Eno, and less nostalgia, that would be perfect. More synths, more electronics, fewer guitars, more aliens, fewer earth creatures ...

Back at the festival, there was only one act left – Gary Glitter. As the lights went down, we saw a giant figure stagger on to stage in the gloom, towering on 8-inch platform boots in front of the two drummers, and the intro to 'Rock and Roll Part 2' started – then, before the lights went up, his entire costume lit up with red LEDs like some weird futuristic space soldier, and his tottering gyrations began. He clearly took up the Roxy performance as a challenge to his showmanship and, simply put, was not going to let them upstage him. Incredibly, his performance was even more popular with the students, who staggered to their feet to dance for the whole set. He appeared to be stratospherically chemically enhanced, with wide-eyed exhilaration veering towards the crazed. Pure physical and musical manifestation of cocaine-fuelled monolithic sound: inject this pure pop narcotic directly into my veins. No one could compete with it, not even stoned hippies were immune. That immense one-day festival remains the most memorable musical experience of my life.

Later, in November 1972, Roxy Music returned to Sheffield to play a little-known student venue called Ranmoor Hall, which only held around 500 standing. By this time, Phil and I were prepared for action. Phil's friend from school, James (name changed), was part of a bad-boy gang led by a sixth-former called Keifer who had recently been involved with the blowing up of the school toilets – he was expelled but unrepentant. Phil and James had been experimenting with LSD, encouraged by the writings in *Oz* magazine, which emboldened a drug-driven revolution, and Phil asked me if I'd be interested in trying acid for the first time. The stories of sitting in the local Wimpy Bar, James and Phil watching each other's faces crawling and shapeshifting into squirming green worms, didn't exactly fill me with encouragement, but I thought, *If I don't try it now, when?*

'Just try half a tab,' Phil said . . .

'Oh, all right,' I said, reluctantly accepting my fate, 'but why don't we wait until the Roxy gig?'

'Good idea,' Phil smirked, as though he knew something I didn't.

As we stumbled towards the gig in our favourite glam outfits – Phil in his *Macbeth* jacket, me in green fun-fur, hair and face covered in sharp, scratchy glitter, tottering on our 6-inch platform boots à la Sweet – we had already dropped the acid at Phil's house (a tiny piece of blotting paper with a peace symbol printed on), and I was nervously but excitedly waiting for the effect to kick in. We must have looked quite impressive in our ridiculous platform boots – I would have been 6 feet 4 inches, Phil nearly 6 feet 7 – so we were fairly confident we wouldn't get into trouble.

As we approached the venue set in leafy Ranmoor, I turned to Phil and said, 'Wow, the trees are looking really green this year.'

'It's coming on' he whispered.

'Oh, OK . . . is that one of the effects?'

'Yep – all the colours will look super vivid, but the best is yet to come . . .'

This sounded great so far, or ominous, or maybe confusing? OK, too late to turn back now anyway . . . As time started to dilate like some immersive sci-fi film, Phil appeared to be moving in slow motion, then flipping back to normal speed.

'This is fucked up,' I muttered aloud.

'This is great!' gabbled Phil excitedly.

I wasn't so sure. By this time we'd found a space in the hall, and the students were starting to resemble slightly mutated creatures as their features bent and slipped on their heads. I was a little scared – I had no idea where this was going . . . 'Just chill out, you'll be fine' – did I say that or was it Phil? Fucking hell, this isn't like dope cakes *at all*. Even the floor was gently swirling and popping with random colours. Heeeellllppppp . . .

In what felt like about three hours later (but was in fact fifteen minutes), the sensations started to become less frightening and surprisingly more familiar, as though every sense amplified to eleven was totally normal. As the fear subsided, I was starting to really enjoy it – it was as though I could see time as a visual representation, as all my senses synthesised. I remember thinking, *Maybe this is what they mean by mystic revelations*, and I started the longest sentence I've ever spoken as I feverishly tried to explain EVERYTHING IN THE UNIVERSE to Phil. He was also trying to talk, but I wouldn't stop – we both had the thousand-mile, wide-eyed stare as we watched each other's faces explode into beautiful patterns. 'I never want this to stop, I want to stay like this forever' – I'm not sure if I said this or thought it – nothing mattered anyway. The world by this time was not dissimilar to the front cover of *Disraeli Gears* by Cream. And then, Roxy took the stage – yowzah . . .

Once again, Phil and I couldn't rip our gaze away from the magnificent Lurex stylings of Eno and his VCS 3. The sounds were causing my vision to pulse and metamorphose, and if only I could paint (or take a photo of my thought-image), I would have created the greatest impressionistic, surrealistic masterpiece ever made. This one event transformed my appreciation of immersivity in art, sound and vision, forever and permanently reconfiguring my neuroplastic mind. I was a changed human, in touch with the *entire universe* . . .

The concert seemed to be over in a flash – to be honest, I had bigger things on my mind. 'When does this stop?' I pleaded to Phil, starting to consider that maybe I would never come down.

'Usually four or five hours, depending on how much and how strong.'

'How do we know?' I mused.

'We don't,' was the sobering response.

I looked at my watch – we'd taken the tab at about 6.30, and it was now eleven-ish. We pulled ourselves together just in time to board the bus back to Phil's.

Thank God, I thought, as we put the Roxy album on in the empty house at full blast, *the walls have stopped moving . . .*

We slept well that night, feverish dreams in the land of lamé, Lurex and glitter . . .

With our newfound insight into what the hell the hippies were on about, my enlightenment picked up speed. The breaking through of the doors of perception thanks to that little tab of acid had finally made sense of the psycho-dramatic brilliance of surrealism and particularly Salvador Dalí and Dadaism's Max Ernst (*The Bride Stripped Bare*), the mind-blowing graphic artwork of Marvel's Jack Kirby and his work on the Silver Surfer and in particular Galactus, the destroyer of worlds, the cartoons of Spike Jones, the work of Italian futurists Carra, Balla, Severini, Russolo, etc., and their obsession with abstractly depicting multi-framed movement and speed. We started voraciously to consume endless amounts of science fiction, with intermittent attempts to scale the impenetrable walls of weightier tomes like James Joyce's *Ulysses*, and the slightly more accessible but even weirder Samuel Beckett and Alfred Jarry's *Ubu Roi* (coincidentally, we would tour later with the band Pere Ubu – lead singer Crocus Behemoth). In music, suddenly Captain Beefheart and Wild Man Fischer made sense, and the king of them all, master sonic surrealist Frank Zappa became a major obsession. We played *Live at Fillmore East* literally dozens of times that year, an album full of stoner rudeness, often while drifting in and out of sleep. Something about the hallucinatory nature of Zappa's work really felt appropriate to dream lucidly to.

I continued to educate myself with regular visits to the only proper rock venue in town – the City Hall – where Phil and I saw The Goundhogs ('Out Demon Out . . .'), Yes, Emerson, Lake and Palmer, The Mahavishnu Orchestra, the magnificent King Crimson,

Faust – where I saw the lead singer Zappi Diermaier stride on to stage and proceed to attack a block of concrete with a pneumatic drill, while the keyboard player played pinball. Five minutes later, an impatient member of the audience shouted, 'Fookin' rubbish, geroff,' at which point Zappi leapt offstage to attack the much larger beer-monster and got smacked. End of concert.

Footnote, *faust* means fist in German – oh the irony ...

Nineteen seventy-two – sixteen with a psychedelic bullet, the year my mind exploded ...

1973–5: Meatwhistle and Musical Vomit

'Teaching the Ethics of Modern Art to a Stuffed Hare ...'

Halfway through year two of my A levels, I decided to give up on my studies – I couldn't see the point of continuing as I had no intention of going to university (despite my teachers urging me to apply to Oxbridge – as if ...), and my family had literally no money to support me. I scanned the local papers with the help of my parents, trying to find appropriate employment, to start my real life and to help out with family finances. Before I left King Teds, there was a cursory attempt at introducing me to a careers advisor, who set me some kind of psychometric test. The results, dryly delivered by the bored 'expert', recommended the job of TV cameraman would be suitable ... *Oh really*, I thought, *loads of those posts on offer in Sheffield*. When I mentioned this to the strange tweedy dude who smelled of tobacco and Old Spice, he replied, 'Ah, I see ... there is always Granada Studios in Manchester.'

'But I don't like Manchester,' I petulantly responded. 'Isn't there anything else I could do in Sheffield?'

His response was a mumbled equivalent to the current trope 'Computer says no.' Another pointless wasted few hours at the hands of my educational torturers.

Despite the common belief that Sheffield in the 1970s was already a post-industrial wasteland, full to the brim with ragamuffins wandering the streets in search of work, I've grown to realise that there was generally full-time work for anyone who wanted it at that time. In those days, part-time work was a rare thing, zero-hours contracts did not exist, and heaven forbid that you should be stigmatised by going on the dole. So it transpired that the very first job that I applied for, I got.

It was advertised in the *Sheffield Star* and the description was as close to hyperbole as you were likely to see on the Sheffield scene (apart from nightclub ads – '2 for 1 student lunches at the Hofbrauhaus – a pint and some chips', and a pitiful, emaciated stripper thrown in for good measure – oh the glamour). The job ad went something like this: 'Dynamic and intelligent young people needed to become Assistant Managers at the Co-op, £1000 per annum. 40 hours per week. Minimum qualifications 6 O levels. Could lead to managing your own branch after training.' Pretty good opportunity, I thought: £1000 p.a. was a good wage at that time for a sixteen-year-old. Thinking about it now, I'm pretty sure my dad didn't earn much more for a sixty-hour week. I applied, was asked to attend an interview and, God bless 'em, my parents took me to Blanchards clothing store on Infirmary Road to buy my first suit on the never-never.

The interviewer was full of evangelical enthusiasm for the potential of the job. 'We need fresh blood in the Co-op, and bright young lads like you are the future!' he gushed.

'What does the work entail?' I asked.

'Oh you know, learning the ropes, how to run a shop, accounts, stock control, etc.'

I had no idea what he was on about, but it sounded important and I was full of unjustified confidence. *Piece of piss*, I thought ...

The initial training took place in the enormous Victorian head branch of the Sheffield & Ecclesall Co-operative Society on Ecclesall Road, ten minutes' walk from my home. On the first day, I met Paul Bower, which was truly a turning point in my life. We got on like a house on fire immediately. We were both smart young things from poor working-class backgrounds, and we both lived for music. We connected over Roxy Music, T. Rex, David Bowie, glam rock in general and a whole slew of obscure outlier bands picked up from my experiences with Phil Oakey. He has since told me that when we first met, he regarded me as 'fearless', but I certainly didn't feel that way at the time.

After two weeks, we were sent to separate branches (much more of Paul later) – and mine was about two miles away at Gleadless Townend in the middle of a huge council housing estate, a part of Sheffield that I wasn't particularly familiar with. This was where I was to become a dynamic young executive, with real command and responsibilities. How wrong I was … in a classic case of mis-selling, the job consisted of taking deliveries, stacking shelves, cutting cheese (I was so bored I used to give old-age pensioners free cheese for a laugh), boning bacon (I nearly cut my finger off one day), etc., while the much-touted 'training' was outsourced to a low-wattage college once a month and was utterly pointless. Put simply, it was for dummies.

I started trying to spice up the boredom by stealing biscuits from the stockroom during break time (Jammie Dodgers usually), while the middle-aged female staff smoked and gossiped in the tiny staff-room. Each of the 'girls' would come into the room and immediately lay out a cigarette for each place around the Formica table. You can imagine the stench of this godforsaken, tiny room, and the women gabbled their way through their fifteen-minute chuffathon. There was one younger girl, Suzy, who I took a shine to in my boredom-driven lustful fantasies, but she was having none of it. God it was dull, dull, dull, but it gave me some financial independence for the first time in my life.

After about six months of this well-paid tedium, the branch manager asked to see me in his office. 'Martyn, I like the cut of your jib – I just wanted to let you know that if you play your cards right, you could have your own branch by the time you're thirty.'

You've got to be fucking joking, I thought. The next day I handed in my notice.

Fun fact: in a bizarre twist of fate, the person who took over from me as assistant manager at the Co-op was none other than Glenn Gregory, whom I'd not met at that time. Small world . . .

Around this time, Paul suggested that I might be interested in coming down to a kind of artsy youth club in the centre of Sheffield called Meatwhistle. (*Sounds rude*, I thought.) I'd had limited success with youth clubs before as I was quite shy. I tended to retreat into the background and let the brash, confident kids take over, sometimes even to the extent of being bullied – so my expectations were low. I was very surprised that everyone immediately welcomed me as an equal at Meatwhistle, and Paul already had a coterie of close friends, who kindly accepted me and encouraged my participation. They were just as weird as me. Everybody feels awkward and a little out of their depth at that age, but very few were as lucky as me to meet such an interesting bunch of misfits. Allow me to introduce the main characters of this timeless crew . . .

The first person I was introduced to was Ian Craig Marsh (or Ozzy as he was known at that time – nope, no idea either). He was a slight, nervous, quiet but very interesting character, with a haircut and chiselled features reminiscent of a young Adolf Hitler. The very first conversation we had was about computers, synthesisers and our mutual love of Roxy Music, and naturally we both clicked immediately. Even better, it transpired that he was in the process of building his own synthesiser from a kit bought in Maplin's electrical store (I think the brand was Dewtron). As I secretly really wanted to be Eno, I realised immediately that we would probably become friends for life. He also lived near my original home in Upperthorpe, and his family were Sheffield Wednesday supporters – job done.

Glenn Gregory was (and still is) Jack the Lad ... relentlessly cheery, cheeky, super smart and full of charismatic bonhomie. A straight-outta-Parson Cross playa. His smile and his energy were overwhelming at first, but he quickly put me at my ease – another Wednesdayite – and I was soon invited to his parents' house, or should I say into his parents' family. Howard and Pauline have always treated me like a son, and I am incredibly grateful for their endless love and support. In fact, since my parents died in the late nineties, I have jokingly referred to them as my 'surrogate parents', and I feel a strong connection to them both. They truly are legends, and they still turn up to every gig possible in their finest going-out clothes – I often joke that Howard looks younger than Glenn (he is in his late eighties and looks twenty years younger, as does Pauline). Glenn was also a huge Bowie/Roxy/glam fan, so we had a lot in common. He even admitted that he'd like to be the lead singer in a band one day. I wonder how that turned out ...

Ian Reddington was even cockier than Glenn (as if that were possible). Meatwhistle had just put on a play at the Crucible (*Marat/ Sade* I think), and Ian was the star of the show – big things were being predicted of his talent as an actor/performer, and this was to come to pass in a couple of years as he succeeded in his very first audition to join the most coveted drama school in the UK, the Royal Academy of Dramatic Art (RADA). His talent and personality reminded me of Malcolm McDowell in *A Clockwork Orange*, all teenage danger, arrogance and charisma, but with emotional and intellectual depth.

He and Glenn made a powerful supercouple, both sexually driven characters with no sense of fear and a great sense of humour. They were so confident in their own skin, and they frequently flirted with cross-dressing and fun transgressions. Put simply, the girls flocked to them. I was less confident (I wasn't sure I had the looks or brazenness to approach many girls, so I tended to wait until they approached me), but within months of hanging out, I realised I could appeal to some of the quieter girls there, and my confidence grew.

Mark Civico was Ian Marsh's best friend, stocky and good-looking, from Italian roots, quite muscular and macho in comparison to the glam-influenced androgyny of Glenn and Ian. He was very friendly, and was the star and prime mover of the proto-punk group Musical Vomit. Vomit was a band formed initially by Mark and Ian Marsh (based on a comment from a review of the band Suicide), which also featured Glenn and Ian Reddington. As Glenn said, 'it was like *A Clockwork Orange* crossed with Alice Cooper, with a generous dash of Sha Na Na'. There was fake vomit used on the stage, and dark theatrics inspired by Alice Cooper's stage show including decapitation and limbs being chopped off. Other members of the band included Jim Ashton, Nick Dawson, Mal Veale, another prime mover at Meatwhistle, and Glenn's and my closest friend at that time, Simon Hall. I was even asked to join at one point, but I felt a little lacking in confidence in the midst of their fearless Dadaist performance art capabilities. In any case, I was probably too 'musical'.

I love this description of Musical Vomit from the Sensoria Festival website about Sheffield's musical history: 'Theatrical subversive rock group. Formed from members of experimental youth theatre group Meatwhistle. Musically inept by their own admission, but contained future members of The Human League, Heaven 17, 2.3 and the cast of *EastEnders* [Ian Reddington, who also starred in *Coronation Street*], they were highly influential.'

Songs usually took the semi-satirical form of traditional blues or doo-wop numbers, and titles included 'I Was a Teenage Necrophiliac', 'Vomit Down the Toilet', 'Denim Mind' (a Status Quo piss-take), 'Self Abuse', a paean to onanism, 'Brassneck Boogie', the touching 'Laxative Lament' and the final song in the set, the rabble-rousing 'Part of That Gang' (inspired by Gary Glitter and The Glitter Band, before we all knew . . .). My first effort at writing a pop song was called 'Wimpy Bar Magnet', written with Paul Bower, but before we had a chance to rehearse (rehearse? ROFL), the band split, so it was mooted for use by Underpants (see below).

Most of the band members had stage names – Mark was Trigae Thugg (vocals), Ian Reddington was Romany Bowls (aural punishments), Glenn was Borstal Communications (three-string bass), Paul Bower was Rocky Coastlines (guitar), Mal Veale was Captain Zapp (sax and pharmaceuticals), Simon Hall had no stage name to my knowledge but played milk bottles, Nick Dawson was Cliff Face (originally banging upturned dustbins with chair legs, but later drums), Jim Ashton was Slick Fakeman (keyboards – good Lord, he actually could read music). When I was thinking about joining, I picked the honorary moniker Art Zero (later to be used as my nom de plume in the fanzine *Gunrubber*).

Mere words are insufficient to describe to horrified reaction of the audiences, most of whom were expecting some kind of spirited comedy malarky, but were compelled to witness a horrifying performance featuring near-total musical ineptitude, shock tactics and ill-advised theatricality all sickeningly coated in intolerable faux-aggression and arrogance. No one had ever witnessed anything so dangerously, unforgivably, insistently childish. It was funny for about a minute. Most costumes seemed to feature semi-nudity. Mark dressed a bit like Sean Connery in *Zardoz* (Google it, you'll be amused), and Reddington would wear as few clothes as possible (a skimpy loincloth would usually suffice). There is sketchy information about the band on the internet, but there is a Wikipedia page, which is pithily droll . . .

Musical Vomit mainly played at the Meatwhistle workshop at Holly Street, but during 1974 they also played shows at the Sheffield University Drama Studio and at Burngreave Church Hall, where they gave their only performance of a self-penned rock opera, *Vomit Lost in Space*, that featured early use of primitive synthesizers. Martyn Ware, a leading figure in The Human League and Heaven 17, was an occasional guest on stylophone but formed a more pop-orientated offshoot of Musical Vomit called Underpants.

Vomit went on to play at the Bath Arts Festival in 1974 and were described by Poly Styrene, who was in the audience, as 'the very first punk band'. They were booed by the crowd but remained on stage despite the bombardment of bottles and abuse, although they never played together again.

As is traditional, this Wikipedia entry is only partially correct – I never played with Musical Vomit, and *Vomit Lost in Space* happened before I met everyone, as did the Bath Arts Festival. Also, a new band Underpants emerged triumphantly, phoenix-like, from the ashes of Musical Vomit and featured many of the same protagonists. But I'm quite happy to be an inaccurate part of the Musical Vomit mythology as it somehow seems shabbily appropriate.

In my effort to emulate my hero Brian Eno, I had bought my first synthesiser, a Stylophone. It was a larger version called the

350s with more notes on the keyboard, various voices, a novel 'wah-wah' effect that was controlled by moving one's hand over a photosensor, and two styluses. This was publicised at the time by another dubious hero (well, not exactly hero) of my youth, the now discredited Rolf Harris. The remaining members of Vomit saw me as a person who just might make them feel a bit more like a proper band that might even one day perform outside the confines of Meatwhistle. However, we soon put paid to that idea by automatically self-undermining any chance of public success with the stupid (but we thought hilarious) name of Underpants.

It was the debut of my live performance career and also my first electronic performance for any kind of audience. My onstage state of mind was a mixture of sheer terror and adrenaline-fuelled power as my inane but weird warblings pumped through the PA. A little bit of me was convinced that I was the second coming of Brian Peter George St John le Baptiste de la Salle Eno, but alas, Underpants flickered into existence for only one fleeting performance and perished, like a mayfly whose sole function is to breed and die within twenty-four hours. As far as I know, there is no documented evidence of the gig, just strange Dadaist memories of Glenn performing on his three-string bass and singing lead vocals. I can't remember the (brief) setlist, but I believe there was a version of 'Sweet Jane' by Lou Reed in there somewhere (it only required the knowledge of literally three chords, so suited our limitations perfectly). But more interestingly, it debuted the first song that I ever wrote, the aforementioned 'Wimpy Bar Magnet', a paean to our love of the only late-night place teenagers could meet in the centre of Sheffield, the Wimpy Bar. The chorus went, 'Wimpy Bar Magnet, I can't let you go-oo-oo-oh' ... It wasn't a classic, even as a comedy song, so it remains to this day the only performance. Probably just as well.

Further bands were created for one-day-only performances as part of a curated series called 'Simon Scott's Kit Kat Club' (Simon Scott was our good friend Simon Hall's impresario alter ego, and the Kit Kat Club was an ironic reference to the club of the same name in 1930s Germany). These one-off events featured some truly bizarre badly-thought-out-but-hilarious ideas (very similar to Reeves and Mortimer's surrealist sketches – it must be a northern thing) such as Dick Velcro and the Astronettes (Glenn was Dick, natch), which featured some girl dancer/singers for the first time. Another was an avant-garde short theatre piece called 'Waiting for Hago' (Hago was Mr Hague, a shop mannequin dressed as John Christie, the famous serial killer creepily played by Richard Attenborough in the 1971 British crime drama *10 Rillington Place*). The set was a makeshift boxing ring with Mr Hague sat on a wooden chair in the centre. In the (thankfully short) 'happening', Adi (Adolphus) Newton taunted and eventually physically attacked the hapless dummy for fifteen minutes, dismembering it in an unforgettably disturbing and faux-psychotic display of random brutality. One of my personal favourite performances was 'Arthur Craven's Tent Band', another Adi creation, with yet another alter-ego Arthur Craven (who looked and dressed like Mr Hague come to life). Adi aka Arthur was manifested as an apparently disembodied head poking out of the top of a tent, with holes cut out for someone else's arms (I think Glenn's) to hold a saxophone and provide the fingering, while Adi blew into the mouthpiece with all his might. In a similar vein was Lister, Greg and Red (a faux folk-pop act). Adi was Lister (yet another character), Glenn was Greg and Ian Reddington was Red. The highlight of their brief but impactful act was a song entitled 'Sore and Red' (parental advisory). Naughty boys.

I even briefly joined a band that had proper musicians in it and occasionally *played for money*! They were called Orion, and I was drafted in for one rehearsal for a potential gig at the Crucible studio as Nick Dawson reckoned I had a half-decent voice (well, could sing in tune). I did the audition, and I sang 'Once Bitten Twice Shy' by Ian Hunter. It went OK, but as often happened in those days, the gig was cancelled, and a few days later, Orion was no more.

Some other detailed Dadaist concepts never evolved into reality at all ... May I present as Exhibit A, members of the jury, 'Ron Moody's Academy of the Occult'? If anyone has any ideas what this might have looked like, please contact me via the publishers of this book. Exhibit B – a drama sketch call 'Flat in Berlin', an angst-ridden piece embodying a hilariously dark and nihilistic duologue in the then-fashionable style of Harold Pinter. Finally, Exhibit C, an unimplemented idea for a didactic pamphlet entitled 'Teaching the Ethics of Modern Art to a Stuffed Hare'. All these ideas from a bunch of working-class, poorly educated dropout kids, none of whom went to tertiary education or art college. Just the purest joy of freedom of expression in a nurturing and excitingly fun environment. No wonder it changed the course of my life – I was ridiculously lucky.

In the summer of 1974, at the height of our exploding social scene, we decided that about twenty of us from Meatwhistle should have a day out in Blackpool. This became one enormous piss-up leading to much queasiness as we recklessly attempted to experience every ride at the Pleasure Beach, including the world-famous Grand National, which is a wooden rollercoaster. It was designed and constructed by Charles Paige in 1935 and is now one of only two surviving wooden Möbius Loop rollercoasters in the world. Look up the word 'rickety' and it probably mentions this ancient ride, which feels like it may fall apart at any moment. I stated my reservations to Glenn (I'm not a big fan of adrenaline rides, especially ancient wooden ones) but he blithely told me that if I was nervous, the best place to go was in the final carriage. Little did I know this was a wind-up. It was precisely the worst place to be positioned as the carriages whipped over the top at higher speed on the way down the precipitous track. Motherfucker.

Dadaism, surrealism, Warhol-esque performance – Meatwhistle was a breeding ground for our daft, northern, vital, irreverent experiments, which ultimately led me and many others to a life less ordinary, a million thought years away from the potential drudgery of life in a northern post-industrial wasteland. We all felt we had nothing to lose and everything to gain – boredom was our enemy. That feeling has pretty much stayed with me all my life, and still drives me on to create, to dare to dream but, most importantly, put those dreams into action without fear of failure.

Outside of Meatwhistle, my social diary was getting very busy – the Penthouse Club next to Castle Market in a very rough part of town was the very antithesis of glamour, but it was our own dive – 10p and 12p drinks (watered-down beer) on Mondays, and a playlist of mainly cool glam-rock classics – loads of Bowie, Lou Reed, Iggy Pop, The Amazing Alex Harvey Band, Mick Ronson, Gary Glitter, Sweet and the prince – Marc Bolan. It was heaven. Wednesday night was Crazy Daizy night – with a similar kind of vibe, but less scuzzy. The Daizy is, of course, famous for being the place where Phil and myself first saw Suzanne and Joanne (later to join the League). But in the early days, the girls were anything but cool in our eyes – they would always be the first on the dancefloor, always dressed head to foot in black pedal-pushers and black jumpers and, strangely, black gloves. They made an odd sight, often dancing out of time with the music and each other, doing the 'futurist sway' as regularly displayed by our old buddy Midge Ure on some of his videos. It was all the rage at the time (not for me, though – I hated following the crowd, still do). Weekends were for house parties and often we would hook up with our friends Stephen Mallinder (Mal), Richard Kirk and Chris Watson from Cabaret Voltaire, who we looked up to as true sonic revolutionaries and a damn good laugh. We would sometimes crash strangers' house parties, discovered on the pre-internet word-of-mouth grapevine, which often led to the classic 'student swap' – take the cheapest bottle of wine you could, then dig in to the best you could find at the party, even taking some away to tide you over until the next party. This was arsehole behaviour, I admit, but we were mavericks, and we learned from the masters, the Cabs. The rest of the week was mainly a tour of the local pubs – the Grapes on Trippett Lane, the Dog and Parrot, the Hallamshire, the Beehive, the Raven – all close to where I lived in Broomhall Flats, and very close to the University Students Union in Broomhall.

Then there were the clothes shops. We were all working in full-time employment, nine to five Monday to Friday, so for the first time had a little spare cash. Our favourite fashion shops were Sexy Rexy (seventies suits), Virgin Rags (hippie stuff and 30-inch-bottom loon pants), Harringtons in the Castle Market (Harrington jackets, suedehead-style Oxford bags with fourteen-button waist-band, of course, Doc Martens, etc.), Jonathan Silver (a bit more upmarket), but, as mentioned, Phil and my secret technique was to shop in the ladies department sales.

Other high jinks from that period included creating fake UFO photos in Endcliffe Park, which was also the scene of a drunken determination to join in with the current craze of streaking, purely on the basis of feeling what the sensation might be like. One of my best friends from school Clive Redfern and I drove in the twilight to the open grass space next to the main road, stripped off, ran across the park and back, realised we were cold, and rapidly reclad ourselves back at the car. I can confirm it was really fun. You should try it sometime. Maybe on a warmer night.

Glenn, Ian Reddington and I experimented with magic mushroom tea, and once again it involved Endcliffe Park, this time on Guy Fawkes Night. I reckoned that, as mushrooms heighten the senses, in particular colour intensity, a huge 25-foot bonfire might be a giggle. We were absolutely right – I've never, ever laughed so much before or since. The colours and the heat were incredible and, thanks to time dilation, I felt like I stood there laughing for half an hour, but it was probably five minutes.

More importantly, my musical influences were still becoming more diverse and interesting, as I moved away from being a pop junkie into more outsider territory. There was a blissful freedom of consumption: there was no distance for me between high and low culture. Mine was an egalitarian approach. Aided and abetted by all my friends, especially Phil, I felt like life was all about culture and creativity, and there seemed to be an endless amount to learn, absorb and enjoy. I still feel this way today.

Intermission:

Sheffield, Politics and Social Conscience

O K, so here comes the controversial section, well, controversial in today's world at least. If you have no interest in politics as a means of helping your fellow man, then you might want to skip it – but I still believe with your open-mindedness and help, we can help each other make the world a better place for all . . .

I am a proud socialist. I was brought up in the self-styled Socialist Republic of South Yorkshire, and my father was a devout trade unionist who regarded the idea of any working man or woman voting Tory as being an offence to humanity which would require committal to an insane asylum. We knew no one who wasn't part of 'our class' when I was young, and the very idea of betraying your roots in the pursuit of social mobility was repulsive. We had an overwhelming loyalty to our community, family and friends. We weren't against making a good life for ourselves, just that, in doing so, you had to look after the people around you, and particularly the working-class and underrepresented people in society. Our strength was our family, our extended family, our neighbours, our people – we had a sense that the security of mutual care and support was a life-enhancing thing. This still existed in large amounts in the UK, particularly in large urban environments, and I thought it always would, and that the Labour Party would always represent those interests.

Then came Thatcher ... it's hard to comprehend the loathing that honest working-class people had (and still have) for this manifestation of middle-class entitlement and evil. She was reviled as 'Margaret Thatcher Milk Snatcher' when she took away free milk from schools. Little did we know what horrors were to come. Her election triumph in 1979 was an enormous shock, indicating an almost incomprehensible shift in UK values. Suddenly, she and her government had tapped into the newly socially aspirant working classes, a significant proportion of whom seemed intent on 'pulling the ladder up behind them' as they sought the holy grail of middle-class financial comfort. *This shit is never gonna fly in Sheffield*, I thought, and largely speaking Sheffield and South Yorkshire stood firm against the divide-and-conquer tactics of the Tories. Then came the turning point – the miners' strike in 1984–5.

Entire communities were starved into submission by the government, supported by police and army, the most painful example of which was the Battle of Orgreave, a violent confrontation on 18 June 1984 between pickets and officers of the South Yorkshire Police (SYP) at a British Steel Corporation (BSC) coking plant at Orgreave, in Rotherham, near Sheffield. I was travelling up the M1 motorway to visit my beloved Hillsborough and see my team Sheffield Wednesday play, and south of Sheffield all the traffic had been stopped. As we strained to see what was happening in the distance we saw a wall of police and police cars blocking all three lanes. *What the fuck is going on? Is this a police state?* We were told by the police to turn off at the next exit and avoid the area – we learned later that they wanted no witnesses to the brutality that was to occur. The miners were physically beaten that night, and over time starved and conceptually smashed. The UK's decades-long descent into a kind of bland, very British tyranny had begun.

I've supported the Labour Party since I was old enough to join (except for a brief hiatus when I resigned due to Blair's support of the Iraq War), and during that time I've been an activist, delivering leaflets, knocking on doors, attending often long and sometimes boring meetings, all because I believe (and still believe) that socialism is the answer. I have seen the benefits first-hand, and those who praise and use the NHS without a second thought for the great socialist politicians who made it happen should be ashamed of themselves in my opinion. It's interesting that when a 'blind' survey asks the general population specific questions regarding policies that would help their fellow citizens, the usual outcome is that socialist policies ring true with the majority – yet somehow the notion, or maybe the term, has become discredited and polluted by decades of state propaganda. Go figure. I'm ashamed to say (but it's understandable) that England in particular has been veering towards a more isolationist, exceptionalist, 'little Englander' mentality as more people benefit from unearned profits on property prices. The prevalent underlying thought seems to be 'I'm all right Jack' and 'the Devil take the hindmost'. This is incredibly sad, in my view, and I will continue to fight for socialist ideals, for my fellow humans, both in the UK and across the world.

In December 1984 I was asked if I'd be interested in co-producing a miners' strike benefit record, initially to raise money for the families who were suffering, but later also for the family of David Wilkie, a taxi driver who was killed while driving two strike-breaking miners. Despite the political content, it made the Radio 1 playlist, and then a live appearance on *Top of the Pops*. Called the Council Collective, the ensemble who made the record included Paul Weller, Mick Talbot, Dee C. Lee, Jimmy Ruffin, Junior Giscombe, Dizzi Hites and musicians from Animal Nightlife and, of course, Heaven 17. The record was a success, raising profile and money for a just cause.

This success led to a more interesting idea, the formation of Red Wedge in 1985 to engage young people with Labour Party values in the middle of the Thatcher era. This collective featured Weller, Billy Bragg, The Communards, Junior Giscombe, Lorna Lee and Jerry Dammers, who all went on tour with Madness, The The, Elvis Costello, Gary Kemp, Sade and The Smiths, among many others, also performing at gigs. Glenn, Ian and I appeared at the House of Commons launch, and Glenn sang on the Red Wedge tour (Heaven 17 didn't perform live at the time). This and a tour of alternative comedians were the high-water marks of an interesting but flawed concept. Ultimately, the Labour leader Neil Kinnock failed at the next election and the idea was shelved.

In today's world of social media, I regularly get trolled for my views, often in the most horrific and disturbing ways, but I won't let that daunt me. If we as the human race are to survive, we need to address world problems in a holistic way – global warming is an existential threat and it's only going to get worse unless we act now. I support underrepresented and victimised peoples around the world. For example, I recently visited Palestine and saw with my own eyes the brutal treatment of innocent people in their own land. I'm also a fellow of the charity In Place of War, a global organisation that uses creativity in places of conflict as a tool for positive change. I've visited Brazil, Zimbabwe and Palestine with them, and I've witnessed amazing results, often from a position of apparent hopelessness.

Greed and the insatiable pursuit of insane amounts of money, combined with the neat abrogation of personal responsibility via the largely out-of-control international markets, all knitted together by the false and unjust tenets of neo-capitalist dogma, mean that the person in the street feels utterly powerless. What is the point of so-called democracy when there is no genuine alternative?

Politics to me isn't a theoretical exercise – it's a soulful, personal, moral duty. I feel compelled to help, for me it's a vocation. I have to thank my family and the good people of Sheffield for my upbringing – it's one of the friendliest and most community-oriented cities in England. Also, I don't subscribe to the fashionable and jaded trope that 'all politicians are the same'. If that's the case, then we may as well give in to anything that is foisted on us. People need to get off their knees and fight for what is right, not meekly accept an unfair world. Join me. We need more hands, and more hearts, and we all need to focus hard on helping each other to 'fight the power'.

1975–8: The Workshop

'Androids Don't Bleed . . .'

The workshop. A place of dreams, of wildness, of parties, of imaginary transgressive Warhol-style pretension. The genesis of a growing belief that somewhere in this confusing but exciting place, if we could find a way to weave creativity and fun in a more grown-up way, then who knows, maybe it could even eventually pay its own way (although we couldn't comprehend what on earth people might pay us to do).

The lease for the workshop in Devonshire Lane was signed, and Ian Marsh, Adi and myself had a room which was our first real studio, even though it only contained a couple of chairs and eventually a two-track reel-to-reel tape recorder, Ian's System 100 synth, my Korg 700S and Adi's EMS Synthi suitcase-model synth and a microphone. That was it. But it was enough for us to inhabit our own private imaginary world, away from reality, where we could develop our weird ideas out of the gaze of any possible criticism. We all need these spaces for intimate free thought – be they garages, sheds, basements – or else how would anyone come up with anything daring and new? The workshop symbolised our joint creative conceptual 'softplay' space where nothing was wrong or doubted, and all was accepted and built upon jointly. This methodology has become accepted in brainstorming techniques worldwide in advertising agencies, large corporations – even large scriptwriting teams – as the way to achieve the most interesting results.

Ian and I were both working long shifts as computer operators, and we loved spending every spare hour we could in the studio as a release from 'working for the man'. I don't think Adi ever had gainful employment, by the way – in his mind he was too ethereal a talent for such mundane activities – but I may be wrong, as he was always a man of mystery. We all enjoyed each other's company so much that creativity was a joy. I've never laughed so much in my life as those times. Glenn Gregory, Paul Bower, Mal Veale and several others had spaces there too, so new people and fresh stimuli were always entering the building.

And then there were the parties – my lord. Glenn Gregory has always been the most gregarious of creatures (excuse the pun), not that the rest of us – even me by then – were exactly shy, so as soon as we settled into the workshop, Glenn and Paul decided that we needed to host a housewarming party. This was a thinly veiled excuse to invite a disproportionate number of girls (most ex-Meat-whistle) in a horny attempt to corner the cool/dangerous end of the party scene. We also had lots of friends we could invite associated with school, work, Cabaret Voltaire, the Sheffield music scene, etc., so this was a great opportunity to trawl for potential ... ahem ... partners.

The workshop wasn't exactly designed for visitors as it only had two outside toilets, both of which were disgusting, but the Olympic-level, grungy, post-industrial chic made up for that. Or so we thought.

The day of the party arrived, and it was a roaring success – there was no one nearby to annoy noise-wise, and Ian Marsh had brought a boombox from home. There were around fifty to sixty guests, of which I would estimate 75 per cent were female – well done Glenn. I know for a fact that he had several sexual encounters that night, apparently in the back yard and, yes, even in the outside toilets (jesus, that must have been grim). Glenn's predilection in those days was for punky girls; in particular, he would prefer, in his words 'thin and wriggly', and there were many of those in attendance. I was less forward, so I just danced and drank the night away, waiting for girls to approach me (which rarely happened – probably not giving off the right vibes).

The following day, the aftermath was gruesome and the place was an insane mess. Apart from the obvious cans, bottles, half-rolled spliffs, Watney's Party Sevens, plastic cups, etc., there was a less savoury piece of evidence sitting shamelessly in the middle of the chaos. Skip the next paragraph if you are of a delicate disposition . . .

There was a large floor-standing vase, about two feet high, that had been used as an emergency toilet. It was full to the brim. Only number ones, thank God, but I was appalled – is this what the world had come to? I asked around to see who might have been responsible, and my suspicions were quickly confirmed. Bower was the main culprit. I made him carry the heavy, piss-filled receptacle down to the toilets outside, berating him at every step, just in case he spilled the contents. Then I sent him to the shop to get some Dettol and cloths, and made him scrub the floor. Dirty bastard.

Another very significant moment in our studio – John Peel had announced on his radio show that he had heard an advance copy of the new Bowie album *Low* (to be released on 14 January 1977), and that it was such an important piece of work that he was going to play the entire album non-stop as a world exclusive. There had been rumours in the press of the album being a major departure, enhanced by Robert Fripp and Eno – this collaboration could not have been more exciting for us futurists at the time. We settled into our studio, had a few drinks, and waited for the lugubrious Peel to enthusiastically introduce the album. John Peel was a man of few words, and generally even less hyperbole, but he could barely contain his admiration for the piece of work he was about to premiere. At that time, we were listening on AM radio, but somehow the tracks sounded even more otherworldly transmitted via this lo-fi medium. We were awestruck by the originality, daring and beauty of the album, and, together with *Diamond Dogs*, it is still my favourite Bowie album. The austere magic of recording in Berlin had certainly had a major impact on the work, and I don't think this kind of music could have been made anywhere else. It is an album of minimalist, crystalline brilliance from start to end – murky and atmospheric, elegant and alien. I've been lucky enough to become friends with Tony Visconti since then, and I always gush about this masterpiece. I can honestly say that it also gave us the confidence to step outside any expectations, and in future give an honest interpretation of the kind of music we felt driven to create.

A very important thread of my life was about to commence. I had met Karen during the famous 1976 heatwave year, and I spent most of that summer at Millhouses Lido hanging out with her and her friends. I fell for her immediately – she was a dancer (tick), a gymnastic specialist (tick), pretty and vivacious in a kind of Ann-Margret kind of way (double tick), and her dark brown hair and eyes were so enticing – I always preferred brunettes to blondes. We flirted and hung out together for a while, but then she had to go away to dance on a cruise liner around the Mediterranean. I was temporarily heartbroken, but I reckoned that maybe the timing was wrong and that we might hook up in the future. How right I was . . .

Meanwhile, our semi-secret messing about with imaginary groups idea was starting to look like it might reach the outside world. One of our beer-driven pub summits was at the Raven, where we discussed forming a kind of proto-supergroup with members of Paul Bower's band 2.3 and Cabaret Voltaire to perform at Psalter Lane Art College as support for a band called The Drones who were from Manchester. We fitted perfectly into the art college's idea of an interesting band – experimental and unique – however, the band didn't have a name yet. Glenn and I suggested The Studs as a sort of pastiche punk name, and we went into full fantasy mode. 'I'll be the singer,' said Glenn, 'and I'll call myself Voice De Kay.'

'VDK and the Studs! Sounds great,' I enthused, and the name was approved.

The band members were Glenn (lead vocals and three-string bass guitar), myself (dual stylus Stylophone and backing vocals), Adi Newton (EMS Synthi suitcase synth), Richard Kirk (distorted guitar, pedals and tape treatments), Chris Watson (I think VCS 3 but I'm not sure), Haydn Boyes Weston (drums). Paul Bower (electric guitar) chickened out days before as he feared there might be trouble from the local rugby-club beer monsters who were rumoured to be coming to the gig. He regrets his decision to this day. It still tickles me to tell people I was in a supergroup before I was in a group.

Meanwhile, the rehearsals were chaotic as we had no idea what we were going to do. We arbitrarily decided to have a bash at the *Doctor Who* theme tune, which was at least recognisable, and also something a bit more punky – 'Cock in My Pocket' by The Stooges (who we were enormous fans of), the lyrics, as the title suggests, accurately summing up many a teenage boy's rather unromantic attitudes to relationships . . .

We were obsessed with Iggy and The Stooges – they epitomised raw, youthful, sexual energy, and Iggy simply didn't seem to give a fuck (I found out later this was indeed the case when we toured

Europe with him with The Human League). Following the excitement of actually deciding which songs we would perform, I got some stickers printed up with the text 'VDK AND THE STUDS – NEW SINGLE – DOCTOR WHO – OUT NOW!' I went to every record shop in town, convinced them that the single was real, and got them to agree to let me leave stickers in their stores to create demand. I also put them on almost every lamp-post I could find in the city centre. Talk about wish-fulfilment fantasies . . .

Showtime arrived, and Haydn from 2.3 had made a special effort – he arrived in a boiler suit with 'CUT STUDENT GRANTS' embroidered on the back (no one was going to argue with him: he was 6 foot 4 inches of muscle) and he entered the building carrying a bucket of pigs' ears that he had taken from his day job as a butcher.

'What are they for?' I asked, bemused.

'To throw at the students,' he said, as though I must be mad for not understanding.

The soundcheck was utter chaos, but we had no worries, as this was more like a 'happening' than a gig. Despite the fact that the organisers were a little concerned, we were mob-handed and I don't think they felt able to pull the plug, so we got to play.

We started with an incoherent version of 'Doctor Who', which was just about recognisable, followed by a spirited but appallingly unmusical and hilarious version of 'Cock in My Pocket', with Glenn hamming it up to insane experimental bleeps and swoops from the Cabs' rig. This was all too much for the manager of the headline act, who walked on to stage mid-song and shouted above the anarchic din into Glenn's ear, 'The Drones want to come on now,' naively assuming that we would comply. The song, however, simply transmogrified into a full-on improvised wall-of-sound jam called 'The Drones Want to Come on Now'. There was no stopping us, but after about ten minutes we eventually ran out of steam and left the stage to a stunned silence, accompanied by the launching of the remaining pigs' ears into the now sparse audience. We were not popular with The Drones either, but I have to say, if possible, they were even worse. Mission accomplished, we agreed 'fuck them' and wandered off into the night . . .

My last attempt at a public outing for an imaginary group occurred at Sheffield Uni where we'd acquired a few good friends who were involved in the Entertainments Committee. They suggested we performed in any guise we wanted as part of a day's series of different arty installations and bands. The gauntlet was well and truly thrown down, and Ian, Adi and I said we'd put something together. All we needed was an identity, and my suggestion was designed to upset the student fraternity and embody a certain direct transgressive charm, while pastiching the daft names of various punk bands – we were going to outpunk punk. The name we settled on was The Dead Daughters, and this immediately found approval from my fellow band members, purely for its anti-commercial, satirical associations.

It says a lot about the quality of the music that must have been performed that night that I can't remember anything, except that it was largely electronic and highly experimental. All I can remember is that Ian Marsh was wearing a full *Rollerball* outfit, complete with American football shoulder pads and, for some reason, a Spider-Man mask. He'd even painted a crash helmet in the colours of Houston, the Energy City (we were a little obsessed with the film *Rollerball* and James Caan's portrayal of Jonathan E. at the time). And he was on roller skates. I can't remember what I wore, but I suspect it was a white boiler suit (later to be reprised when I played our first Human League gig at the Limit in Sheffield).

We were approaching lift-off creatively, if not yet for our careers . . .

1975–8: The Future

'Looking for the Black Haired Girls . . .'

As we developed our techniques and ambitions, and we finally had a fully functioning (if somewhat limited) studio room in the workshop in Devonshire Lane, we started to believe that we were on to something creatively unique. There were certainly no other bands in Sheffield that were similar in any way to our synthetic cottage industry, and I really don't think there were any that were on our, admittedly uncomfortable and untrodden, path. Maybe in Berlin or Düsseldorf or New York there were musicians as devil-may-care, but that was of no concern to us, and we were determined to be as unrestricted as possible in our creativity. We had no one to report back to, no one to please apart from ourselves.

I also was convinced that we had the tools for the job – only a couple of weeks previously I'd had yet another epiphanic moment, reading a two-page article in the *New Musical Express* interviewing Brian Eno (my hero . . . swoon) where he contentiously declared that rock and roll, and in particular guitar-based rock, was a dying artform, and that the future was about musicians seizing the means of electronic production. He claimed that all young, future-facing music makers needed was a synthesiser, a microphone (good old Shure SM58 – rock and roll!) and a two-track reel-to-reel tape recorder (he said a Revox, but they were pretty expensive). With this simple setup, you didn't even need a mixing desk, you simply recorded a musical part on to one channel of the stereo tape, then copied that across to the other side while adding another element, and so on. What we didn't appreciate at the time was that the quality declined with every 'bounce', so after five or at the most six bounces, the original recorded elements were thoroughly sonically fucked – and of course the end product was in mono.

We didn't let this deter us, and a lot of our early experiments were created using this technique. Ian bought a cheaper Sony reel-to-reel two-track with sound-on-sound capability (£400 as opposed to £900 for a Revox – Eno must have been loaded), but more importantly he'd already bought a Roland System 100 modular synthesiser on the never-never, and I had bought my first proper synthesiser, the Korg 700S, also on hire purchase. By this time, Ian and I saw ourselves as fine, upstanding members of society, with a regular full-time salary, and we were both happy to rack up some debt – in fact, we found it hard to believe that financial institutions would trust us to pay it back ...

I had bought my Korg at one of the few consumer music gear shops in Sheffield, the imaginatively named Musical Sounds on Abbeydale Road. Both the Korg and the Roland were mono-phonic, ideal for non-trained experimental musicians such as us. When I say 'experimental', I mean incapable of playing more than one note at a time without fucking up, but in our excited and demented minds we were suddenly capable of producing sounds that no other human being had ever considered possible, let alone heard.

Every second we had available we would spend in our home-made recording studio, which by this time was clad with purple fruit trays from the local greengrocer to help control sound reflections – a free alternative to expensive acoustic tiles. I even had my bedroom at home in our council flat clad in the same stuff as I thought it made the room feel like the TARDIS from *Doctor Who*. It mystified my mother, who thought it was an indication of my forthcoming descent into drug-addled hell – that combined with my sudden predilection for joss sticks. One day, Mum politely knocked on my bedroom door and timorously asked if the scent was a kind of drug (I think she got confused as someone probably told her that joss sticks were there to cover up the smell of dope). 'Nope, I just liked the smell,' I honestly admitted. I've always had a special relationship with scent throughout my life. It must have been something to do with having two older sisters and their perfume collections, which seemed a fantasy world away from the normal odours of our house – fag smoke, wax polish and, back in the days of the two-up two-down, stale piss.

The staff at Musical Sounds were typical failed-musician types, eager to enthuse about the butchering of 'Stairway to Heaven' on a multitude of cheap Gibson or Fender copies played through astoundingly loud amplifiers to the chagrin of those customers waiting their turn. Occasionally they'd whip out a half-decent acoustic guitar or, if they were feeling adventurous, a mandolin or even a lute. However, progress is progress, and these same dudes had obviously been railroaded into selling the new technology which *clearly* wasn't rock and roll (unless you could play 'Frankenstein' by the Edgar Winter Group, or 'Catherine Parr' by Rick Wakeman, or even the outro of 'Lucky Man' by Emerson, Lake and Palmer). These toys might eventually threaten their musical priesthood status, and were the subject of deep mistrust in the hair brigade, the kind of guys that usually hung out in the rock tavern the Wapentake in the city centre (or 'town' as we called it). We were definitely more interested than they were in the manuals for the synths that they showed us, which claimed that anyone could recreate a realistic 'Funky Frog' or 'Large Audience Applauding' or, amazingly, 'Alien Sounds from Outer Space'. This led to some sub-voce tutting from the staff and general disapproval when we freely admitted we couldn't really tell our arses from our elbows technique-wise, couldn't read music and, most importantly, that we couldn't care less what they thought ...

Suddenly we found ourselves in a position to create soundscapes that would transport us all into alternative worlds, and for now that was enough. But within weeks it was clear that we wanted to start sculpting the experimental sounds into a shape that at least resembled album tracks, maybe even singles with a conventional structure. This proved to be a significantly difficult thing to achieve – you know what they say, you don't know how much you don't know ... Armed with enthusiasm and a near-bulletproof belief that we were bravely exploring new and exciting frontiers, Ian and I nonetheless decided to form a band somewhat presumptuously entitled The Future. In for a penny, in for a pound.

We immediately enlisted our old friend, the aforementioned Adolphus 'Adi' Newton, a crazed avant-garde artist whose real name was Gary Coates. Adi was obsessed with Dada, surrealism and in particular Samuel Beckett and Alfred Jarry, which was quite unusual for a dropout working-class kid from the wrong side of the tracks in Sheffield. Here is an excerpt from the biography on his website – this should give you a feel for his character: 'One of the Founder members of The Future. Founder of ClockDVA & TAGC (The Anti Group). Artist, Painter, Sonic & Kinetic Engineer, Konstructor, Konnectionist, Pataphysical Pantheist, Meontological Mycologist & Existentialist Super-naturalist Traveller.'

Adi was unlike any other person I'd ever met. He was a true outsider with a whiff of the charismatic charlatan, who seemed to be constantly in debt, being chased by people he had promised to pay back. He was also fascinating in a way that I presume must have been similar to the artists that he absorbed and transmuted into his own inimitable character. He was based at the Devonshire Lane workshop and possessed the most coveted of devices, the EMS Synthi AKS, a gorgeous experimental synthesiser that came in the form of a mysterious James Bond–like suitcase. It couldn't really be played musically in any conventional sense, but that wasn't impor-tant: it looked the part. We asked Adi to join our new venture The Future, and we started to feverishly plan our Frankenstein's monster of an art group. Please don't get the impression that we were seek-ing world domination – this was simply a more grown-up version of the messing-about groups we were part of at Meatwhistle. Ah, that glorious period of our lives when all seems possible before hitting the brick wall of reality, full of unassailable optimism.

As we looked out over the wild electronic musical landscape, we were living inside our own experimental bubble, and we simply didn't care at all whether or not people understood or even liked what we did. We were doing this all for serious fun and art, the kind of art that we could talk endless bollocks about in our protracted pub sessions on West Street, usually with our mates from Cabaret Voltaire and Paul Bower's band 2.3. After a few weeks, it became clear that to realise our 'important' vision, we were being hobbled by our lack of recording technology.

One late evening, while listening to John Peel's show, Ian said, 'Why don't we buy a four-track machine? Think of the arrange-ments we could record.'

'That's all very well, but we're already up to our necks in debt,' I replied.

We both knew that Adi never had any money, so it was pointless getting him involved in the conversation. It would only end up with another creditor chasing him (and probably us) down the street ...

'I know – I've got it – do we know anyone we can record with? Who's got a four-track? Are there even any recording studios in Sheffield?' I asked.

We knew no one from that world, and what's more we couldn't afford a professional recording studio, even a cheap one. So, we decided to advertise in the local paper, the *Sheffield Star*, in the small ads. Amazingly, we received a reply from a retired ex-Radio Sheffield recording engineer called Ken Patten who said he had an Akai four-track recording facility in his home, and that he was experienced and, more to the point, dirt cheap.

We excitedly prepared and rehearsed our shtick, knocking our esoteric musique concrète ramblings into some kind of shape in demo form in anticipation of the big day. We had four pieces prepared – 'Blank Clocks', 'Looking for the Black Haired Girls', 'Cairo' and 'Pulse Lovers' – none of which remotely resembled a song, or indeed anything familiar at all (these are described in detail in the appendix). The lyrics for these pieces were largely created by our newly invented, quasi-random lyric generator with the cute acronym of CARLOS (Cyclic And Random Lyric Organisation System) – a tribute to our inspiration Wendy Carlos, who composed the music for *A Clockwork Orange*. This simple formula generated lyric sentences based on random parts of speech, e.g. 'The outrageous fox smarmily shot the dancer in a bag' or 'A fast blue car disguised my scented broth' – endlessly and meaninglessly regenerated until a gem emerged (which was rare). It was a kind of homage to William Burroughs and his cut-up technique, much admired in our circles, and used among others by David Bowie and Brian Eno. The results also reminded me of early Zappa or Captain Beefheart lyrics in a dark, sardonic but amusing way.

The day arrived, and we headed to what seemed to us quite a posh part of suburbia on the outskirts of Sheffield to meet Ken Patten, who we hoped was to be our George Martin. What confused and surprised us is that he didn't actually have a studio at all, and when we were shown the location of where we hoped the magic would happen, it was in fact a chintzy, flowery front room complete with voluminous armchairs, brocade curtains and deep-pile carpets. The open-plan design led to the kitchen at the end of the ground floor with a huge coffee table dominated by the aforementioned Akai four-track tape recorder, accompanied by a small mixing desk.

'Err – where shall we put our synths?' I asked, confused by the layout of the homely lounge.

'Oh, you can put them on the floor by the coffee table,' Ken replied confidently, as though this was the most normal situation for a recording studio.

'Would you lads like a cup of tea?' chipped in Mrs Patten.

'Ooh, yes please, Mrs Patten.'

Not really very similar to recording at 'Hansa by the Wall' in Berlin.

'Biscuits?'

This was luxury beyond compare in our world. We greedily polished off an entire cake stand full of cookies then we got down to work.

Our fully rehearsed efforts at laying down our ideas were going really well, accompanied by kindly but bemused comments from Ken. Then, at 6. p.m. sharp on the first day of our two-day session, Mrs Patten brought a halt to proceedings by declaring that Ken's supper was on the table, and that it wouldn't wait. The fact that we were mid-take of recording Adi's vocals on a song evoking the crazed serial killer Son of Sam stalking the Manhattan streets wasn't really important compared to the gastronomic delights of sausage, egg, chips and beans going cold on the family table, mere feet away. This was the most Sheffield thing ever.

We were buzzing with the progress that had been made, but it was a bit of a shock to be chucked out so abruptly without warning. Not in a rude way, you understand, it's just that in this household, it was obvious that mealtime would always take precedence over art. Ken may have had some medical condition that required sustenance at exact times – who knows? We quickly packed up, stashed our synths in the broom cupboard, thanked them both, and ordered a taxi to home base at West Street to celebrate with a couple of pints of Magnet, leaving the Pattens to their private domestic bliss.

The following day we completed the remaining recordings, including the instrumental 'Cairo', featuring Adi's portentous rendition of an excerpt from J. G. Ballard's *The Atrocity Exhibition*, 'This Venus of the dunes, virgin of the time-slopes, rose above Tallis into the meridian sky, diffused upon its crests into the wind', commendably performed but the meaning strangely mutated by Adi's thick Sheffield accent. But we loved the daftness of it all. The sessions finished in a flourish, recording the truly bonkers 'Pulse Lovers', featuring vocals by all three of us, the lyrics spat out by CARLOS, sometimes inspired, sometimes nonsensical.

Pulse ... pulse ... pulse ... pulse
Pulse lovers feel gently
Their bodies hold fear
His love feels fear
Their feelings hold anger
Their pulse feels stronger
Pulse bodies feel fear ...

... and so on ad nauseam. (Lots of fear, I notice now.)

It's easy to see how this semi-randomly generated bollocks can be interpreted in many ways, and gets the lyric writer out of jail creatively. I still sort of admire our devil-may-care attitude of the time, and we were well pleased with ourselves, but God knows what the average working men's club band would make of this approach – something like 'What the fuckin' 'ell are they on about?' But to be fair, their imaginations generally only used to stretch as far as 'Smoke on the Water' or 'All Right Now', maybe Zep and Maiden if they were feeling adventurous.

Within a few days, Ken had mixed the four-track recordings and laid them on to two-track tape, which he then delivered into our feverish hands at our studio. Nervously, we laced the tape on to our two-track machine and played the mixes. We were super chuffed and, for a brief moment, I think we all saw the potential for something we could be proud of. Armed with our magnum opus, we decided to contact major UK record companies for the first time. I went to the Central Library in Sheffield, got a list of addresses of the main fifteen, including all the big ones, and proceeded to design a flyer on the mainframe computer I was working on at Lucas Industries just off West Street in Sheffield. We'd been advised that sending tapes without explanation or context was pointless as they'd probably end up in the bin, so I sweet-talked one of the punch-card girls to help (in this Jurassic age, this was how data was input – literally punched holes in a card).

I wanted our presentation to be innovative and futuristic, so I went all-out and printed the flyers on our giant dot-matrix printer on continuous-feed computer paper (usually used for payroll or reports). I liked it because the result reminded me of all the great sci-fi series like *Space 1999*. Also, we were going to withhold the cassette tape itself hopefully to generate curiosity. The content of the flyer was something like this: 'Meet The Future ... The Future of music is here, now. The Future will be visiting London and this is your chance to meet the men behind

The Future and hear their creations', yadayadayada. You get the idea.

Amazingly, we received twelve responses from fifteen invitations, and all bookings were to be face-to-face meetings with real A&R dudes! This was unprecedented, as most Sheffield bands constantly moaned that 'them London twats never come up to Sheffield' (as though they would randomly turn up at St Philip's Working Men's Club or some scruffy rehearsal space). The truth is, we dared to try, and at least we'd have some fun out of it. What did we have to lose? Bear in mind we'd never yet visited London, let alone a record company. There were a few companies we felt a connection with as consumers, our favourites at the time being Virgin Records and Island Records, but EMI, Warners, Atlantic . . . these were big and scary multinational institutions.

We copied the masters of the songs on to 20 cassettes to take down with us, planning our meetings carefully re timings and tube journeys (this took days). Then, our first train trip to London was booked, and we'd arranged with Glenn Gregory (who had recently moved to London to seek his fame and fortune) to doss on his floor at his tiny basement flat in Oxford Gardens, Notting Hill. This was all impossibly glamorous for three working-class lads from Sheffield . . . it was really happening.

The day arrived, but the first five meetings didn't go exactly to plan. We'd rashly given Adi the responsibility of making the reel-to-reel copies. Adi had somehow managed to fuck up the recordings, so that he'd copied the stereo masters on to some existing four-track tapes that looked identical, presumably to save money. The net effect of this was that when we finally started to play the tapes at the first meeting, there was a mysterious song being played simultaneously – this turned out to be Elvis Presley performing 'In the Ghetto', backwards. The look of bemused incomprehension on the face of the first A&R executive was horrifying – I'm pretty certain he must have thought we were some kind of candid camera show. After embarrassed and profuse apologies, Adi whipped out the cassette backup, and we unconvincingly played back the cheap-sounding proper mix. This seemed to be equally confounding to our exasperated executive. For the remainder of the meetings, the response to our masterworks went like this:

- After about thirty seconds, they would ask to hear the next song.
- After twenty seconds of song 2, they would make a 'spin-it-on' gesture.
- Song 3 – usually ten secs or less.
- Song 4 – our planned 'big finish', but they usually didn't make it this far.
- The executive makes an excuse that he's late for another meeting, and before leaving utters one of two phrases . . .
  1) What is this?
  2) Please go away and write songs with structure and a melody.

Rude bastards, I thought, *but I suppose this is what the real world is like . . .*

Disheartened, we trudged to our final meeting of the day, at one of our favourite labels, Island (Roxy Music!). On the tube, we gave ourselves a pep talk, saying that we needed to stay positive in the face of the oncoming onslaught – more or less 'it's their loss' – but we all suspected we were whistling in the wind. When we arrived, the vibe was instantly different, less corporate and more relaxed with hot, hippie-looking receptionists and more open plan and welcoming. Cups of tea, biscuits, warmth, all really needed after a near-suicidal day of brutal reality. And our feet hurt . . .

A kindly, hippie-ish, middle-aged tanned guy welcomed us. 'Hi, my name's Chris, and yours?'

Chris, Chris? Could this be *the* Chris Blackwell who signed Traffic, King Crimson, Emerson, Lake and Palmer, Jethro Tull, Cat Stevens, Grace Jones, Free, Fairport Convention, John Martyn, Sparks, Nick Drake and Roxy Music? Holy shit.

He and his staff showed us great respect by treating us like established musicians whom they might one day want to sign, and this was before he'd even heard a note! We were guided around the offices and introduced to all the departments. We were amazed and confused.

Then the moment of truth – he was the only person in those meetings to carefully listen to the full length of all the songs and give them his full attention. His kindly demeanour turned serious for a moment, and I feared the worst . . .

'How many more songs do you have?'

We looked at each other, and I said, 'That's it.'

'Well . . . it's a great effort, but they definitely need some work. These are really quite experimental, which I like, but we also need to sell some records.' I appreciated his candour. 'Look, why don't you go away and finish writing an album's worth of songs, then come back and we'll talk some more?'

Then I plucked up the courage to ask, 'Do you have any feedback about how we can improve?' *Probably a mistake*, I thought as the words left my mouth, *but hey, we may never be here again.*

His response was similar to the others, but delivered much more sympathetically. 'Tunes . . . more sung melodies . . . more hooks.'

There were plenty of experimental groups out there who had record contracts but clearly he was more interested in selling records – bloody sell-out. But after consideration, we all knew he was right and he was trying to break it to us gently that we needed to keep the creativity and innovation, but add pop/rock songwriting intelligence (if we had the talent, of course). I will thank him until the day I die for his advice. It changed the course of my career.

Day two's meetings brought more of the same – it was pretty clear that the consensus was that we needed more melodies, more structure, more songs, more singing in the traditional sense. It appeared we'd missed the mark on pretty much every metric. There was, however, a general (sometimes grudging) appreciation of the level of innovation, and support and interest in our bulletproof belief that the future was electronic. For fuck's sake, even Faust and Wild Man Fischer got a record contract. So not all was lost.

When we returned to Sheffield to unpack the intense experiences and learnings, it became clear in private conversations with Ian that we needed to find a lead singer who could actually carry a tune (as opposed to a Jim Morrison-style mumblescape). This unfortunately meant that there would need to be a clean break with Adi. Although he was slightly built, we were concerned that he may lose it when told he was surplus to requirements, so we took the precaution of asking our mutual friend Mark Civico (a gentle but imposingly muscular presence) to be lurking in the background to intervene should it all kick off.

When we sat down to discuss and deliver the decision, he sat there shocked and very upset, almost in tears. We explained our reasoning, and to his eternal credit, he understood that he wasn't a good fit for what Ian and I wanted to do going forward. This made Ian and I feel (justifiably) very guilty and a little bit regretful, but the deed was done. While things became chilly for a short while, no punches were thrown and we have remained good friends to this day. Adi did insist, though, that he had equal rights to the name The Future, and, not wanting to get involved in any future legal stuff, we decided to retire the name and start a new group. After all, this was our MO during the Meatwhistle years: group identities would come and go like buses.

The main problem was this: who did we know who could replace Adi? I could sing but I've never wanted to be a frontman, so who? We didn't want to advertise and audition, we wanted someone we knew who we could trust. The ideal person would have been our mate Glenn Gregory, but he was in London and already in a group called 57 Men, later to become Wang Chung. (The name 57 Men was inspired by Glenn's inexplicable belief that he would die when he was fifty-seven. I'm glad to say that deadline has now passed.) Ergo, Glenn would have been the original singer of The Human League – I wonder how everything would have turned out but for this twist of fate?

Between us, we knew very few conventional musicians as our group of friends was largely personae non grata among that cliquey world, and to be honest we had no interest in it anyway. Just as we were resigned to the boring option of advertising in *Melody Maker*, I had an idea ...

'How about my mate Phil Oakey from school? He looks like a pop star, but I've never heard him sing.'

Phil had never been part of the Meatwhistle crew, except he and his girlfriend (soon to be wife) Anthea had joined us all briefly for a Meatwhistle outing to London Zoo. The general feeling was he was a good-looking oddball, and a little awkward socially. In other words, he didn't feel like 'one of us'. He was my best friend, though, and when I wasn't at the workshop/studio, I'd be hanging with him.

Ian whooped, 'Yeah, good idea, why not?' and I realised that Ian probably identified with his outsider, maverick nature and appearance.

'OK, let's invite him to the studio, and play him that new track – what's it called?'

'It doesn't have a title yet – do you mean the one inspired by Parliament/Funkadelic?'

'Yeah, that one,' I replied.

Phil visited the studio, we played him the track and suggested, as a form of audition, that he should take away a cassette and write some lyrics and a melody. We gave him a week. Within two days, he called to say he'd done it and he'd be ready to sing it for us.

There we were in the studio, excitedly awaiting Phil's audition. He started to sing in a low monotone . . .

Listen to the voice of Buddha, saying stop your sericulture . . .

'Whoa, stop the tape,' I interjected. 'Do you have the lyrics there? What the fuck does "sericulture" mean?'

I present this hilarious extract from Wikipedia: 'The lyrics (described as "bizarre" and "confused") combine a protest against silk farming with a vague mention of oriental religion – ("Listen to the voice of Buddha/saying stop your sericulture"). In Japan, the sound of bells are referred to as "the voice of Buddha".'

Ian's response was much more elegant and to the point: 'You've got the job.'

'Being Boiled', and soon The Human League, were born.

Intermission:

Why Electronic Music?

G ood question ... it seems to be a little bit of a given in the context of the rest of the book, so I think it's probably worth more detailed exploration and explanation. There are several interesting factors here: the space race; a proliferation of science-fiction programmes in film and on TV; the abject absence of any reasonable prospect of the old ways providing a means of escape from Sheffield's lovable but limiting possibilities; the growing presence of synthesisers in popular music; but most of all the sheer thrill of hearing sounds that evoked spaceships, aliens, other worlds – in a nutshell, the future.

There were very few purely electronic pieces of music that someone from my background was ever likely to come across. The earliest examples were from the 1956 film *Forbidden Planet*, featuring the most alien of pure electronic experimental soundtracks by the husband and wife team of Louis and Bebe Barron. Their role in the score was originally as an enhancement to a more traditional orchestral recording, but the film's producers decided that their work was so convincingly bizarre and alien that they got the exclusive gig for the whole movie. The score was not only futuristic, but largely didn't attempt to interpret the onscreen action, almost as though the music itself was a metaphor for mesmerising but incomprehensible elements, perfectly blending the worlds of sound effects and avant-garde musical composition. The net effect was one of mystery, discomfort and glorious, devil-take-the-hindmost daring. It is also worth noting that their work isn't really synthesised per se, it was created by using a variety of analogue techniques – they sculpted their soundscapes with custom-designed circuits, which they sampled and processed manually. The American Federation of Musicians at the time claimed that the composition couldn't be considered to be 'music', which led to the credit on the film's titles being changed to 'electronic tonalities'. They even forbade Louis and Bebe from joining the federation, and this in turn meant that they could not be considered for major industry awards, including the Oscars. Even more appalling, they never composed another soundtrack for a Hollywood movie.

This charismatic and mysterious sound world planted the seed that led to my eventual career in pop, and sometimes in abstract composition. Later I became dissatisfied with bands and pop groups that made no effort to use interesting sounds as part of their work, and the increased availability of synthesisers made this even more inexcusable in my eyes. Other early influences were the TV series *Space Patrol*, which was transmitted in the UK from 1963. It was similar in style to many of Gerry Anderson's Supermarionation TV programmes featuring puppets, but the atmosphere of the whole programme had an entirely more disturbing and alien tone, as embodied by the bizarre electronic soundtrack. Even stranger, the series was created and written by the prolific polymath artist Roberta Leigh, the first woman producer in Britain to have her own film company. Leigh herself composed the theme tune, and she used electronic equipment bought from a local store after asking an assistant for anything that made interesting noises. F. C. Judd was responsible for creating the electronic music for the series; he was an early British electronic experimenter, amateur radio expert, circuit designer, author and contributor to many wireless and electronics magazines from the 1950s to the 1990s. There is no doubting the obvious *Forbidden Planet* influence, and my seven-year-old mind exploded with excitement at the prospect of a weekly dose of off-planet activity. 'This is what the future will be like!' I convinced myself, and it seemed feasible for the year 2100. Each of the characters had its own leitmotiv, and my favourite (and scariest) was the robot who had a disturbing atonal rhythmic loop to accompany its gangly gait.

Then there was the *Sparky's Magic Piano* record (1947) – a children's story that was terrifying and thrilling in equal measure. If a piano can come to life, what else might happen? Great early use of a vocoder (a sound source filtered using a second sound source – often this would take the form of vocal formants, hence the 'talking' piano). The Beach Boys' 'Good Vibrations' featured the eerie Theremin sound, so in my eclectically open mind that also qualified as futuristic. My teenage years bore much more of this strange fruit – White Noise (featuring David Vorhaus and Delia Derbyshire from the BBC Radiophonic Workshop) was the natural successor to the Barrons, using similar bespoke tape manipulation and analogue electronic techniques to create otherworldly simulacra of pop/rock songs. Their masterpiece in my opinion is 'Love Without Sound', which David Vorhaus later explained was composed of over nine hundred tape edits! Progressive rock was also highly experimental in the late sixties and early seventies, and the futuristic and mysterious stylings of King Crimson, Van der Graaf Generator and, ultimately, Roxy Music and Eno's ultra-glam androgyny lit a fire in me that was inextinguishable.

The musical influences that had the most impact on me, however, were connected to my friendship with Phil Oakey. We both discovered and voraciously consumed everything that Walter/Wendy Carlos had produced after we were blown away by the soundtrack for *A Clockwork Orange* – her album *Switched-on Bach* still stands as a masterpiece of synthetic design and arrangement. Phil also introduced me to Isao Tomita and the gorgeous *Snowflakes Are Dancing*, a selection of whimsical classical reinterpretations, much more experimental than the rather formal approach of Carlos. One could say that viewing Western classics through the lens of Japanese perception created an intoxicating, if occasionally bizarre, concoction.

Eno deserves a chapter to himself, but I'll keep it brief. No Eno, no career for me. Apart from his work with Roxy Music, his solo albums were fantastically out there as pop artefacts, but really his legacy is his advocacy for the relatively new genre of ambient music – and his work with Robert Fripp on 1973's *(No Pussyfooting)* was a game-changer for me. I later shamelessly appropriated his more purely electronic series of albums, including *Music for Airports* and *Music for Films*, for the BEF albums *Music for Stowaways* and *Music for Listening To* (let's call them a 'homage').

A full list of my top 100 electronic music influences can be found in the appendix, but my main influences in the 1970s and early 1980s (which have remained with me as the bedrock of my taste since then) were Giorgio Moroder and black American dance music in general. Both of these fitted perfectly with my 'fuck you' attitude towards the trends of the time, as the major tastemakers backed away from disco and black music in general – in other words, the UK musically was becoming much 'whiter' and more appropriated by the European version of the dance scene. My view has always been that the progenitors of house music, for instance, originally from Detroit and Chicago, championed simplicity and organic non-machine-based musical arrangements. Listen to 'Love Can't Turn Around' by Farley 'Jackmaster' Funk – it's really technically sloppy (the piano timing is clearly not programmed and is very loose timing-wise) but it has soul and funk, and has gospel elements. This was rapidly largely rinsed out as soon as house music became 'whitened' throughout Europe and, before we knew it, we were all slaves to the quantised computer rhythm – and in my opinion we all were the losers from it.

Back to Giorgio Moroder, 'I Feel Love' still sounds like the future to me, and I defy anyone to argue that this masterpiece isn't the greatest electronic dance track of all time. Come at me, and I'll fight you. This and dozens of other productions, particularly with Donna Summer, still thrill me to this day – I love the *Once Upon a Time* Album, and 'Working the Midnight Shift', 'Now I Need You' and 'Queen for a Day' are pure electronic genius, all driven by Moroder's exceptional Moog Modular programming. There are too many significant influences to mention here, but special kudos goes to my good friend Daniel Miller/The Normal and his master-work 'Warm Leatherette' (interestingly another song inspired by futuristic fantasy literature, in this case J. G. Ballard's *Crash*, which was also an inspiration for an early Human League track I wrote), and also to the fabulous *No. 1 in Heaven* album by Sparks, which was produced by, you guessed it, Giorgio Moroder. The mysterious and psychologically disturbing song 'My Other Voice' showed that electronic dance music could also have intellectual depth.

Philip Glass was mentioned by David Bowie as one of the artists who signposted the future, and his albums *Glassworks* and *Koyaanisqatsi* made me determined to maintain a thread of experimentation in whatever future direction I chose. To this day, I believe I should be doing film soundtracks, but for whatever reasons the opportunity has never arrived. Ah well, there's still time ...

Regarding the underestimated influence of electronic music that emerged from the American black dance scene, I must recognise the pioneering work of Stevie Wonder, Quincy Jones, Michael

Jackson and Cameo in particular. Stevie's work with the duo of Bob Margouleff and Malcolm Cecil (who originated from their own unique band Tonto's Expanding Head Band) was ground-breaking – they worked together for four years from 1972 and were responsible for over 240 collaborations in total, including on the albums *Music of My Mind* (1972), *Talking Book* (1972), *Innervisions* (1973) and *Fulfillingness' First Finale* (1974). Stevie then went on to produce his own *Songs in the Key of Life* (1976). This put the final nail in the coffin of the argument that electronic music had no soul, or even no place in emotional extemporisation. He used Margouleff and Cecil's expertise as a broad-minded leavening agent in his work, which moved the perception of his songs into a more futuristic frame – listen to 'Have a Talk with God', complete relaxed brilliance. Later with Heaven 17, this is the kind of stylish hybridisation we aspired to, and sometimes, occasionally, we got close.

Kate Bush, Scritti Politti, William Onyeabor, Ryuichi Sakamoto, Prince, George Clinton, Laurie Anderson, Japan, Soft Cell, Yello, Cabaret Voltaire, Space, Sylvester, Scott Walker, even Weather Report, etc. – so, so many artists to whom I feel grateful for having an impact on my creativity. I will never stop keeping a lookout for new artists who stimulate me ...

Electronic music is my life, and I'm proud to say I've devoted my career to championing this noble cause. Although electronically generated music has now become ubiquitous, I still get a thrill when new artists create sound collages and more melodic works using analogue or virtual instruments. Creating brand new expressions of emotion and feeling will always be possible in the world of electronic music.

1977–9: The Birth of The Human League

'Your time is due big fun come soon ...'

Picture the scene: Ian Marsh and I were ensconced in his new abode, a council flat he shared with our old friend from Meatwhistle, Okko (David Oxley). On the kitchen table was our main creative synthesiser, the Roland System 100, the sequencer's twinkling red lights flashing away while issuing forth a pretty funky white-noise-based rhythm patch. Oh, how many hours of experimentation and hypnotic mind melding took place in that tiny room ... The demise of The Future obviously meant that we needed a name for our brand-new enterprise.

As we idly considered various unconvincing options, Okko suggested we have a look at his geeky new strategy board game called StarForce. At first glance, it looked futuristically exciting, but in reality the game itself was dull beyond belief. An examination of the dense and unpromising rulebook, however, revealed a series of 'scenarios' which could be played. If I remember rightly Scenario 6 was entitled 'The Rise of the Pan-Sentient Hegemony and The Human League'. I immediately recognised that artistically we were on a mission to prove that electronic music could be as emotionally engaging as any other form, and the word 'human' combined with 'league' definitely chimed. Even better,

The Human League sounded like a superhero team from Marvel or DC comics.

After a few days of indecision and after sharing the idea with a few trusted friends, we decided to nail our colours to the mast. The Human League was born, shiny and new, fresh from the ether. Now the real work could get started . . .

'Being Boiled' turned out surprisingly well, considering it was our first serious attempt at writing a pop song. After signing the recording to Bob Last's Fast Records, it was released in spring of 1978, and it immediately started to draw attention in the music press and on John Peel's extremely influential radio show. It was single of the week in *NME* and *Melody Maker*. John Lydon (later to become a friend and collaborator) was guest hosting the *NME* singles column, and he denounced our efforts with a simple two-word critique: 'Fucking hippies.' Obviously he'd not really listened to the song, and I presume his forensic analysis was based on the use of the word 'Buddha' in the opening line. Fortunately, it had little effect as the general consensus was that this single was adventurously curious, and at best revolutionary. Yes, the same single that was recorded in mono, bouncing from track to track, adding elements as they occurred to us, on a reel of tape that cost £3.50, copied on to a cassette costing £1.50, was causing a stir as a potential future direction for UK popular music. Fucking excellent.

Also, I had co-designed the cover in Letraset with Bob Last (it took me bloody ages), and we were both very pleased with it as a piece of cover art. The lyrics were also printed on the back of the sleeve, as we always felt they were at least as important as the music.

John Peel played 'Being Boiled' at least once a week on his show – this was very good news indeed as he was Radio 1's primary tastemaker for new music, and before long the record had sold five thousand copies by word of mouth alone.

One day, Bob excitedly called us explaining that he'd been inundated with enquiries from major record companies about our availability. We thought he was winding us up at first, but when he told us the companies involved we sat up and took notice. Virgin and Island were the two labels who had originally promised to keep tabs on our progress, and now Virgin had opened initial discussions with Bob in an effort to steal a march on competitors. We were hot property, and we could barely believe it – all those local bands who had been desperately straining to be signed up by record labels were going to hate us for the relative ease with which three 'non-musicians' were going to be thrust into the limelight.

Among the other labels sniffing around were the newly formed Fiction Records and EMI Records, one of the traditional giants of the UK music business. Chris Parry, the owner of Fiction, invited us to a meeting. When we arrived there was just an empty office with no furniture, but with a huge stereo system. 'Let's all sit on the floor,' Chris suggested

'Um, OK,' I replied, looking quizzically at Phil and Ian. We would never have done this in the workshop in Sheffield as we would probably have caught something.

Chris proceeded to outline his world-domination plans for Fiction, and gave us a sneak preview of his first signing, a jangly indie pop band called The Cure. 'This is called "Killing an Arab",' he jauntily exclaimed, and I'm pretty sure we were all thinking the same thing – what a wanker, and what the fuck was this depressing garbage. But being the nice, friendly Sheffield lads we were, we politely listened and, as soon as we could, we made our excuses and left.

On the other hand, the EMI meeting was in their luxurious but bland London offices. It was clear from the outset that this wasn't a good fit for us. There was no vibe, just money, and we all felt it would have been a miserable experience to sign with them.

A couple of weeks passed and Island's interest had cooled, but thanks to Bob's negotiating skills, Virgin had come up with a firm offer, which he presented to us.

'Six-album deal, first album thirty-thousand-pound advance, fifteen thousand recording budget, with five thousand advance escalations for every album. If we do well, they'll want to renegotiate with better terms, trust me.'

We were so giddy at the prospect of signing for our favourite label that we'd have signed there and then. But then came the stinger.

'But they also want you to sign a publishing deal with Virgin,' Bob cautiously added.

What's wrong with that? we thought. *More dosh.* But we were very naive, and put all our trust in Bob and our lawyer Brian Carr's hands. The terms for the publishing deal were OK, but length of the deal was 'in perpetuity' – in other words, forever. We are still bound by these terms in 2021. Stooopid, but quite commonplace in 1978.

Bob continued, 'I suggest that I should be co-signatory to the Human League bank account, and that you pay yourselves a wage of £30 per week each.'

That was half of what Ian and I were earning as computer operators! It was going to be a hard sell to my mum and dad, but I knew that I had to take this opportunity. The sweetener was Bob suggesting that we set up our own proper recording studio, and that we could spend part of our recording budget on new equipment. Shit, this was the dream! The terms were agreed and three weeks later we were invited to a signing ceremony in London on board Richard Branson's luxurious houseboat in Little Venice. The deed was done. We were now bona fide recording artists, and we were full of bulletproof ambition and optimism. It all seemed so easy and straightforward that we could barely believe our luck.

In the coming years, we would see Branson regularly, especially at the Earl of Lonsdale pub on Portobello Road on a Friday evening, where he would cheekily ask his A&R co-ordinator Gemma Caulfield to pay for drinks on his behalf. Our first ever Human League gig was at Psalter Lane Art College in Sheffield (scene of the one and only VDK and the Studs gig). To this day, I can't imagine anything more boring than watching the three of us on stage – Ian and I totally static, rigid with fear, with no performance smarts whatsoever, and Phil, a hospital porter who had never performed at all, ever, in his life. We didn't even have proper stands for our synths, so we had to borrow Formica tables from the refectory, and, in an effort to look arty, we bought a few old TVs from junk shops and had them showing static in the background, as a sort of nod to what we thought Andy Warhol (or our mates Cabaret Voltaire) might have done. The performance, complete with the first appearance of the two-track tape machine onstage, proudly demonstrating that much of what the audience was hearing was pre-recorded by necessity, remains in my memory as the most nervous I had ever been in my life. When I left the stage, my mouth was full of blood due to unconsciously biting the inside of my cheek. But the performance seemed to go OK, and Phil had remembered all his lines – hell, considering that Ian and I even got all the manual rewiring and patch changes on the synths right, it was close to a miracle.

On 25 July 1978, we played the Limit Club in Sheffield. The Limit was Sheffield's equivalent to Eric's in Liverpool – it was the best place to see new bands on the independent tour circuit. They would also stage regular local band nights, which would usually be sold out. We were excited to be on a bill with some Sheffield bands who were starting to make names for themselves. This was the first gig for Def Leppard, whose music we regarded to be the essence of old-fashioned, no-hoper, Cro-Magnon heavy rock. It just goes to show how poor our judgement was, as they went on to sell 70 million records.

For some reason, that night we decided we wanted to make a strong impression so Ian and I performed in white boiler suits, and the three of us called ourselves A, B and C. The reason for this is lost in the mists of time, but I think it was influenced by the excellent performance art pop of Devo's live shows (they also wore boiler suits, but theirs were made of paper and were yellow).

These were early days for the Human League, so to be asked to record a session for the John Peel show was an honour and a major step forward in credibility. Our visit to London in August that year saw us at the BBC Maida Vale studios, home of huge orchestral recording spaces, but also the legendary BBC Radiophonic Workshop, which we were given a guided tour of. This was the equivalent of visiting NASA for space geeks, and our awestruck behaviour must have been something to behold as we witnessed in operation dozens of mythological synths that we thought we'd never get to be near. *Doctor Who*, for fuck's sake! Racks and racks of massively expensive modular synths, rare experimental synths, one-off homemade contraptions – it was Aladdin's cave, the likes of which I would not see again until I produced Erasure at Vince Clarke's studio in Chertsey in the early 1990s.

When we were ushered into the studio, we had to quickly set up our synths (no tech assistants for us), and then we were introduced to producer Bob Sargeant, who had recently had chart hits with The Beat. He was pleasant enough, but it quickly became apparent that he had little interest in the session, and proceeded to spend 90 per cent of the time on his phone, barely speaking to us. It was left to us to buddy up with the engineer and record the four-track session, virtually as live with few overdubs, just as if we were a normal rock band – and due to Musicians' Union rules, we only had three hours to do it in. Considering our creative process (and the fact we were technically *very* basic performance musicians) meant we usually took days per track to record a song in our own studio – but these were the BBC rules, and the end result was just about acceptable.

During this period, we were performing all the time, refining our act, and gaining a reputation as a curious but crowd-pleasing act. Phil and I had metamorphosed into much more animated performers, and Ian maintained his mysterious, insouciant charm as the enigma of the group – a kind of mix between Eno and Ron Mael of Sparks. Gigs in London and Liverpool followed, but the biggest break was being invited as a support on to a major national tour with Siouxsie and the Banshees in September 1978. We were nervous at first as we realised that their audience consisted of not just gothic indie types, but in the wake of punk had also attracted a huge skinhead following. What the fuck were they going to make of us? Would we get bottled off stage, or even attacked? (Yes, this sort of thing actually happened back then.) The venues were much larger than anything we'd encountered before, so we were hoping this would really help grow our audience. One thing we didn't really understand at the time was that Virgin had to pay the tour promoters to let us do the support slot – I think it was in the region of £20,000 – and that this would be added to our unre-couped debt (in other words, we were ultimately paying). To be fair, this was standard procedure at the time, but this meant that we were unknowingly racking up the debt which would cause issues later, as you will witness . . .

The punk audiences reacted to us in various ways ranging from hostility ('Geroff, weer's Siouxsie? GERRRROOOOOFFFF!)

and indifference to curiosity, genuine interest and increasing appreciation as word of our weirdness spread. There was one particular gig at the less-than-luxurious Hanley Hall near Stoke-on-Trent – a big old standing-room ballroom, about 1500 capacity, that had a reputation for being, shall we say, challenging from an audience perspective. We set up as usual, various screens with imagery controlled by Adrian Wright (who by this time had joined the band as a permanent full-time member to look after the visuals), and as the strains of 'Circus of Death' cinematically introduced us to the audience, a hail of spit was projected from the skinheads in the front rows. As Phil and I were stationed at the front of the stage, we were the main recipients of the expectorating. Ian had prepared for this by building a stand with a Perspex shield, but we were unprotected and therefore covered in gob. The repulsive hailstorm of spittle reached a climax during our sensitive and tear-jerking duet of 'You've Lost That Loving Feeling', but there was a certain 'fuck-you' pride in not letting this affect our performance, or even acknowledge it, and the majority of the audience seemed to be won over by our stoic professionalism.

As we finished our set and left the stage, a concerned Bob said to me, 'Are you all right?'

Full of adrenaline, I said, 'Yep, I think so . . .' It was then that I looked in the mirror in the dressing room – my face and clothing were spattered with blood. 'What the fuck is this?' I was horrified.

Bob told me he was watching one particular skinhead from the wings, who was smashing the bridge of his nose on to the edge of the stage, swallowing the resultant blood, and spitting it at me, which had covered me from head to foot, together with my keyboards. How I never contracted hepatitis during this tour is still a mystery. By the way, a big shout out for Budgie, Siouxsie and Steve for their generous friendship and encouragement – they are very caring and nurturing people. Thanks for making our touring experience so memorable beyond a gory drenching.

Around the same period we performed several gigs at the Factory in Manchester (Tony Wilson's venue), which were notable for the mainly male audience's preference for wearing trench coats and RayBan glasses, while showing as little reaction as possible. The general vibe was 'impress me', and I think they all imagined themselves as stars in some kind of avant-garde Berlin film. Maybe it was just a Mancunian thing, but it didn't sit well with me – it all seemed very pretentious and 'look at me'. The opposite was true at Eric's in Liverpool, where we always had a good, authentic, enthusiastic audience reaction. I know it's a bit of a cliché but Liverpudlians wear their hearts on their sleeves and are enormous music fans for obvious reasons. (Side note – give The Beatles a fucking rest will you? It's fifty years ago. *wink*) Our early gigs there were really exciting, enhanced by the nature of the black-painted, beer-and-piss smelling, sticky-carpeted, low-roofed glory of the subterranean room. The roof was so low that if (like many of the bands at that time) we'd pogoed to any of our songs, we would have knocked ourselves out. I've been told since that time that several bands were influenced by our early performances, including Orchestral Manoeuvres in the Dark, who later went on to include a backing tape machine onstage as a named member of their band.

But our really big break was our first major headline show in London at the Electric Ballroom in Camden on 28 October 1978 – coincidentally I now live five minutes from there in Primrose Hill. In those days, London was the place to be to influence the music press, and Camden seemed like the epicentre of punky cool. Our show was rammed and went down a storm, and more to the point received great reviews and gave us growing confidence that we were heading in the right direction. In the feeding frenzy, promoters were also now sitting up and taking notice, and the gig offers started to flood in – *My God*, I thought, *we might even start making some money instead of endlessly racking up debt with Virgin.*

We were now a fixture of the indie rock circuit, which led to some very odd one-off gigs. In February 1979, we were scheduled to play a gig at Notre Dame Hall in London with the Transmitters and a fellow Fast Product band, The Scars. We arrived ready for duty but never performed as apparently we withdrew for 'moral reasons'. I have absolutely no memory of what they could have been, although it may have been some kind of dispute over billing, or that the Transmitters were arseholes – that rings a bell but who knows?

Two gigs in that period were notable for very important reasons. Firstly, we were booked into a tight, atmospheric 'pub-rock' venue called the Nashville Rooms in London for two nights. On the fateful evening of 15 February 1979, we were sitting in the scuzzy dressing room (which had no door and was covered floor to ceiling with graffiti), half an hour before stage time, when Bob Last excitedly entered the room. 'There's somebody here to see you,' he mischievously twinkled.

'Oh for fuck's sake, you know we don't want visitors before we go on,' I grumped nervously.

Before he could reply, David Bowie casually entered the room unannounced, smoking a cigarette, followed by his entourage of about six people.

Words cannot express our shock – it was as if God himself had appeared before us. Why was Bowie in this shithole? To see us? Oh my God, the pressure, the expectations ... He was really friendly and surprisingly down to earth, and someone even took a photo of me talking to him, mainly because I'm certain no one would have believed it otherwise. Our idol told us he'd heard exciting things about us, wished us luck and joined the packed throng out front. We then had ten minutes to prepare for what was now the most important gig of our lives so far. God help us ...

Fortunately the gig was rapturously received, and the following week Bowie was quoted in the press as saying that The Human League were 'the future of music'. David Bowie, our guiding light for all things musically innovative and future-facing, the compass that we used *every day* to show us the way we should conduct our creative practice, not only liked us, but thought we were 'the future'. Our lives were complete. In our minds, we had definitely arrived. It may even have gone to our heads a little ...

As our reputation grew, later in the year we performed to sell-out audiences on two nights at the world-famous Marquee Club in Soho. No air conditioning, sweaty, humid – conditions guaranteed to cause problems for delicate electrical equipment – and this meant enormous oscillator-drifting tuning problems for my poor Korg 700S, which sounded like it was dying. We stormed through the edgily raucous and somewhat tuneless performance, however, and people adored it. We were at the peak of our electro-punk phase – loud, distorted and strange. Recently, a long-time fan told me that there were a couple of unexpected people who rocked up to the second night, and the overzealous bouncers refused them entry as the venue was packed to way beyond fire capacity. The disgruntled visitors (who wandered off into the Soho night looking for fun) were David Bowie and Iggy Pop. Fucking bouncers.

The second notable gig from spring 1979 was a bill featuring a bunch of incongruent acts, which we were headlining: The Mekons and Gang of Four were fellow Fast Records acts, but there were also two punk acts, The Good Missionaries (previously ATV) and Stiff Little Fingers. As you can imagine, The Human League were the odd band out of this lot (to be honest, we were always the odd band out), and the audience was predominantly punk. We did OK, but I definitely sensed some form of resentment from the other bands, probably because we threatened their more traditional rock stylings. I've since become good friends with Gang of Four's lead singer Jon King, but they were quite sniffy at the time. We never let this kind of behaviour put us off – we maintained a dignified cheeriness and friendliness, which often didn't sit well with the more 'edgy', po-faced rockers. But inside, we knew we would have the last laugh.

We were doing a lot of travelling during this period, and as we were trying to save money we would often travel with the equipment in the back of a transit van. One day, as we were returning to London, our driver was chatting to us and decided to throw his chewing gum out of the window. Unfortunately we were travelling in the outside lane at 75 mph at the time, and as he launched the gum, he lost control of the steering wheel, over-corrected, and hit the central reservation. The van careered 180 degrees, coming to rest in the centre lane, with suitcases, equipment and synthesisers sprawled across the fast lane. Miraculously, no one was seriously hurt, and no articulated lorries crushed us, but we were thoroughly shook up. We decided that, whatever the cost, we had to be securely seat-belted and in proper seats from now on. Dying young was a bit too rock and roll for us.

Two weeks later, I was travelling back to London from Sheffield with Glenn in his girlfriend Karen's car when we had a similar accident just 200 yards from the scene of the previous near-death experience.

I've never had a crash since, but I'm always a nervous passenger on the M1. Fun fact: I still don't drive . . . never saw the point. I've always lived in city centres, so the costs always outweighed the benefits. I'm glad to see that more and more people are feeling the same.

The tours with Siouxsie and the Banshees were incredible – sold out every night, brilliant musicianship and crazy audiences. But nothing in my touring life could compare with the opportunity to travel around Europe supporting Iggy Pop. When Bob told us, we could barely contain our excitement. This was it, the apogee of our live experiences. Apart from all of his records being high on our playlists, he'd only recently finished promoting *Lust for Life* and *The Idiot*, both of which were tremendous pieces of work – brooding, menacing, psychotic, intelligent genius. The tour was to promote Iggy's new album *Soldier*, which wasn't in the same league as those two albums, but the opportunity to see the emperor of real punk do his stuff night after night was too good to miss.

All those stories about him leaping into the audience, cutting his chest with broken bottles, being the 'real wild child' – there wasn't a single punk or post-punk band that didn't regard him as a demigod. Thankfully, I can confirm that Iggy had lost none of his edge. As we toured around Europe – Paris, Brussels, Amsterdam, all over Germany – we were in awe of his energy, showmanship and stamina. He and his band were all friendly and accommodating, and we would voraciously consume his ever-changing nightly onstage cavortings, which mesmerised us.

One night in Berlin, he was particularly animated before going on and collared me, and for some reason started to explain his views on the British political scene. 'You need a strong leader, someone like Margaret Thatcher,' he incomprehensibly drawled in his inimitable Michigan accent.

'I didn't realise when he sang "I'm a Conservative" that he meant it,' I muttered to myself under my breath, but there was no point in arguing with his views: this conversation was strictly one-way traffic.

As stage-time approached, he stopped his grandstanding for a moment, picked up a full bottle of Jack Daniel's and proceeded to glug it down *in one* ... I was dumbstruck, but apparently this was standard procedure pre-stage. As you may suspect, this ensured a dynamic start to the show, which was never the same two nights running.

Iggy had a very impressive and terrifying stage trick, which was to climb to the top of one of the freestanding PA towers either side of the stage, and then start to rock them towards the audience. There were no safety chains, so if he'd have misjudged the rock (maybe thanks to a certain Mr Daniel, or other enhancements) then there would have been serious injuries, but I'm pretty sure Mr Pop would have emerged unharmed, flying higher than your highness ...

Another feature of the tour was the presence of the original 'China Girl', who was his personal assistant. Apart from tending to Iggy's needs, her job was to identify suitable female fans and invite them back to Iggy's hotel for late-night frolics. We always joked that the short straw would be to have the hotel room next to Iggy. He definitely found plenty to keep him occupied through the night, as I found out after the gig in Parma, Italy, where I happened to draw the short straw. I bore auditory witness to a seemingly endless night of passion and couldn't resist having a peek into the corridor: there was an orderly queue of pretty girls, all about to become part of the emperor's harem. After very little sleep, I blearily made my way to breakfast, where Iggy was already eating, cheerily welcoming all-comers as though he'd had the best night's sleep in months. It was at this point I realised that he was not human.

Later in the tour, we performed at the Paradiso in Amsterdam to a near-catatonic and totally stoned hippie audience, who were sat cross-legged on the floor *for Iggy Pop* for fuck's sake! It's not the Grateful Dead, it's the reigning champion of heavyweight punk! We'd already performed our set to kindly but restrained applause, and we had naturally assumed that they'd go bonkers for Iggy, but when the audience's polite but unexpired response showed no sign of changing after a few songs, and despite a determined Iggy pulling out all his normal stops, he lost his rag and started berating the semi-comatose audience.

'WHAT'S WRONG WITH YOU JUNKIE MOTHER-FUCKERS? GET UP AND DAYANCE!'

This had no significant effect, and their indifference to his howling just served to make Iggy more determined to piss them off. Nobody ignores Iggy. The venue was 'policed' by the local Hells Angels gang, and they were less than impressed by Iggy's insult to their friends in the audience. Iggy finished the gig and returned to our shared dressing room, where Ian, Phil and I were hanging out, only to be confronted by six of the biggest Hells Angels I'd ever seen. The discussion was short and to the point – they informed Iggy that unless he went back onstage and apologised to the audience, they would kill him. He had changed into his ruby-red satin boxing gown by now, and foolishly tried to face the giants down, but one of them immediately, and without warning, hit him square on the nose, causing a copious nosebleed. Discussion over, he went back onstage post-haste.

'I'd like to apologise to anyone I may have offended in the audience, it wasn't my intention.' Iggy's whipped-dog act may well have saved him a severe beating that night. So much for the reckless, fearless, brave Sir Iggy. He ran away. I can't say I blame him though.

We also did a brief tour with the mightily eccentric avant-rock band Pere Ubu. On paper, we shouldn't have been a bad match, as Wikipedia's description suggests: 'Describing their sound as "avant-garage", Pere Ubu's work drew inspiration from sources such as musique concrète, 60s rock, performance art, and the industrial environments of the American Midwest. While the band achieved little commercial success, they have exerted a wide influence on subsequent underground music.' But it would be gilding the lily to say this tour was an enjoyable experience. While I admired the uncompromising approach of their leader David Thomas, the live gigs were less impressive, and my impression of Thomas was one of arrogance and aloofness, to the extent that he refused to acknowledge our presence, let alone offer any encouragement.

This disappointment was quickly counterbalanced by the excitement of our first trip to America, to perform at the Palladium in Manhattan as part of filming for a forthcoming movie entitled *Urgh! A Music War*, featuring many early performances of 'New Wave' acts which would go on to achieve world fame: Orchestral Manoeuvres in the Dark, Magazine, The Go-Go's, Toyah Willcox, The Fleshtones, Joan Jett & the Blackhearts, X, XTC, Devo, The Cramps, Oingo Boingo, Dead Kennedys, Gary Numan, Klaus Nomi, Wall of Voodoo, Pere Ubu, Steel Pulse, Surf Punks, 999, The Alley Cats, UB40, Echo & the Bunnymen and The Police. Unfortunately, our performance didn't make the final cut, but our love of New York and all it had to offer was born on that trip.

We stayed at one of the most famous rock band hotels in Lower Manhattan, the Gramercy Park Hotel, a big, sprawling but very rundown place, full of character and musical history. Our suite – glamorous title but really beaten up – had an air-conditioning unit that was so old and noisy that we decided we'd rather swelter in the 92-degree, 90 per cent humidity heat than tolerate the racket. It's where we drank our first Budweisers and watched live baseball for the first time, and it felt like we were in an episode of our favourite

US comedy, *The Odd Couple*. I think we all secretly felt that we'd like to move there one day.

Alongside the extensive and exhausting touring schedule, we were recording our first records for Virgin Records. Sometimes for London gigs around that time we stayed at the Colombia Hotel in Lancaster Gate, an ex-glamorous, cheap hotel with big rooms, but definitely past its best. We recorded the famous flexi-disc there, which was included with our first Virgin recording, the esoteric *The Dignity of Labour* 12-inch EP, released in 1979 and featuring atmospheric electronic instrumentals inspired by Yuri Gagarin's return from space.

Although by this time we had our own studio, Virgin were reluctant to let us produce our first album without help or supervision, so they insisted that we used a co-producer/engineer, and that, after approving the demos, we should record all the tracks from scratch at Virgin's Townhouse Studios in Shepherd's Bush, London. Colin Thurston was hot property at the time, having just co-engineered Bowie's *Heroes* and Iggy's *Lust for Life* albums.

Thurston got the gig, and we were given three weeks at the Townhouse to record *Reproduction*. The studios were brand new and excitingly full of top-quality, state-of-the-art recording gear. The large, soundproofed recording studio area featured a full-size Steinway grand piano – what joy! Even better, the studio had accommodation in-house, so we were treated like honoured guests complete with on-demand food from the kitchen. God knows how many toasted BLTs we ate in those three weeks. It was all very cool and almost like a hippie commune.

The details of the recordings are documented in the Appendix, but the overall vibe was one of focus, super-hard work and excitement that our destiny was about to be fulfilled. The monitors in the studio were astoundingly loud and clear, so everything sounded impressive to us – in essence we had no option but to place our trust in Colin's expertise in making everything sound as good as it could be. But what we didn't realise was that *Reproduction* would be only his second album as a producer and that he had little experience with recording purely synth-generated sounds, which required a specialised skill. The songs were faithfully re-recorded and they sounded pretty good, but our vocal performances maybe felt a tad hesitant at times as we explored our capabilities and experimented in this new recording environment for the first time. It was all a bit of a blur – shoot first and ask questions later, no time for reflection until it was finished.

We had a playback party in the studio after we'd assembled the album, and the A&R people at Virgin seemed impressed and approved with no notes or comments. We were all happy, relieved and exhausted, and travelled back to Sheffield for some well-earned rest and recreation.

The first night back, I excitedly suggested to my girlfriend Patricia that she could be the first person to hear the new album. After an uninterrupted forty minutes, I asked her opinion.

'Yes, it's really good,' she half-heartedly opined.

I was disappointed – I was expecting something a little more enthusiastic. 'Does it remind you of anything?' I egged her on.

'Erm – oh yes – it's a bit like early Led Zeppelin.'

Not quite what I had in mind, but she was a hippie chick, so this was an attempt at praise, God bless her. I don't think she knew what we were aiming for.

There was more relevant feedback from most of our other friends, who seemed to be very impressed at the attempt to find a unique sound and vision, but there was something bugging me ...

We'd done a lot of live work by now, and I always liked the contradiction of the purity of the synth-generated sounds combined with the roughness of live performance through a PA system. An analogy would be an electric guitarist putting his signal through an amp to give it colour and character, as opposed to direct injection into the mixing desk, which is cleaner but less charismatic. Colin Thurston had chosen the direct-injection route, and so therefore the songs we'd been performing live, which were electro-punky and spirited, now sounded almost like a polite synthetic chamber orchestra. This worked really well for some songs ('You've Lost That Loving Feeling', for instance), but for songs like 'Almost Medieval', it was far too polished. And it wasn't just the mixes – we had virtually no experience of mastering then, so we had to rely on Colin's experience (which we now know was not much more than ours). The net result was that the vinyl cut sounded thin and weedy, which was quite an achievement (and not in a good way). It was only in the 2000s when the album was remastered using more contemporary equipment that the true emphatic and powerful beauty of the original tracks was revealed. So please seek out those remasters, as that is how the album was always meant to sound.

Directly after finishing recording *Reproduction*, we embarked on our first headline tour of thirteen dates to promote our magnum opus. The tour was an undoubted success, selling well, getting great reviews, with an expanded visual setup – more powerful projectors, bigger screens – and we were making good progress. Our reputation was increasing, but news was starting to seep through that our live success was not translating into the kind of record sales that Virgin were hoping for. The attempt at a break-through mainstream chart single had not happened with the release of 'Empire State Human' (which we were all sure would be a top 20 hit), so for now, it all felt more like consolidation and slow growth rather than firework-like explosive success. This was the first setback of our career, but we were starting to worry that it could become a slow-burning nightmare if we didn't turn it around soon. In today's music business, we'd have almost certainly been dropped, but thankfully Virgin seemed to have faith in us. We were pretty sure that they'd cut us some slack, and roll the dice again with a second album and tour.

As 1979 drew to a close, life was looking good. I had reunited with my girlfriend Karen, we were going steady, and this time I was determined not to let her go. I suggested to her that maybe we should live together, and she agreed, but was a little concerned that her parents might object. 'Nah, it'll be OK,' I said, as I tried to brush off her concerns, but she was right. Karen asked her dad, and he threatened to disown her if we moved in together without getting married.

At first I was outraged, but after a couple of days of careful thought, I said to Karen, 'Fuck it – I don't believe in marriage anyway, so if it keeps your parents happy, let's do it – but no fuss, just at the register office, close family only.'

I was secretly pleased at this turn of events, as I was devoted to Karen, and wanted to make sure we would always be together. We were happy and, apart from anything else, I needed emotional support through the coming maelstrom of what I hoped would be world-famous success. Little were we to know how long we would have to wait . . .

1979–80: The Human League – *Travelogue*

'Someone wants my job, it is someone in this building . . .'

Everything seemed to be going well at this point, and I felt we were pretty much in the groove creatively and privately – writing material for the next album in our freshly equipped Monumental Studios on West Bar in Sheffield, and busy juggling multiple elements of my professional career. I should make clear at this point that our studio was less than monumental, with the room painted sunshine orange for some reason (to keep us awake probably). The most characterful feature of the whole place was the derelict kitchen next door to the control room, which served as our live recording area and vocal booth. It had the unique acoustic benefit of the presence of approximately two hundred empty glass milk bottles (which for some reason we never removed), creating a very bright presence which accidentally turned out to be perfect for recording vocals that would stand out in any mix – serendipity in action.

We loved that studio, however decrepit it appeared to be. I can't overstate how important it is for a young band to have their own private, creative sonic laboratory. We learned so much by trial and error, and that is how we rapidly and organically developed our own process and style.

We had some help from an engineer friend of Bob Last's – Tim Pearce – and as a thank-you we helped him to record his passion project, a song he'd written called 'C'est Grave', the title being a play on 'C'est Chic' by Chic. It was a very strange, upbeat electronic reimagining of the funeral march in the style of *The Addams Family* theme tune. Tim wrote and 'sang' the lead vocal, and the end result can still be heard on a couple of rarities compilations, although it hasn't aged well, to be brutally honest. After a few months of living in each other's pockets, Tim finally flipped one day and said he couldn't stand working with us any more, especially me! This came as a total surprise, and when I asked Glenn what had triggered him, he said it was about 'my attitude to women'! Yes, I had the raging hormones of a teenager and the sexual appetite of any young man, and I haven't shied away from being honest about that in these pages, but that doesn't mean I have ever wanted to demean any woman in any way, shape or form. Anyone who knows me would testify that I have always been very un-macho in my relationships with women and, of course, I've always been a strident advocate for women's rights. To this day, I've no idea what the fuck happened – none. In any case, I suspect it was a simple clash of personalities, but we never exchanged a cross word, ever. People are weird.

On a more positive note, word was beginning to spread that we now had a close-to-professional recording facility, leading to offers coming in for us to help with demoing various up-and-coming, newly signed artists. The first of these was a couple of friendly and talented guys from Blackburn, Neil Arthur and Stephen Luscombe, who called themselves the daft name of Blancmange, but there was no denying the quality of their songs, which included their future hits 'Blind Vision' and 'Living on the Ceiling'. The demos we recorded sounded great, and I got paid, but I was somewhat

(above) My first faltering
steps helped by my doting
sister Janet and her friend.
This is the house where I
grew up: 34 Hope Street
in Sheffield. *(Courtesy of author)*

(right) Coquettish look and
a not very straight fringe.
I must have been around
eight years old.
(Courtesy of author)

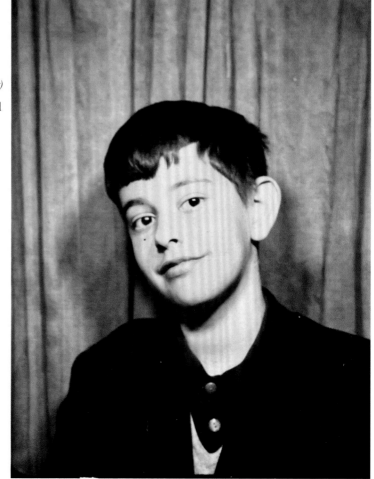

(above) The 1993 Cup Final, Sheffield Wednesday V. Arsenal (we lost of course). We hired a Winnebago. Friend on the photo include Glenn Gregory, Spike Denton, Marcus and Tish Vere, and Ian Reddington.
(Courtesy of author)

(left) Kitty and Jack in their front room, 1983. They proudly displayed the gold and silver discs to all concerned, including postmen, doctors etc.
(Courtesy of author)

Hard at work in Townhouse studios making *The Luxury Gap* album with talented co-producer Greg Walsh. *(Courtesy of author)*

Relaxing in the shade in Venice on my first ever visit in 1982 – the start of my lifelong love affair . . . *(Courtesy of author)*

Just prior to the split from The Human League. We were a happy bunch – mostly . . .
(above: Goddard Archive portraits/Alamy Stock Photo; left: Courtesy of author)

Our third ever gig with The Human League at The Limit Club on West Street in Sheffield. The boiler suits were inspired by Devo's stage outfits. Fun fact: the three of us were labelled A, B and C for this gig! I also designed the backdrop. *(Courtesy of author)*

Curious photo – I know we were going for the industrial angle, but I'm not really sure to be honest ...
(Glenn Gregory)

These were taken at one of our several early gigs at Bar 2 in the Sheffield students' union building.
(Courtesy of author)

Our first session with Earth, Wind and Fire's Phenix Horns at London's Air Studios 1 – me, Don Myrick, Louis 'Lui Lui' Satterfield and Greg Walsh. *(Courtesy of author)*

At home on Chepstow Road, Notting Hill in 1982. I'm with my favourite toy: a state-of-the-art BBC B computer. *(Virginia Turbett/Getty Images)*

With good friends Rob Whittaker, Ian, Jane Whittaker and Beverley Hills. Sadly, Rob and Jane are no longer with us. *(Courtesy of author)*

The one and only Spizz in 1981. We toured together extensively with Spizz Oil and Siouxsie and the Banshees from 1978 to 1979. We have remained good friends to this day. *(Virginia Turbett)*

One of many Sheffield parties, this one around 1984. From left to right: Sue Bower, Lindsay Crisp, Mick Clark, Nick Dawson, Mark Civico, Sue Clark, Corinne, Liz, Glenn, Howard Willie, Dave Bower and me. *(Courtesy of author)*

Smouldering. Working the Al Pacino Italian gangster vibe.
(Janette Beckman / Getty Images)

surprised when I wasn't approached to produce their album. I've remained good friends with Neil, and often playfully jibe him about this, and he always apologises unnecessarily – he has no need, of course. They are still a fantastic live act, and, as we are all devoted footy fans and have similarly underwhelming football teams, we regularly tease each other about Blackburn and Wednesday's perpetual lack of success.

Another exciting opportunity emerged to perform live supporting a rising new US band called Talking Heads on their first UK headline tour. I'd seen them a couple of years earlier when they were supporting The Ramones in Manchester – to be honest, I was a little underwhelmed as they appeared to be a bit light on originality (what do I know?). As Phil, Ian, Adrian and I discussed how to outshine and upstage the headliners, I came up with an idea. 'You know the Kraftwerk robots, and the fact Kraftwerk aren't actually onstage ... how about we go one better, and just have the slide show and the music, but to avoid people thinking we're taking the piss, we guarantee to be in the audience every night. It's like the ultimate in breaking the fourth wall: we'd be actually with the audience watching our own show!'

We were convinced that the notoriously art-installation-loving David Byrne would applaud the audacity of the idea. The whole concept made us laugh, which is the usual green-light within the band, and we nervously shared the idea with Bob. He thought it was ironic, funny and artistically interesting and so he agreed to present the idea to Virgin. Surprisingly, they loved it (presumably because it would create a stir), and plans proceeded in a state of feverish anticipation. Also, for once, we could all participate in designing the slide show. Advertising in the music press was arranged, designs were approved, costs were agreed ... Just one thing: nobody told Talking Heads.

I suspect that Virgin were hoping that if they avoided kicking the hornet's nest, it would be too late for them to object even if they didn't dig the idea. How wrong they were. As soon as the unique 'performance' had been announced and advertised, their management immediately ripped up their agreement with us and threw us off the tour. We were gutted, but we've learned since then that typical US music managements love to play hardball over just about anything as it's in their cultural make-up (as in 'no one fucks with us, we fuck with you') – different cultures. Our attitude, however, was that Talking Heads talked the talk re 'avant-garde' and irony, but in reality they were just another corporate rock band, and this caused us a significant amount of disillusionment. Yet another 'sod 'em, we'll show 'em' moment, but looking back, on balance it was a big open goal missed. Regrets, I have a few, but then again …

During this period our recording skills were getting pretty good. All the love of experimental and diverse types of music, and the way that these sounds and elements were created, started to pay dividends as we strode out into this seemingly endless new musical landscape. While our first loves were synthesisers, we were also obsessed with tape manipulation techniques – we had a ravenous appetite for experimentation. All those years of listening to Frank Zappa's weird sound-collage techniques, including varispeed, micro-editing, musique concrète, tape reverse and found sound – also experimentation with pumping the various sounds through multiple signal paths, guitar pedals, inappropriate equalisations and channel overloading – all of it was now within our grasp. And in the words of our guru Brian Eno (I paraphrase) 'it is essential to keep an element of randomness in compositional practice'. This really stuck with me, and to this day is one of the main reasons I moved away from creating purely on digital audio workstations. Onscreen interfaces engage a different part of our creative processing, and subconsciously pull you into regular *anti-random* patterns, which in turn hinder innovation. We put all this Enoesque dogma to good use, recording with the engineers John Leckie and Richard Manwaring, who helped us make sense of our excitable ideas and focus them into solid form. They were both gentle sorts, full of suggestions and experience.

Our second album, *Travelogue*, came out in May 1980. Twenty-odd years later, I claimed in an interview with *Mojo*, 'Tracks like "The Black Hit of Space" are way ahead of their time. Pumping the synths through massive distortion and overloading the desk. How prescient is that? The ethos of what we were doing was to kind of future-proof it all. We were envisaging people playing this music in ten or twenty years' time.' Some people were actually playing it back then too, as it entered the album chart at number 16 and spent a long time in the chart even after Ian and I had left The Human League.

Much of the engagement for the listener on *Travelogue* I'm pretty certain is due to a more organic experimental approach. I know this seems counterintuitive, but once you realise that all this shiny, exciting new technology is just another set of tools (but with more or less endless functionality), the more you can relax into what the whole deal is about – which is this . . . *content is king.* All the exciting sounds in the world will not compensate for a lack of core identity of your creation. That's it, that's the statement right there. As The Human League we had created a happy, functional and unusual set of professional content creation tools in Monumental Studios – in a rundown, mostly derelict, ex-veterinary surgery in a dilapidated part of ex-industrial Sheffield. This, as it turned out, proved to be a surprisingly productive place.

The cover art of *Travelogue* was originated by the band and included the first piece of work for us by our long-time collaborator Malcolm Garrett, who is still my go-to graphic designer – he created great and seminal artwork for Buzzcocks, Magazine, Duran Duran, Simple Minds and Peter Gabriel. As for the genesis of the album's identity, we were running out of time to find a title and 'look' for the album. Ian turned up at the studio one day with a stack of *National Geographic* magazines, and our research turned up a highly evocative photo of a dog-sled trainer and his dogs on a frozen lake in Canada, all low sun and long shadows coming towards the viewer. We instantly loved this photo and its allusion to isolation, mystery and beauty.

Why should this resonate for us? It was probably because we felt a bit isolated and mysterious, maybe even beautiful?

'Perfect,' I said, 'what should we call the album? Something to do with exploration or travel on a wild frontier, that's the journey we're on isn't it?'

We decided we wanted a one-word title (as in *Reproduction*) and I'm almost certain that the word 'travelogue' was my idea. I like the similarity to the word 'analogue' – almost as though 'travelogue' was a portmanteau of 'analogue travel' (as in travelling in imaginary terms, i.e. analogous to travel). So there you have it, let's face it, I'm a fucking genius . . .

The Polaroid images on the back were taken by the band, and we told Malcolm that we wanted to incorporate the Microgramma Bold Extended font that was used on *Reproduction* (yes, we were font geeks since designing the 'Being Boiled' Letraset cover; that's why we got on so well with Malc). We also wanted the colour choices to be strong, hence the deep orange of The Human League title and the sunshine orange used on the back sleeve – we wanted these to give a subconsciously non-cold, non-traditional visual ambience.

At the same time as all this was happening, we were building up our live following, which included various trips to the smoke. Supporting the Rezillos (or perhaps they were the Revillos by then) at the huge old venue the Music Machine (later Camden Palace and Koko) was a gas, and we saw first-hand the excellence of future Human League band member and co-songwriter Jo Callis, with whom who we became good friends. A little later we headlined for the first time at Camden's Electric Ballroom, which was an unexpected success – we were flattered that people seemed to be into us, not just as a curious support act for more popular bands. The momentum was building nicely. We were in the music press almost every week, in features, news items or generally enthusiastic fan letters. We were becoming a hip act internationally, and a name to drop. Tony Wilson, the famous Mancunian impresario, was always ahead of the game: he had given us our first break on TV when he asked us to perform on 'What's On', his slot on *Granada Reports*, which was filmed live at his club the Factory in Manchester. Tony was good friends with Bob Last, and I'm almost certain that a major reason for being selected was Tony's sexual attraction to Phil – it certainly seemed that way whenever we met. Phil was happy to play along, I'm glad to say, and it led to further opportunities with Tony as his empire spread.

In my private life, before getting back together with Karen, I had moved into my first flat away from home with my girlfriend Patricia – the sense of freedom was palpable. Even though it was a less-than-luxurious studio flat with peeling wallpaper, it was treasured. But our relationship was destined not to last, and pretty soon I had to do a runner due to unpaid rent (I was skint and owed £600). Don't do it, kids – apart from being illegal and immoral, I ended up with a court order against me, so I ended up paying the arrears owed plus legal costs. I learned my lesson, and from then on I played by the rules – in fact, I've never lost a legal dispute since (and there have been *a lot*). Also, in my haste to run away before capture, I decided to abandon my precious collection of around five hundred American (mainly Marvel but some DC) comics in the flat, which probably ended up in a skip. These included several early *Spider-Man* and *Fantastic Four* editions, which in current prices would probably be valued highly. I had *Spider-Man 4*, which is worth at least $2000, so the whole collection would have been worth at least $25,000 now. Crime doesn't pay ...

All in all, we were at peak confidence about our creative direction, and the likelihood of major national, and hopefully therefore international, success. We were definitely no richer financially but that wasn't our motivation at this point. We wanted to be recognised as artists, like all the magnificent influencers that we'd grown up with – some would say that was the peak period of popular music diversity and imagination, ranging from the 1960s hippie revolution, through to the experiments and pop rock and glam of the 1970s. We wanted to be, literally, in the avant-garde of not just a fashion or a 'scene', but a movement – to change the direction of popular music in some small way. But our carefree electric troubadour days were numbered and we would soon be forced to face a different kind of challenge: commercial reality.

The View Outside: Richard Manwaring, engineer and co-producer, *Travelogue*

Wow, *I thought to myself*, what is this? *as I first entered the disused building in Sheffield that was the location for The Human League's studio. I had started engineering in commercial studios: Wessex, IBC, A&M and now, in 1980, Virgin Records' residential twenty-four-track studio outside Oxford, The Manor. So the eight-track studio The Human League had set up on the first floor above an abandoned veterinary practice was a change of recording environment for me. I was looking forward to it. I had been asked by Simon Draper, Head of A&R at Virgin Records, to produce the tracks (apart from 'Being Boiled') that became the* Travelogue *album.*

I met Martyn as well as Phil, Ian and Adrian in March 1980. Martyn and Ian executed the practicalities of the songs as they created and programmed the sounds and played the keyboards. Martyn was very good at setting out the context of the songs. In 1980, mobile phones were yet to be available and there was no landline in the studio. I remember one occasion when Martyn was a particular help. Late one evening I was asked to take a call at the minicab office across the street. There was no electricity in the building apart from the studio itself and, as I stumbled down the stairs to the totally dark ground floor, I was met by what I remember as an extremely bright torch beam. My mind still on the current song, I was taken completely unawares, so shocked by the light in my eyes that I fell back against the wall and slid to the ground unable to utter a word. The torch beam came from two police officers investigating why people were coming in and out of a disused building. Luckily Martyn heard the commotion from upstairs and immediately understood the situation. He was very reassuring as he made sure I was OK, which took quite a bit of time, while explaining to the police the circumstances of us being in the building. Once recovered, I got to my feet and managed to make it over to the minicab office. I have no recollection what the phone call was about. We never talked about it at the time but I'm forever grateful to Martyn for his presence of mind.

1980–2: The Split and the Birth of BEF and Heaven 17

'I'm moving back to the age of men ...'

Anyone who comes from a large family knows that families argue, and The Human League family – Phil, Ian, Adrian, Bob and me – were typical in that respect. We were intensely committed to our craft and our work, and would theorise and passionately defend our corners, usually in a friendly 'who-finished-off-the-cornflakes?' kind of tone, but occasionally more intensely. Almost all of these discussions ended without resentment (certainly on my part) and often were resolved by a trip to the local pub. After a few pints, mysteriously nothing seemed to be as much of a problem.

But ... various factors were coming into play that were exerting stresses on our usually happy crew, many of which I didn't understand (or want to understand) at the time. Firstly, Bob Last was in constant contact with Virgin, and we naively assumed he was working exclusively on our behalf as a unit. Unbeknownst to us, and confirmed many years later on film, he had been in clandestine discussions with Simon Draper at Virgin because the record company had not been able to break the act internationally, despite our cool and credible 'pioneer' status within the industry. Virgin saw Phil as a potential mainstream, traditional 'pop star', whereas they viewed The Human League as a bit too niche and uncomfortably edgy for crossover pop tastes. In other words, we didn't fit the mould.

At the same time, Virgin's negative cashflow was a powerful motivator to extract maximum value from us and many other bands on the label at the time (XTC, for instance). The lack of breakthrough from any of the more recent signings was beginning to make the company's financial controllers more and more nervous. This wasn't exclusively our fault, of course, but fear of failure spreads like a virus and can cause rising panic behind the scenes. The 'North Sea oil'-style windfall from Mike Oldfield's *Tubular Bells* in the mid-1970s, which fuelled the exponential growth of Virgin Records, had almost run out, and financial reality had hit the executives like a brick wall.

Virgin never indicated much was amiss at the time and, to be fair, Bob probably felt it was his duty to protect us from the pressure. After all, we were doing our best creatively, enjoying our work and preparation for our first full-scale European headline tour. Everything seemed to be going reasonably well from my perspective but just not fast enough for the record company – our attitude was, 'Ah, but they're greedy bastards; we'll never sell out our creative integrity, we are artists, etc.' But Bob's subtle hints that, pretty soon, we'd need to have a top 40 chart hit or there would be trouble on the horizon were taken seriously. We all respected Bob's opinions, especially on business strategy, so we focused hard and discussed what could be done in the short term. We came to the conclusion that we should release a very direct attempt at hitting the charts head on, and stop fucking around.

Our version of going for the pop jugular was the EP *Holiday '80*, to be recorded in our own Monumental Studios in Sheffield, and produced by the very experienced John Leckie (who had just been working with bands we loved: Simple Minds, Be–Bop Deluxe, Public Image Limited, etc.). The EP would be a highly desirable (we thought) double-gatefold picture sleeve, with a photograph by me and co-designed with our mate and famous post-punk graphic designer Malcolm Garrett . . .

1. 'Marianne' (Marsh/Oakey/Ware) 3:17
2. 'Dancevision' (Marsh/Ware) 2:21 [performed by The Future]
3. 'Being Boiled' (Album Version) (Marsh/Oakey/Ware) 4:22
4. 'Rock 'n' Roll/Nightclubbing' (Gary Glitter, Mike Leander/Jim Osterberg, David Bowie) 6:22

We were determined that this collection of tracks, featuring all the right cultural references (Bowie/Iggy/Grace Jones/Glitter – yes, he was still 'antihero cool' at the time, before anyone knew of his awful crimes), would quell any record company doubts about our sales potential in a super-cool fashion. Surely people would love our new composition 'Marianne', which was our preferred lead track, but Virgin agonisingly didn't agree and thought it was too weak. I still believe it was the peak of our songwriting output at that period. It sounded futuristic, confident, stylish and melodic – the story was engaging, the vocal arrangements were on point (I mean, a three-part, interweaving polyphonic counterpoint in the chorus? Give us the Ivor Novello Award now, for God's sake). But they were convinced that 'Rock 'n' Roll/Nightclubbing' had a much stronger shot at convincing *Top of the Pops* to give us a break: we'd never been selected before, and it was regarded as a prerequisite for chart success – together with A-list playlisting on BBC Radio 1, which we'd also never achieved. Plugging (promoting records in person direct to radio and TV show producers) was a murky, dark art in those days – there were several key pluggers who could give the record company an increased (but not guaranteed) chance at being on *TOTP* and Radio 1, but they were very expensive and massively oversubscribed. A record company radio promo exec told me that, one week, a famous plugger turned up at Radio 1 with a pile of eighty 7-inch records, all of which he'd been paid to plug, but obviously only a few would reach playlist nirvana. Money was being wasted on an industrial scale, but the potential rewards were so great that the record companies regarded it as the equivalent of buying a ticket to one of those 'Win-A-Ferrari' raffles. Bizarre in retrospect. I never did find out if these costs were charged back in any way to recoupable debt – it wouldn't have surprised me.

When a record is released, the record company sales team subscribes to private industry information regarding how sales are going nationally (which determined chart position at that time). Say the record was released on a Thursday – there would be a 'midweek' position, post-initial weekend sales, which would indicate possible success when the actual public UK Top 75 was announced on the Sunday. The 'midweek' for *Holiday '80* was only 72, which was devastatingly disappointing as *Top of the Pops* would normally only consider songs that debuted in the top 40. Virgin tried to assure us that there had been some kind of distribution issue, and that there would be an improvement, but we were gutted. All that optimism and hard work, and in all likelihood *Holiday '80* would be consigned to the remainder bin of history.

What's even worse is that we thought it was probably the most commercial we could be – and I include Phil in this as we were all in agreement. (You'll understand why I mention this now, at a later point.) As we slunk back to our studio, resigned to continuing work on the arrangements for our forthcoming tour, we were sure we'd done our best, and that nothing else could have been done – it was just fate . . .

Then, out of the blue, an excited head of promotions at Virgin called. 'You're on *Top of the Pops*,' she screamed.

'What the fuck! How is that even possible?'

'We did a bit of a quid pro quo with them: we told them they could have an exclusive film by another act.' I think it may have been Devo but I'm not sure.

So, for the first time in *TOTP* history, at least to our knowledge, a record that debuted at 72 was allowed on to the show. We were ecstatic, and immediately rang around all our relations and friends that had supported us from the outset. I had finally achieved something that my mum and dad could comprehend as success – we were now going to be household names. 'Oooh, our Martyn is ont' telly!' crowed my mum to almost anyone she would meet in the street, and also postmen, dustbin-men, electricity and gas meter readers, the doctor, etc. No one would be in any doubt how proud she (and my family in general) were of having a real-life pop star in the family. To her, this was the equivalent of being in a Hollywood movie. She would have bragging rights for life, and I'd like to think that my success at this time (Kitty was sixty-eight and my dad was seventy-three) made their remaining years on earth happier ones. As my success progressed, I always made a point of getting an extra silver, gold or platinum disc dedicated to them, which they mounted in their front room, making the whole place resemble a downmarket but very successful tiny record-label waiting room.

Nineteen million people – that's around one in three humans in the UK – would religiously tune in to *Top of the Pops* in 1980. Now that's what I call event television. A great performance could literally catapult a record into the upper reaches of the charts in a matter of a few weeks, and at that point nobody could ever again argue that you weren't a pop star. They could always say you were a 'one-hit wonder', but they could never take pop-star status away ever again. Even more exciting was the fact that in those days, UK top 30 success was a trigger for many other international radio and TV producers to give the green light. The UK chart was almost as significant and prestigious as the US Billboard chart, and could potentially ignite the giant firework display that was world music business success.

An awful lot was riding on this performance, and although we were by this time very experienced as live performers, we were very nervous as we were much less experienced on TV. We'd done a few arty late-night shows (usually commissioned by Tony Wilson for Granada), but *TOTP* was a horse of a different colour entirely. It was make or break time – no exaggeration. Phil washed and conditioned his hair until it was gleaming. Ian, Adrian and I picked our best/coolest clothes, as befits newly born pop stars (until then, we dressed more like a student band, except for Phil who always dressed like a star). We really had little idea about stagecraft and the fact that we were in 'showbusiness'. That smelled a little too much of desperation – we had a 'too-cool-for-school' vibe, obviously a ridiculous stance with the benefit of hindsight. But we certainly made up for it later with Heaven 17.

The show was exciting and we performed well, and it was a curious experience watching the performance the next day back at Ian's house (he was the only one of us with a VCR). It felt to me like I was watching an alternate reality version of myself, with all the frantic hooting and cheering and dancing from the audience, our energetic and awkwardly animated performance apparently driving the crowd wild. Oh, and Ian being as chilled as always, chiselled handsome features, enigmatic, inscrutable, in the way that maybe Kraftwerk or Ron Mael from Sparks (without the irony) would be. But in any case, we didn't look or sound anything like any act I'd ever seen on the show, and I'd been watching it every week since I was about six years old. I felt satisfied and proud, not just for me but as a justification for the risk we all took to take a 50 per cent pay cut to live a frugal lifestyle and dedicate ourselves to our long-term career. This was going to be the start of something big, I could feel it in my bones.

The expected leap up the charts never materialised. The EP peaked at 53, way short of expectations. Virgin were very disappointed, as were we, but we could always blame it on the record company. The main reason that the *TOTP* performance didn't do the trick was that, despite much effort, Virgin's pluggers just couldn't persuade the playlist committee at Radio 1 to A-list *Holiday '80*. No A-list meant the gains from the week of the *TOTP* performance would die on the vine, instead of Radio 1 keeping us in the public eye for weeks – sometimes months – marching forward and solidifying our presence in the national popular-culture consciousness.

Even back in 1979, Virgin had suggested that we might abandon our 'synthesiser only' purity by employing some of their most favoured session players, as they felt we had to 'think outside the box'. This was sold to us as our opportunity to experiment with a different genre. All the band loved disco, especially as the alternative white music press in both the UK and US had thrown the whole shebang under the bus (a bit too black and gay for them perhaps), and the chance to have a go at creating an authentic-sounding disco classic was too tempting to refuse. But we had a condition – we refused to dilute the manifesto of The League, so we suggested putting the track out under a pseudonym (Bowie had done something similar by experimenting under the guise of Arnold Corns, and if it was good enough for Bowie, it was good enough for us).

Bob and Virgin agreed to the idea, so we had to come up with a name. We thought it would be ironically funny to parody the macho nature of many disco groups, and I think it was Ian who came up with the beautifully elegant name The Men. That was it. Phil was even more excited when he realised that the lyrics could be as direct and banal as we needed but, as usual, we managed to make the story more difficult. There always had to be a twist: it was in our DNA to be contrary buggers. So Phil came up with the idea of the chorus, which was 'It's cruel, but it's true, I don't depend on you' – based loosely on his whirlwind relationship with his then young wife Anthea (who I had a crush on). In the spirit of all the best disco tunes, the chorus had to be hooky and repeated, and in this case tagged at the end with 'go back to the end of the queue'. Here's the twist – the verse of 'I Don't Depend on You' would be sung by Phil, and the chorus would be a pre-girl-power female backing vocal chant. .

The first verse is a work of tongue-in-cheek beauty . . .

The night
So young
You could lose
You could gain
Your temperature's rising
Better pull into the outside lane
You always say you're not the jealous kind
Then you tell all your friends that I've got one thing on my
    mind . . .

Then the killer blow, a pre-chorus that could be the chorus, sung by the female character in the narrative as embodied by Lisa Strike and Katie Kissoon, with curious and slightly menacing parallel thirds, and it presages the title's use in the chorus . . .

127

I've played this scene before, you had one foot in the door

But there's always plenty more, don't try to use me

I don't depend on you, I've got my own friends too

I'll never be your wife, don't try to use me

I've played this scene before, you had one foot in the door

But there's always plenty more, don't try to use me

As *NME* commented later in 1990, the song was 'Utterly commercial, the irritating bleep-content is all but lost under lashings of catchy Euro-Pop sheen (with prophetic female backing to boot). The Human League were quite clearly ahead of their own time, never mind anyone else's.' Utterly commercial it may have been, but it didn't chart.

The concept was completed by the artwork featured on the picture sleeve – an androgynous female model posing in a business suit and tie in a typical suburban kitchen. This was meant to symbolise the evolving nature of women's roles in domestic environments (i.e. female empowerment), and I think we pretty much nailed it. It certainly didn't resemble anything else on offer in the marketplace, but it was clearly an ironic nod towards the subservient representation of women on many disco record sleeves (Ohio Players, *et al.*).

Looking back on this recording now, I can see that this was almost like a pilot for what The Human League could have become, and definitely the template for Heaven 17 – use of real instruments combined with synthesisers, predominant use of girl backing singers, more of a focus on danceability, and most importantly, glamour, style and fantasy (admittedly all a little difficult to achieve with a band of weird, studenty-looking indie guys who bought their clothes from charity shops and army stores). Enlisting women in the band enabled an entirely different vibe. Heaven

17's fashion template was the kind of style popularised by the best R&B bands in the US (including Chic, whose style was ironically influenced by Roxy Music), and we fancied that we might make half-decent gangster types (à la *The Godfather*). This would come into full effect later as stylists were employed by Virgin to make this happen, as exemplified on the cover of the 'Penthouse and Pavement' single, clothes courtesy of a film and TV supplier called Contemporary Wardrobe ... but the ramifications of all this are to be revealed later.

Meanwhile, back in 1980, the commercial failures of *Holiday '80* and 'I Don't Depend on You' were jointly the tipping points of Virgin's patience with us, and this was probably when the clandestine plotting started between Bob Last and the A&R execs at Virgin. Simon Draper, who had always been a massive supporter of us, was now forced into a corner. All of this was invisible to me, there was not a hint of anything other than 'Oh well, it's a bit of a setback, but we'll regroup and press on', but somehow the atmosphere had subtly changed. Phil and I seemed to be rubbing each other up the wrong way more often. Ian diplomatically stayed out of any personal arguments but was never short of an opinion on creative matters.

The truth is that Ian and I held common beliefs and intuitions, and Phil was, and still is, a contrarian (perhaps before the word was even coined). The dynamics of the group had changed when Adrian joined, although I didn't realise it at the time. Adrian was an interesting and quiet lad, quite eccentric and very arty and agreeable, but a lot of friction was starting to happen between Phil and me as Phil insisted that not only should Adrian be a full-time member of the group, but that he should be an equal partner in all the rights associated with The Human League. I couldn't see the logic of this – right from the start we had decided to split all rights equally three ways to avoid arguments. It's very easy to determine majority view in a three-person unit, but as soon as it becomes a four-person unit, inevitably there will be 2 v. 2 factions as a possibility. I argued that Adrian had no role in writing, and frankly a less important role in performance. I also argued that Adrian could just as effectively perform his duties out of the public gaze, as a kind of media/lighting director, next to the actual lighting director by the mixing desk. I admitted that I liked Adrian being onstage – I thought it was unusual and interesting, but not essential: I regarded our erstwhile 'visuals co-ordinator' as virtually set dressing. Phil and Adrian were outraged at this admittedly somewhat indelicate, bald and honest opinion, but Ian (quiet though he generally was) openly agreed with me. Why should we water down our shares in this enterprise when Adrian was contributing less on the recording side? Why should he get 25 per cent of our recording and writing royalties? It was dogmatic nonsense. I had nothing whatsoever against Adrian, but he was getting paid well for his work and this was a step too far.

Phil and Adrian backed down, but I felt that their simmering resentment remained, bubbling away just beneath the surface, an infection that very slowly started to poison the laddish, good-time, 'all for one and one for all' bonhomie that we had always enjoyed in The Human League and every band I'd been involved with previously. After all, Phil had been my best friend since fourth form at school, Ian and I had been close at Meatwhistle and other manifestations since 1973, but Adrian was a charming Johnny-come-lately art student who was really good at slides but didn't have a musical bone in his body. A nice enough guy, but honestly couldn't really be regarded as being on the same level (or paygrade) as the original members, who were responsible for writing and performing the songs.

Work continued on prepping for the European tour, which

was zooming up less than eight weeks away. After a strategy discussion with Bob Last and the whole band, I suggested that it might be a good idea for us to see Adrian's planned image programming by setting up a Kodak projector Carousel array in the studio, with mini versions of the four screens we would be using. We'd always left Adrian to get on with his job without supervision, as we didn't want to be back-seat drivers, but in the newly febrile, self-critical world we were drifting into, we felt it might be a good idea to know what we were letting ourselves in for. As the live slideshow was behind us on stage, and this was before the world of video recorders in your pocket, we'd never actually seen a full show, only snippets from TV shows (which were usually set up differently anyway).

The day arrived, Adrian set up what seemed to be a huge amount of gear, and a few hours later we were ready for the show. It felt very awkward, a bit like we were examiners at a university presentation, but we made light of it, darkened the lights, and got our pens and paper ready to make notes as Ian started the backing tape arrangements of the set list. What happened next was totally unexpected. As Adrian diligently activated the various Carousel projectors, what became clear was this: he was completely insane. There was little to no relationship between the imagery and the themes of *any* of the songs: it was as if the visuals were being controlled by a random image generator. Don't get me wrong, the chosen images looked good and interesting, it was just that they had no thematic connection at all. We were in an avant-garde installation version of Adrian's massive image and toy collection. We all looked at each other after about three or four songs, by which time it had become abundantly clear that there was no sense to what we were seeing. It was all just decorative, and any meaning the crowd might derive from these images would be purely down to the belief that 'it must mean something'.

Wow ... where do we go from here? Do we ask Adrian to focus his themes a little? As soon as we plucked up the courage to discuss this with him, he railed and said, 'If I have to reprogram this it will take me weeks.' So we decided to allow the dice to fall where they may, and let it ride. But I was secretly convinced from that moment on that Adrian was at least part full of Art Bullshit™.

The increase in overall niggly antsy-ness proceeded apace, fuelled by the Phil/Adrian axis's probable sense of injustice about the quarter-share knockback. We were arguing about many more insignificant things – what food to order, how much money to spend on equipment, when should Adrian be in the studio, etc. As far as I was concerned, there were no hard feelings and the matter was closed but, behind the scenes, bad faith actors were in motion ...

Our manager's secret discussions with Virgin must have been proceeding apace behind the scenes, and I can only assume that at some point Phil was brought into their nefarious confidence to test the water for future plans and what he would and wouldn't accept. Malcolm McLaren (the infamously Machiavellian Sex Pistols manager) was Bob's mentor and friend, and he may have influenced Bob. I'd met McLaren a couple of times and, far from admiring him, I mistrusted his smirking, charismatic arrogance. I wouldn't have trusted him as far as I could spit. He would have made a great Tory politician. I can imagine the kind of conversation that might have been happening behind my back – something like ...

Bob: Phil and Martyn aren't getting on – what should I do? Oh, and add to that the record company are putting pressure on me to sort it out. They want their money back for all the effort, marketing and tour support – they're hundreds of thousands unrecouped.
Malcolm (with a knowing nasal snark): In every negative situation there are myriad creative opportunities. Phil should be a glamorous pop

star. He needs to ditch the visually unaesthetic part of the group, that should do the trick. While you're at it, get some proper pop songwriters in – never mind all that trendy cerebral sci-fi stuff, it's just too niche. You'll never make any money like that – you need a hit! Do you know anybody who can write songs that the average person can relate to?'

Bob: We can't just throw Martyn out, he founded the group!

Malcolm: Time to grow up, Bob . . . Virgin will love this. Tell Martyn to leave, offer him some compensation to give up his rights to the name, off he fucks and forms another group, you've got rid of the problem, replace him with some real musicians, maybe some girls, *et voilà!* Virgin have two bands for the price of one!

Bob: Hmm . . . I have a few people in mind who might fit the bill. I have to think about this and discuss it with Virgin. It's not a stupid idea, but poor Martyn . . .

Malcolm: It's a shit business . . . but necessary.

I've no idea if this ever happened, but Bob has since confirmed (on film) that the bare bones of this subterfuge actually occurred. I'm also pretty certain that Phil's ego was being massaged by Bob and Simon, culminating presumably in asking him directly if he'd support throwing me out of the band. Heartbreakingly, he must have agreed in advance of the fateful meeting that he would be prepared to throw me under the bus to make his dreams of becoming a famous pop star come true. It's worth mentioning that never, at any point, had Phil intimated that he was discontented with the direction of the band, or that he was unhappy with me as a friend – we were still hanging out and socialising, apparently 'brothers in arms'. I was shortly to find out this wasn't the case . . .

I arrived at the studio a little early, as always (I'm fastidious about timings), for a 'strategic band meeting' called by Bob at our studio. When I arrived, I was surprised to see that Bob, Phil and Adrian were already settled in. Strange, but I thought nothing of it at the time. Bob led the conversation . . . this is as close to an accurate, word-for-word record of proceedings as my memory will allow:

Bob: Sit down, Martyn, we have something to tell you . . .

Me: Huh?

(Ian and Phil are looking a little sheepish, and I don't understand why. Have I done something wrong?)

Bob: We want you to leave the group.

(A chasm of disbelief opens up in me. This isn't just a shock, it is completely without any warning of any description.)

Me (gasping): What are you talking about? What's happening?

(I look at Phil, my oldest and best friend, who looks ashamedly at the floor – Ian looks drained too . . .)

Bob: We think it's for the best . . .

(I can barely speak. Seconds become stretched as I attempt to comprehend what has just happened. I can't believe that my best friends on earth would betray me. I just don't understand why. Then, from deep inside, anger emerges, combined with a blazing sense of injustice . . .)

Me: You can't throw me out of The Human League, it's my group! I'm not going . . .

Bob: We'll compensate you for giving us the name.

Me: I'm keeping the name, I'll see you in court! *(I've heard this on the telly.)* Phil, Ian, what is going on? Did you know about this?

(Nothing, silence, shame.)

As though in a nightmare, as my mind was racing, trying to figure if this was really real, Bob was mumbling on in his posh drone about 'breakdown of communication', 'musical differences', 'change of direction' and other such bullshit platitudes. All of this, *all of it*, was totally unexpected and news to me. I felt like I'd been blindsided and punched in the head in a cowardly action from behind. By my friends. My best friends. I was losing my livelihood, my passion, but, most hurtfully, my most trusted brothers. All in the most cruel way possible, by a method that I wouldn't use on my worst enemy. It was too much to take; I began to sob with rage and frustration.

Bob: You have to relinquish the name, we have a European tour in three weeks, which if we cancel now will bankrupt everyone, as we'll be sued.

Me: I don't give a fuck.

(In that moment, I want to scuttle the ship – if I can't have The Human League, then no one shall! Then, a bolt out of the blue: Ian utters his first words in the meeting . . .)

Ian: If Martyn is thrown out, I'm out too . . .

Wow, what a turn of events . . . through a cloud of tears I thanked Ian from the bottom of my heart for his support. Bob, Phil and Adrian were stunned. Complete silence for a few seconds, as Bob processed the shifting terms of the chess game. They'd fucked it – Ian, he later told me, had been privy to the secret discussions for ages, and was undecided until this meeting which way to go, but the realisation of the awful injustice was just something he didn't ultimately want to be part of. Ian and I were close musical collaborators from the beginning, and it was us who brought Phil into the group. I think Ian also believed that our musical direction was just beginning and potentially had a long, successful future. I'm not sure he felt the same way about what was to be revealed as the new version of The Human League, obviously planned ahead and presented as a fait accompli.

135

Of course, all this was sold to the press as 'plucky underdogs left with no musicians cobble together a band and triumph over adversity', with Ian and myself somehow 'spun' as abandoning the group: in other words, as though it was our doing, and our idea in the first place! Let me put on record that it was their plan that failed thanks to Ian's loyalty, and that Ian and I were the victims of a botched plot. The account of the split currently on Wikipedia says this ... all of the items highlighted in bold are wrong ...

> The relationship between Oakey and Ware had always been turbulent, and the pair often quarrelled over creative **and personal matters**. The lack of success compared with the success of Gary Numan's work at that time had brought matters to a head. Ware insisted the band maintain their pure electronic sound while **Oakey wanted to emulate more successful pop groups**. The pair clashed continually, **with Ware eventually walking out**. Taking Ware's side, Ian Craig Marsh joined him.
>
> **Manager Bob Last tried to reconcile both parties**, and when that proved impossible various options were suggested, **including two new bands under a Human League sublabel**. Eventually it was agreed that Oakey would continue with the Human League name while Ware and Marsh would form a completely new band, which became Heaven 17

The best bit is 'Manager Bob Last tried to reconcile both parties' ... I can only assume that Bob himself wrote this utter crap in a delusional state. The exact opposite is true, and he has since admitted as much. Bob's best friend Jo Callis (whom I'd always got on with since we supported the Revillos/Rezillos in London) had been slated to take over as traditional pop songwriter/guitarist/

keyboardist. Ian Burden from alternative Sheffield band Graph was drafted in on synths and bass. But the apocryphal myth that Phil, in a moment of desperation, had a flash of 'common people' inspiration to ask Suzanne and Joanne to join the group one night in the Crazy Daizy nightclub after being left in the lurch by the evil Martyn and Ian is utter rubbish. This was planned in advance of the split, then revealed afterwards. Adrian somehow managed to convince Phil that he should play synth and help the songwriting in the group. Madness.

The day after the meeting, and after discussions over a pint with Ian, we decided to meet again with Bob to break the impasse. We had decided, essentially, that there was no possibility of reconciliation, and that Ian and I would start a new band; we would relinquish rights to the Human League name in return for compensation. What we wanted was a share of royalties on the next Human League album. We agreed with Bob (Phil and Adrian were absent) that the deal could be done if Ian and myself received 1 per cent royalty each on the retail price of the album. He agreed, and also he astonishingly suggested that he would be happy to remain our manager and help us with whatever our next venture might be. I've never been a grudge-holding kind of person, and his offer seemed genuine enough, so we accepted. Bob then invited myself and my girlfriend (soon to be wife) Karen up to his home in Edinburgh to brainstorm some ideas about what to do next. At least this was a compassionate move, I felt at the time, and things started to feel a little less earth-shattering.

Once in Edinburgh, still reeling in a state of shock at the split a few days earlier, Bob suggested an idea that really appealed to me: the concept of Ian and me forming a production company that could maximise our passion for working in the recording studio. He had obviously had preliminary discussions with Virgin, and intimated that they might be open to this innovative structure. The idea was that we would re-sign to Virgin Records on a six-year deal (standard in those days) as an umbrella production company, and that we would write and produce up to six albums a year, all with different group identities – a bit like a mini-Motown production line (PWL later formed a similar entity for their artist roster). I loved the idea, and we quickly moved on to brainstorming a name. I intuitively felt that it would be fun to conceptualise the production company as a kind of bland, corporate institution – you know, the kind that feels like it's been around forever, but you've never noticed, and ambiguously could be massive, or not.

'How about something like the BBC? Umm, British Electric Company has a ring to it.'

Bob called his lawyer to ask for advice, and he came back to the table. 'We can't imply we're a public utility, so can't use "company". However, there are other organisational words we can use apparently – Institution [I didn't like that, reminded me of the Women's Institute, sounded too conservative], Association [nah, too bland], Society [nope, sounded like a building society] – how about something that sounds more educational?'

'Foundation! That's it ... The British Electric Foundation!'

It sounded as though it was important, timeless and had always been there, even if you'd never noticed it. I was excited – I could visualise the logo. 'It should have a caps typeface which is kind of roman but appears to be carved into stone or embossed on an ageing brass plaque. Also, maybe just the initials BEF – more mysterious.'

Bob loved the idea, got it approved by his lawyers and, together with his partner Hilary Morrison, started to design the logo (Hilary and he co-designed many of his record label Fast Product's sleeves). I asked him to make the logo look like it might have been designed in the 1930s, and his creation is an excellent piece of design, incorporating a large tape reel as a key image.

Karen and I returned to London in much better spirits but still very deeply hurt by the whirlwind of events and emotions that I'd had a week to unpack. I arranged to meet Ian to share the exciting news, and as we brainstormed ideas, I casually mentioned that I'd always liked the idea of forming a band named after a fictitious group in *A Clockwork Orange* – The Heaven Seventeen. It was number 4 in the chart on the wall of the record store as Alex chatted up the two lollypop-sucking girls. These are the fictitious bands in the top-ten list and real bands that were named after them . . .

Heaven Seventeen (Heaven 17)

Johnny Zhivago (punk band from Essex, active 1999–2002)

The Humpers (garage punk band from Long Beach, California,
    active 1989–98)

The Sparks (rock/pop band from Los Angeles, California, active
    from 1970)

The Legend (English heavy metal band/Shadows tribute band/
    Christian rock band/ rockabilly band)

The Blow Goes

Bread Brothers

Cyclops

The Comic Strips

Goggly Gogol

We were quite keen on Goggly Gogol as well, and other suggestions included Monolith and The Wordmasters. We settled on Heaven Seventeen and told Bob, who immediately insisted that we should turn 'Seventeen' into '17' as it would internationalise the name (and it simply looked more snappy and contemporary). He was right. It was impossible to dislike Bob, he was a socialist like us, but also a creative entrepreneur, which both Ian and I admired and aspired to be. His Fast Product label was highly influential and artistically credible. Even to this day, I have a big soft spot for him, notwithstanding his role in the split.

The next job was to find a lead singer. 'How about Glenn, is he still in London?' said Ian.

'I suppose I can ask, I'm not sure what his plans are,' I replied. The last I knew he was still lead singer in 57 Men, which were being mooted as a possible signing by several record labels, but it all seemed to have gone quiet for the last month or so. As I mentioned earlier, Glenn would have been our first choice as Human League singer had he not moved to London, so this seemed to be a karmic possibility.

I now felt a great deal more optimistic than I had before I went to Edinburgh. I found out Glenn had just returned home to Sheffield and got straight on to the phone. Here is a transcript of how it went . . .

Me: Hi Glenn, how's it going?
Glenn: Good, Mart. Fancy a drink?
Me: Always. How about that pub opposite Meatwhistle?
Glenn: Five o'clock?
Me: Deal!

I didn't want to ask such an important question over the phone: I needed to be able to persuade him in the flesh, after a pint or two . . .

I needn't have worried. It seemed like the stars were aligning, everything felt right, the timing, the fact that my band had split and Glenn had returned to Sheffield. He was ready, we were ready, we were two pints of Ward's Best Bitter into our session, so I took a deep breath and popped the question.

'I want you to be the lead singer in our new band, it's going to be called Heaven 17, like in *Clockwork Orange*. Are you up for it?'

Before I'd finished the question, Glenn said, 'I thought you were never going to ask – I'd love to!'

And so Heaven 17 was born. It was that simple.

Bob negotiated the 'leaving members" terms with Virgin Records and Virgin Publishing, and soon Ian and I signed the innovative British Electric Foundation production deal. Potentially six albums a year (crackers), all different identities (double crackers), with the possibility that any of the created recording identities would have their own separate budgets and contracts. Over six years this could have led to thirty-six bands, all with their own budgets and contracts! Insanity but, at least in theory, very exciting. In addition, one of the initial albums we wanted to release was under the BEF identity but as a separate creative unit!

We started organising and recording immediately, both *Music of Quality and Distinction Volume 1* (the cheek of it, as though we were about to take over the world), and the first BEF band Heaven 17's debut album. Imagine recording *two* debut albums simultaneously on night shifts while, in the same studio during the day, Phil and the new Human League band were recording demos for what was about to become *Dare*. All in Monumental Studios, a filthy, part-derelict, ex-veterinary practice in an abandoned part of industrial Sheffield. Never in the history of recorded popular music has such historical creativity emerged in such a short space of time from such a shithole. But it was our shithole, and it was us against the world . . . and The Human League.

Our first BEF recording session together was a kind of de facto 'pilot' recording – Ian and I were starting to record the BEF first album and we wanted Glenn to cover a classic song we all loved, Jimmy Webb's 'Wichita Lineman'. It was to be an evocative, fully weird and electronic, hauntingly sparse version, largely centred on the bleep hook in the pre-chorus, but it ended up also featuring Glenn on saxophone (which he could barely play) and our friend Dave Lockwood on acoustic guitar. Glenn's immature but impressive baritone suited the mood of the piece perfectly, and it rapidly became obvious that he was a recording 'natural'. There is a saying in the music industry that the recording process 'loves' certain singers, i.e. the characteristics of their voice, the evenness of tone and volume, pitching, timbre, etc., are suited to the recorded medium, and Glenn needed very little processing on his voice to make it 'sit' in the mix. We 100 per cent knew that we were on to a winner.

An additional benefit was that Glenn's range and Bowie-influenced delivery was not a million miles away from Phil's voice. This meant that the early instrumental sketches that Ian and I had been working on the next Human League album would almost certainly suit Glenn's voice just as well. These later became the completely electronic second side of *Penthouse and Pavement* – 'Geisha Boys and Temple Girls', 'Let's All Make a Bomb', 'At the Height of the Fighting (He-La-Hu)', 'Song with No Name' and 'We're Going to Live for a Very Long Time'. It's interesting to imagine how these songs would have developed as Human League lyrics – I'm almost certain they wouldn't have been as diverse and compelling.

The really cool thing, though, was that Glenn slotted into our creative process as though he'd been with us for years – it felt absolutely natural and confirmed our belief that he should have been the original singer for The Human League. We will never know if that would have worked or not, but Heaven 17 was absolutely the right home for Glenn. All those years of playfully messing around with real-but-imaginary groups seemed to be paying off. The metaphor that has always stuck with me is this: when you buy an authentic Chinese wok, you have to 'season' it several times (oil it, heat it, wipe it off and repeat) before it is ready for use. Musical Vomit, Underpants, Dick Velcro and the Astronettes, VDK and the Studs, The Dead Daughters and The Future were all leading me to this point – if you want me to be pretentious, let's call it fate.

We were on a mission, an arms race, to beat The Human League to the punch. I was energised, full of righteous anger and a desire for revenge – this was the white-hot fuel that drove us in the coming weeks, months and years to work seven days a week in our shared studio, The League working between 10 a.m. and 10 p.m. and BEF/Heaven 17 working nights, 10 p.m. to 10 a.m. This suited Ian and me as we could fit this into our work schedules as computer operators. The scene was set, and the wok was ready to cook up a storm . . .

Intermission:

Art, Books, Cinema and Comedy

Not a single iota of my career could have happened were it not for my inexhaustible love of culture and humour. Right from the very start, even before Meatwhistle changed my life, as a child I was fascinated with music and television. It was a window into an unimagined world of possibilities, of glamour and fun, a galaxy away from the utilitarian council flats that seemed to be my inevitable destiny.

Apart from my sister's huge collection of records (which had a great influence on my future career), we had virtually no books – so the enormous Sheffield Central Library was like an Aladdin's cave for me. I wasn't particularly interested in traditional children's books (although I was very fond of *Little Women*, which seems to have been an indication of my lifelong empathetic relationship with the opposite sex), but I had a voracious appetite for knowledge and new subjects. To this day, I have little interest in fiction, except for science fiction, but I couldn't get enough about science and technology, the world around us (geography and anthropology), and anything associated with the future. Growing up in the sixties, the space race appeared to this child to be impossibly romantic and optimistic, and therefore anything at all connected with a 'bright new future' was consumed by my sponge-like mind. I was always obsessed with fantasy, which was understandable to a certain extent considering there were some legendary shows on the TV then – *Bewitched, The Munsters, The Addams Family*, the great Warner Bros cartoons, *Boss Cat, Yogi Bear* ... The entire swathe of sci-fi fantasy series, *The Outer Limits, The Time Tunnel, Lost in Space*, etc. tapped into (or created) my love of imaginary worlds and times. The magnificent Gerry Anderson series had an enormous influence too – starting with *Four Feather Falls, Torchy the Battery Boy, Supercar, Fireball XL5*, then *Stingray, Thunderbirds* and *Captain Scarlet and the Mysterons*. After that I gradually lost interest, but the die was already cast.

Of course, I was quite typical of my age group then. School breaks were often spent excitedly discussing the previous evening's episodes, and this was all reinforced by the enormously popular weekly magazine *TV21*, which was linked to Anderson's Supermarionation series. It featured an interesting take on the normal comic format, i.e. the front page was laid out as though it was a newspaper in the present tense, which fascinated me.

The proprietors of *TV21* were very clever – they would regularly have special free gifts physically included in the magazine. This encouraged kids to pester their parents to subscribe at the local newsagent's (in case the free gift was lost in transit). One week, the free gift was a tatty piece of plastic, which could enclose a cut-out pennant. This in turn could be attached to your bike (which we couldn't afford, but anyway ...). The smell of the strange plastic has stayed with me to this day, and still triggers the memory of unconfined happiness.

Film was a great working-class escape also – and the 1960s had its fair share of classics. The first film I was taken to was in 1963 when I was seven years old: *Summer Holiday* with Cliff Richard. This was far from a classic, but did feature one bit of cinema magic – the opening sequence was in black and white, and then, to my young eyes at least, magically transformed into full CinemaScope and

Technicolor. I couldn't believe what I was witnessing. The rest of the film unfortunately was dull as dishwater, and I quickly became bored and politely asked to go home so I could play football with my friends. Soon after that, I was given a second chance with the strange but epically bonkers *Those Magnificent Men in Their Flying Machines* (which I managed to sit through and enjoy) and the three-hour-long fantasy epic, *Chitty Chitty Bang Bang* (time just flew – excuse the pun). Let's face it, I was hooked.

My love of film grew during the 1960s, and my friends and I managed to sneak into several X- or AA-rated films (we were around thirteen at the time). In 1971, there was a sex education film on at the local Odeon, which created enormous excitement for pubescent teenagers. It was called *Growing Up* and featured sex scenes, including male and female masturbation. We were in heaven. There was very little in the way of sex education either at home or at school, so all this openness and naked flesh was a revelation. 'When can I get started?' was my all-consuming thought.

In the wake of the growing influence of the Women's Liberation Movement, there were some very strange movies which reached the light of day on general release. My friends and myself were always on the lookout for any films which might reveal any form of illicit nakedness, and one such film that we sneaked into was *Prudence and the Pill*, which portrayed the conflicting and comical attempts by five couples to avoid pregnancy by using contraceptive pills. All of their efforts are ultimately unsuccessful, with the result that all five of the women give birth the following year. It wasn't quite what we were looking for. Although there was a modicum of nudity, it was more of a failed social comedy, and we left unimpressed with the low percentage of naked breasts on show.

One of my most significant memories is of a visit to the children's library when I was around ten years old. I was looking for new subjects to try and wanted to make sense of the world around me, and I came across a section called 'humour' – maybe this could help me understand why I was so curious about comedy and laughter. One book was entitled *The Anatomy of Humour*, and was a dull, academic tome which tried to dissect the mechanism of what makes us laugh (it wasn't this book, for starters). At the same time, I borrowed a book by James Thurber, the American cartoonist, author, humorist, journalist, playwright and celebrated wit. This all was terribly out of my depth for the time, and, although the books were almost indecipherable to me, I was determined to crack the puzzle of why these dry tomes were in the humour section. I never did. Humour was an enormous influence on my creative development; in fact, it might even have been the most important influence. The Goons, Monty Python, *The Young Ones*, or more mainstream transatlantic comedy – *Rowan and Martin's Laugh In*, *The Smothers Brothers*, *The Flintstones*, *My Favourite Martian*, *Car 54, Where Are You?*, maybe even the tongue-in-cheek irony of Adam West's *Batman* TV series. All of these were crucial building blocks of irreverent but popular comedic intent, which become a filter through which my creative work was fed.

Art has always been central to my being. From the early days in Sheffield at the Graves Gallery, through to temporary exhibitions of avant-garde artists and immersive light installations, all forms of art have been a massive inspiration to me in not only my musical career, but the accompanying graphic design. I now understand after travelling the world that the UK needs more creativity and colour generally, and I must have intuitively understood this from an early age. In every city I visit, my first port of call is almost always an art gallery, and of course my love of Venice (I lived there on and off for twenty-seven years) means that I always witness the Venice Biennale – one of the world's most important contemporary art festivals. I simply cannot imagine how impoverished my life would be without my love of art of all descriptions. And I can't draw or paint or sculpt for toffee, dammit.

I can, however, express my artistic compositional appreciation using photography as my medium. I am a relentless hunter of striking images and compositions. Since 1980, I must have taken at least 200,000 photos, most of which I have access to on demand in my digital library. One day I would like to exhibit the best of these as a kind of abstract visual autobiography, but we shall see. I think it's so important to have an easy and regular creative outlet to help maintain mental health and wellbeing. Otherwise, what are we on earth for?

The epiphanic moment for me regarding film as a major influence was in 1977. Imagine the scene: it's 7 a.m., Paul Bower, Ian Marsh and myself are all queuing outside the Gaumont cinema in Barker's Pool, opposite Sheffield City Hall. We are near the front of the line, and we've been there since roughly 5 a.m. We are all knackered but overexcited. What would cause us to sacrifice our precious sleep? This is the UK-wide simultaneous premiere of the most anticipated film of the decade – *Star Wars* (retroactively titled *Star Wars: Episode IV – A New Hope*), and, in a unique marketing gimmick, is set to be launched at 7 a.m. across the country (and the world). Here I am, proudly wearing my silver plastic waist jacket, thinking I am somehow more futuristic than the rest of the normal people in the queue. In these pre-internet times, the hype has been spread by word of mouth and mainstream media, but there are no leaked clips or even images, just the advertisements, which suggest this is a major moment in cinematic history, and our imaginations are running riot.

There was a reporter, presumably from the local paper the *Sheffield Star*, who was approaching several people in the queue for quotes. I was still a little shy, but eventually (probably attracted by my loud jacket) the reporter approached me. 'Are you excited to see this movie?' What a stupid question, why would I be here otherwise? 'Of course, we're all big science-fiction fans, so this should be fantastic,' I gushed. I gave him my name, then he asked, 'And what do you do for a living, Martyn?' I think for a second – computer operator sounds dull, so I blurted out, in an awkwardly arrogant way, 'I'm in a band called The Human League, and we're going to be very famous!' The reporter is laughing in a pitying and patronising way. 'Well let's hope so young man,' he smarms. *We'll show you*, I thought, and thankfully, eventually, we made it happen.

It is hard to describe the impact this film had on us at the time. It had a great story, of course, but the attention to detail was incredible – simply put, it felt real. The worlds were brilliantly realised in obsessive detail, but most impressive was the genius touch of imparting almost every character and piece of machinery and technology with the patina of age. Until now, in all science-fiction films, the sets and characters were squeaky clean, box fresh, but these guys and objects had lived a little – they had seen life, alien life, and we felt privileged to witness such a convincing reality. The *coup de grâce* was the final act where Luke Skywalker's X-wing fighter squadron attempted to destroy the Death Star, while being pursued by the Empire's TIE fighters. Special effects of this complexity and detail had never been attempted before, it was all so thrilling and mesmerising. This was clearly one of the greatest and most significant movies of all time.

This section cannot be considered complete without reference to the most important film director in my list of influences – Stanley Kubrick. His inimitable vision, his technical excellence, his daring and prescient futurism, completely embodied an artistic panoply of aspiration for me. *A Clockwork Orange* is still my favourite film, not only for its stunning imagery, but for the strength and daring of its conceptual depth. Of course, we named Heaven 17 after an imaginary band both in the film and in Anthony Burgess's brilliant book. But in reality, the film that had the most influence of my world was *2001: A Space Odyssey*. It's immutable calmness, brilliance of imagery (many contemporary space films have still not lived up to its production values fifty years on) and strangeness of narrative create controversy and mystery to the current day. Then there is the sheer beauty of the 70mm print in Cinemascope, ultra-wide aspect. I recently saw a non-digital restored original celluloid print shown at the BFI Southbank, and I can confirm that it has lost none of its magic. This film demonstrated to me that creative bravery (or 'thinking outside the box') could also be massively commercially successful. This is a credo that I've followed for my entire career – be as creatively brave as possible, and the rewards will follow. It doesn't always work, but it has almost always worked for me, and it is *so* much more fulfilling. People often underestimate the role of humour in Kubrick's oeuvre. Would *Lolita* or *Dr Strangelove* have even worked as movies without a generous swathe of black absurdity, or the bone-dry ironic humour of HAL 3000's demise singing 'Daisy, Daisy' – or Alex's dry, northernish observations as running commentary to his appalling thoughts in *A Clockwork Orange*? The answer is no.

Thank you, Stanley Kubrick, you have inspired so many creative lives.

The View Outside: John Wesley Barker, BEF and Heaven 17 orchestral arranger

As I write on 12 December 2020, it's my birthday and one way and another, my birthdays remind me of Martyn. In 1980, my friend Rene Rice gave me Reproduction *by* The Human League *for my birthday. I played 'You've Lost That Loving Feeling' over and over. The minimal synth backing absolutely blew me away. The release of* Penthouse and Pavement *was the flowering of a solid synth groove and was the long-awaited arrival of happy, groovy, meaningful, popular electronic music. Then amazingly, through a set of lucky events, Lost Jockey gigs, and while playing for the Metamatic sessions, I found myself actually working with Martyn on the album* Music of Quality and Distinction *in John Foxx's Garden Studio in Shoreditch. I mean, what an amazing way life works out!*

With the simply astounding voice of Billy Mackenzie (we miss you Billy), I made an orchestral backing to the huge 'It's Over'. During the sessions, there was a mention of a forthcoming second album from Heaven 17. 'Make the orchestra sound like Big Country,' that's all Martyn said. What a spec! Then a few weeks later, on my birthday in 1982, we recorded the orchestra for The Luxury Gap *in AIR Studios. Martyn has a big heart – he's my kind of musician and very prolific, endlessly creating and writing and encouraging others, always striving for new and interesting ways to make music. We had fun in the studio and the creative atmosphere suited me. Martyn and Glenn and Greg [co-producer Greg Walsh] got really into the harp during the sessions. An AMS DMX 15-80S digital delay processor in the control room became a whirling dervish filled with harp glissandi. We ran two twenty-four-track machines in sync using a Q-Lock for the orchestral sessions. Looking through the handwritten manuscripts for* The Luxury Gap *orchestra sessions (yes, in 1982 I didn't have a computer, just pencil, paper and a cassette deck), one of the songs was called 'Tony Benn': on release it was called 'Temptation' and became a hit. Thank goodness, cos my sessions were expensive but, now we know, worth it.*

1981–2: BEF's *Music* . . . and Heaven 17's *Penthouse and Pavement*

'Here comes the daylight, here comes my job . . .'

It's hard to describe our febrile mood during that insanely creative and motivated period. At that time, for understandable reasons, I now disliked the traitorous Phil and wanted nothing more than to see The Human League Mk2's first efforts at recording a hit single fail. Their first live gig with the new lineup was pretty weak, but not a total embarrassment. Glenn went to the gig (at Doncaster Rotters, I think, which was a long-arranged warm-up gig for the European tour), and, always the diplomat, said it was OK, but that we didn't have a lot to worry about – he thought that the novelty of the girls might be a temporary thing, that they couldn't really sing or dance in time with each other – generally Suzanne was in time with the music whereas Joanne appeared to be dancing to someone else's tune on headphones, and that the other newly recruited musicians had saved the day (we suspected that Jo and Ian would work out for them).

One day in the studio, we were preparing to record a rough mix, and we had run out of ¼-inch tape. We found an unlabelled reel which had been left on the machine, but thought we'd better ensure it wasn't any kind of important recording before we overwrote it. What we heard was astonishing. It had obviously been used as a tape delay by The League (i.e. there was recording of live singing on it, unmixed). Normally both camps were paranoid about ensuring tapes were removed from the studio so there could be no spying on what each other was up to, so this was a coup.

It was *awful*. It revealed an attempt by Phil and the girls to sing the chorus of what was to become 'The Sound of the Crowd'. We were in ecstasy – if this was the best they could come up with, then surely we were going to win this war. And it was hopelessly funny, with the girls childishly and consistently out of tune. My God, there were even some muffled comments on the tape between takes, with Phil encouraging them to try harder. We pissed ourselves, then replaced the tape on the machine so Phil wouldn't know anything was amiss, giggling like naughty schoolchildren who had left a whoopee cushion on the teacher's seat.

Of course, we made sure we never bumped into The League in the studio. At the time, we hoped that there might be further hilarious bloopers to cheer us up, but alas this never happened again. Our naughtiness knew no bounds. Glenn and Ian decided to ask Suzanne and Joanne out by way of an apology, ostensibly because, in the previous week, we had unintentionally slagged them off as 'dodgy boilers' in an *NME* piece by Paul Morley. This was a drunken off-the-cuff, cheeky comment which we thought was off the record. It clearly wasn't, and we never made that sort of mistake ever again. The real reason for asking them was to wind up Phil (I think it was probably Ian's idea), and much to Ian and Glenn's amazement, the girls accepted. They took them for a meal, and it was apparently all very civilised, but I was concerned this would raise the bar regarding our rivalry. To Phil's credit, he didn't rise to the bait.

Around this time, Karen and I decided to move in together and finally permanently leave Sheffield, moving to Notting Hill (which we'd grown to love while staying at Glenn's flat in London). All we could afford was a tiny attic studio flat, which required us to duck our heads as we moved towards the edges of the room. It was *really* small. When Karen's mum came down for her first visit, she had a horrified look on her face as we climbed the narrow staircase to the top floor, passing a Filipino family who were very fond of cooking with extremely pungent fish sauce, which saturated the air and made our eyes sting. I like all kinds of world food, but the staircase stank, it really was something. We proudly opened the door to our tiny abode, and Karen's mum, crestfallen and disbelieving, said, 'Is this it?' as though it was possibly some form of anteroom leading to the real apartment. Clearly we hadn't managed expectations very well, as she spent the rest of the afternoon close to tears. All would end happily in a couple of years, however, as the royalties for my first major production success, Tina Turner's 'Let's Stay Together', enabled us to buy a really fancy split-level apartment just off Westbourne Grove (heart of the 'front line', and site of the world-famous Notting Hill Carnival, the biggest street party in Europe on August bank holiday every year). God bless Tina. The descriptions of the hearty parties, especially the legendary open-house Carnival 'home club nights' lasting forty-eight to seventy-two hours, that we hosted at the Westbourne Park flat could fill a separate book – they were happy, happy times, with very few cares in the world.

Around this time, I met two of my oldest and best friends – Spike Denton and Mick Clarke (rest in peace). They both were from the club world and both dance music aficionados – Spike and his friend Neville were Soho habitués, part of that demi-monde, and this opened a whole new world of fun and excitement to me. Spike introduced me to the Groucho Club, where I am sitting writing this at this very moment, and he also introduced me to the

Wag Club, where I met Robert Elms and the guys from Blue Rondo à la Turk – Chris Sullivan and Christos Tolera are good friends to this day. Our gang's taste in music was different to the New Romantic scene as epitomised by the Blitz crowd – ours was more cool, rare and groovy, generally black or Latin music, made for dancing rather than posing. This suited me perfectly, given my soul-loving background. As an added benefit, the Wag was also an attractant to some of the most beautiful girls in the club scene in London, and an excellent place for people-watching, flirting and more, and that's pretty much all you need for a great night out.

Back at our tiny new flat, it seemed that there was always something creative happening between Glenn, Ian and me, mainly daft ideas that seemed a sound idea at the time. I had just bought an early hand-held video recorder (the size of a small microwave), and we were obsessed with filming everything – it was almost like we were trying to recreate our time at Meatwhistle. But this time we'd blue-sky comedic ideas for imaginary TV pilots, and actually film them. One such idea was 'Pink Peter', which was a risqué gay version of the children's programme *Blue Peter*, in honour of our very gay friend Robert Bond (who has since touchingly confessed he wanted to sleep with Ian, Glenn and me). I wish those tapes still existed: they were embarrassing but almost certainly hilarious. We were also obsessed with the novel world of computer gaming, and I was the only one of our crew to possess a BBC B computer, for which there were many very basic but entertaining games – I miss the simple engagement of those types of games, it's all a million polygons and photorealism now, not as much room for the imagination any more.

Meanwhile, our writing and recording work was getting serious. Stories from our first London recording sessions at the Townhouse are detailed in the track-by-track appendix later, but suffice to say that this was the most exciting period of my life so far. Opportunities seemed to be randomly flying towards me at a rate that I could barely comprehend, but with the energy and optimism of youth, I was ready to take on allcomers. Not only were we recording and mixing *Penthouse and Pavement*, but under the aegis of BEF, Ian and I were about to embark on not one, but two more album projects, the cassette-only *Music for Stowaways* and the vinyl LP version *Music for Listening To*.

Stowaway was the early name for the Sony Walkman – and better I reckon. As a tech enthusiast (I didn't get enough toys as a child), I bought one of the earliest models in the country. I was so impressed with the brand-new idea of walking the streets in my own private film, complete with personal choice of soundtrack, that I wanted to release a suite of electronic music specifically for this purpose, thereby riding on this massive paradigm shift (and Sony's huge marketing budget). The fact that *Music for Stowaways* was cassette-only was highly pretentious on our part, but I've always believed in the 'collectable artefact', and to this end we insisted that each cassette was uniquely numbered. I was heavily influenced by Tony Wilson's Factory Records approach, where each release was numbered and given the respect usually accorded to works in the art world.

I love this from Wikipedia: 'Largely ignored upon release, the music has been praised in retrospect, with critics crediting both the cassette and LP versions of the album as being prophetic of later musical styles.' On AllMusic, John Bush calls it 'One of the few synth-pop records of the era – instrumental or otherwise – that attempted to develop the universe of possibilities inherent in the form ... It's not even a matter of sounding dated; *Music for Listening To* sounds decades ahead of its time and could easily be taken for music produced 20 years later.' And apparently, according to the

Quietus in 2013, Moby rates *Music for Stowaways* as one of his favourite albums and says the track 'The Decline of the West' helped inspire his incredible career.

We reluctantly agreed to allow the release of the vinyl version after Virgin complained that foreign licensees couldn't afford to manufacture the cassette. This was total bollocks, I now realise. The real reason was that they hoped to sell a lot more on vinyl. There was one stipulation that we made: that it couldn't be sold in the UK. This was unenforceable, however, as record shops simply imported them. Well, at least we tried. As was typical of our awkwardness at the time, we also insisted on adding a couple of different tracks unavailable on the cassette – 'A Baby Called Billy' and 'BEF Ident', which we still use as a walk-on piece of 'sonic branding' for Heaven 17 live concerts. I wanted every release we put out to feel like it was something to be valued, both musically and visually, some highly collectable that would be treasured in the future. This was to be an ongoing theme in future years: the huge ambition to create work that could be regarded as 'timeless'. At one point, I even considered changing the name BEF to 'Timeless Productions'. I'm glad I didn't.

As if all this wasn't enough, I was approached by Carol Wilson from Virgin offshoot label DinDisc to see if I'd be interested in producing the debut album for Hot Gossip, the extremely popular and sexually provocative dance troupe from Kenny Everett's TV show, which was essential viewing at the time. I was dumbstruck, as this would be my first third-party production, and I wasn't sure if I could handle the responsibility, but what swung it was that Arlene Phillips (the famous choreographer who created Hot Gossip) was a huge fan of the first two Human League albums and wanted to cover several of our songs! I couldn't believe it – what on earth would they do with such unusual and frankly less-than-commercial songs? What would they sound like without Phil and me? But Arlene was very keen on the dramatic and cinematic qualities of the different songs' narratives and felt they would be perfect for videos and maybe even live choreography.

I agreed, cut a deal, and I met the members of Hot Gossip for the first time on the first day in the studio. We had a mere fourteen days to record and mix the album from scratch, and I had to quickly assess the relative strengths of the different singers. Helped by engineers Pete Walsh and Nick Patrick, we recorded versions of songs we wrote included 'Soul Warfare', 'I Don't Depend on You', 'Geisha Boys and Temple Girls', 'Morale', 'Word Before Last' and 'Circus of Death', together with a Sting song called 'I Burn for You' and 'Houses in Motion' by Talking Heads.

The girls were hot, very hot, so hot that Glenn found any excuse to hang out at the studio and work his irresistible charm. I'm still not sure whether he managed to seal the deal with any of the girls, but I know he would have kept it to himself even if he had. The boys were hot too, and vocally all of them had been stage-trained, which is a different feel to a more untrained, raw rock/pop style. Performance-wise, this caused me a bit of trouble as getting anything out of them that sounded authentic and passionate was not easy. But a shout out in particular goes to the beautiful redhead Kim Leeson for her sensitive performance on 'I Burn for You'. Fun fact: I used a Synclavier sampling keyboard for this track, which had the first realistic sounding string samples available, and I played all the parts manually.

The album didn't do much sales-wise, but it was well-paid work and a fascinating insight into this new, highly lucrative world of production. I was proud of what we achieved despite the obvious limitations. The videos for 'Circus of Death' and 'I Burn for You' are still on YouTube, and are totally indicative of that period, both good and bad ... make your own mind up ... I like them.

My second effort at outside production came along almost immediately, with a Belgian band called Allez Allez, who wanted a trendy producer, and I apparently fitted the bill. They were fronted by a beautiful female lead singer called Sarah, and – surprise, surprise – Glenn managed to scrape into the recording sessions, and quickly lured Sarah under his spell (or was it the other way around?). In any case, they fell madly in love, and within months they unexpectedly got married. For whatever reason, the marriage didn't last, and I believe that the break-up broke Glenn's heart – for a while at least. The songs and our new versions were interesting and critically well received, but the band split up after the first album, which was a real pity.

The initial idea of *Music of Quality and Distinction Volume 1* (I intended this to be a series from the outset) was to establish us slap bang in the middle of the public pop consciousness. The deliberately self-reverential, ironic title was post-modernist before the term was popular outside the fine-art world, but in fact was copied from a vintage shirt box, as indeed was the concept for the album cover, which was a faithful pastiche. The photo shoot even used the same location, the Royal Garden Hotel on Kensington High Street. Ian and I were also desperate to establish a production 'house style' as bait for future lucrative outside productions, so it was crucial to attract as many 'names' as possible to participate. Fortunately, Virgin loved the audacity of the concept as much as we did and opened their contact list to us – however, it was me and my big mouth that did most of the talking and persuading. The artists we approached must have felt they wanted to help out a ludicrously inexperienced but extremely enthusiastic novice in the field, or maybe I'm underselling myself. Maybe it was a combination of both, but between me and Virgin's A&R department (take a bow, Gemma Caulfield), we had a high strike rate. Of course, some we approached more or less laughed at us (not in a cruel way) – Bowie, Ferry, Steve Harley, etc., but we did pretty well.

It was important to us to create a juxtaposition, a friction, between the electronic music interpretation of famous songs and ensuring that the artist seemed an excitingly unusual or in some cases inappropriate choice. Early enthusiasts who immediately signed on the dotted line included the glorious Billy Mackenzie (what a scoop), Paula Yates (famous for presenting *The Tube* TV show and partnering Bob Geldof, not so much for her voice), Glenn, of course, and the magnificent Sandie Shaw (who was married to one of the Virgin directors at the time, Nik Powell). I know it's now controversial, but I was a huge fan of Gary Glitter and The Glitter Band, and I was determined to create the first recording session where they all played and sang live together in the studio (it was normally their producer Mike Leander who played most of the parts), and I was thrilled that they agreed. Bernadette Nolan, from Irish middle-of-the-road singing group and Saturday-night TV regulars The Nolans, had just left her sisters and was looking to start a solo career. I'd always been a fan of Paul Jones from Manfred Mann, who nailed 'There's a Ghost in My House', and it turned out to be a huge bonus when I was told he was one of the UK's leading harmonica players, and his perfor-mance on 'Ball of Confusion' was incredible.

Much of the recording took place at John Foxx's Garden Studio in Shoreditch and we loved its bohemian vibe. John himself was a gracious host, whose music and approach we greatly admired. The house engineer was Gareth Jones, who, thank God, was one of a rare breed: an engineer who understood and loved electronic instruments, and knew how to record them. He went on to produce many famous acts including Depeche Mode and Erasure, and most of the acts on Daniel Miller's Mute label. We also brought in a young but experienced engineer called Nick Patrick, who went on to be nominated for Grammys for his work on the fiftieth anniversary recording of *West Side Story*. He was a quiet but interesting guy, particularly strong on orchestral recording, which is exactly what we needed. One small caveat, however – I was very strong-willed and always insisted I knew best, and I was in charge at every moment of recording, mixing and mastering. With the benefit of hindsight, a lot of these mixes are too bright and brittle, and I mixed some of these complex forty-eight-track recordings with a massively arrogant attitude ('if I can't hear an instrument, then push the volume up to eleven'). I was bluffing, but I think Nick secretly fixed many of my bolshy errors.

Plans for an attention-grabbing release were cooked up, and Virgin really pushed the boat out re marketing and formats. I had the idea to release the album as a boxed set of five double-A-sided singles, and again Virgin's marketing department loved it. These sets are now much sought after forty years on. Virgin suggested a big launch party at Kensington Roof Gardens, and I asked Glenn (my fashion guru) to advise on a new outfit for the do. He suggested Johnson's on King's Road, and I bought my first ever glamorous, showbiz suit – a shiny, blue, slubbed raw silk two-piece with shoulder pads, which was the style at the time. Of course, Glenn got the real thing, an Antony Price suit which made him look a million dollars (which is roughly what it cost), but we all looked great at the launch. There was a sound system for the playback of the album, which unfortunately sounded terrible due the appalling acoustics of the space, but everyone was so drunk I don't think they noticed. This was the first obvious example of a terrible curse I suffer from, namely that I automatically analyse every acoustic space I enter, whether I want to or not. It can be useful, but usually it's a pain in the arse. Most of the artists were there – Sandie Shaw,

Billy Mackenzie, Paul Jones, Bernadette Nolan – no Gary Glitter (probably just as well, as he would have upstaged all attending) and no Tina Turner as she was based in LA at the time.

It was decided that the first single off the album would be Tina's incandescent version of 'Ball of Confusion', and we were very happy with that. Unbelievably, however, Tina was almost regarded as a has-been by the youth-obsessed playlisters at Radio 1 and *Top of the Pops*, so it made little impact. If only they knew what was to come a couple of years later. The next effort was Sandie Shaw's beautiful and emotional version of 'Anyone Who Had a Heart' (the Bacharach/David song originally made famous by her then-rival Cilla Black), but once again, the ageist radio and TV producers failed to grasp the post-modernist idea.

Although we were disappointed at the lack of chart success, there was no denying that the album was well liked for its originality and daring, and our risk-taking quickly led to further offers of production work, including Tina's new album – so, the job was a good 'un, as we say in Sheffield. We were far from downhearted, we were just getting started . . .

The View Outside: Pete Walsh, co-producer and engineer, *Penthouse and Pavement*

Penthouse and Pavement *was not only pivotal for Martyn, Ian and Glenn as the debut album in their new constellation; it was also a hugely important album for me at the beginning of my career. It was my first recording session as a freelance engineer after leaving Utopia Studios; my first experience working in the New Wave synth-pop genre. It gave me my first top 20 hit and a gold disc to hang in the studio. It also gave me a name within Virgin Records, which directly led to working with Simple Minds and China Crisis. Martyn gave me the time, freedom and confidence to experiment with the sound and was generous enough to give me my first production credit as 'Assistant to the Producers'. Up until then I hadn't had a lot of experience working with the new technology of electronic music, so it was quite an eye-opener. The concept of the album was intriguing – they'd recorded the Pavement half of it in Sheffield already, and I was brought in to polish that part and to record the Penthouse side of it in London. Maison Rouge was a happening studio in the New King's Road. Eighties Fulham had a real buzz about it, and it felt like we were working on something ground-breaking, sitting in the centre of the scene, as it were. It was great fun and a lot of hard work.*

I remember Martyn huddled over a LinnDrum machine at one side of the desk, programming the tracks, and Ian almost disappearing behind a vast bank of synths and sequencers on the other side of the room. Both worked tirelessly into the early hours of the morning to create the distinctive rhythm patterns and sounds that shaped the album. Glenn was always upbeat, a really funny guy with lots of personality. He always brought a lightness to the atmosphere when he came in. In contrast to the others' quite concentrated and insular roles, Glenn had the freedom to just rock up and sing these incredible vocals that gave the music its human touch. When we took a break, it was to drink cocktails at the studio's in-house bar – there were always lots of other artists and musicians hanging out there. London studios back then were very vibey. Glenn's vocals and additional instruments were recorded at Townhouse Studios in Shepherd's Bush, which boasted table tennis, snooker and its own restaurant. The artwork on the album includes the guys in the corridor at the Townhouse, as well as Penny the studio manager on the phone at the SSL desk.

Some memories stand out particularly. Moments like recording John Wilson's bass guitar on 'Penthouse and Pavement' and the freak-out solo on the outro. At first, I wasn't sure what to do with it, it was difficult to find a perspective on it. It was like a burst of energy, so extreme. Then we realised that it could almost be seen as a kind of fight between instrument and machine – and came up with the concept of the Linn fading out and the bass winning. How mad was that? Recording the whistling on 'Play to Win' was also a hilarious episode that I remember well. The synth was the basis of the whistling theme and we wanted to put a human whistle on top of it. We tried to audition who had the best whistle and kept getting the giggles. Have you ever tried to whistle and laugh at the same time? I actually cannot remember who won, but it may even have been me. I later continued my eminent whistling career on Scott Walker's 'Face on Breast' (Tilt, 1995). The sessions were always fun and pretty relaxed. I think Martyn had found a new lease of life, a new vehicle to express his musical ideas since leaving The Human League, which probably brought an element of excitement to the whole approach. I felt like we were all pushing the bar higher to come up with new effects and new colours to define a new direction of music at the time. We definitely felt like we were the innovators, searching for a fresh sound and attitude.

1983–4: Heaven 17 – *The Luxury Gap*

'Like all the dreams you've never known ...'

In my personal life, these were the happiest of times – a new apartment, a loving wife, a great bunch of friends, enough money to have holidays and fun, the best food, travel, hotels, etc. I even found time to take my delayed honeymoon with Karen, to Venice via the Orient Express, arriving on the Grand Canal and immediately and permanently falling in love with the most incredible and romantic city on earth.

Released in 1981, *Penthouse and Pavement* didn't produce any hit singles and only reached 14, but the album went gold and was in the charts for over a year. Then, at the start of 1983, Bob Last informed us that it was time for him to relinquish his role as manager for BEF and Heaven 17. He felt his work here was done and it was time for us to look after our own affairs, but the reality was that Human League Mk2, following the success of *Dare*, were taking up all his time and energy.

Likewise, Heaven 17 was taking up all of our time now and we were in full control. During the romance of this whirlwind period of our career, and despite the less-than-exceptional chart performance of the singles, I could sense that we were about to find out whether or not we were going to succeed on a global scale. Virgin were initially disappointed, but when we came to discuss writing and recording the normally difficult second album, they gave us a huge confidence boost by not even requesting a provisional recording budget. In other words, we could use the best studios, engineers, musicians, collaborators – they believed in us. Little did we know that Virgin were in some financial difficulty, and that we were one of the bands who they were relying on to solve their major cashflow issues. But still they protected us from this pressure, and encouraged and supported us, which in turn allowed us total creative freedom. We were also still highly motivated to compete with the stellar success of The Human League's huge international acclaim with *Dare*, and the white heat of vengeance still burned brightly. There were to be no half-measures, no pusillanimous attempts at second best, all efforts that could be made would be made. This was the start of a period where we had no holidays for nearly three years. We worked and worked and worked, and we loved our recording home at AIR Studios on Oxford Circus. If there had been sleeping accommodation there, we might not have ever gone home.

Before we took to the studio, most of the demos were created at Glenn's flat in Notting Hill, including the musical arrangements and most of the toplines and lyrics. We wanted to work with Pete Walsh again as co-producer, but after initially agreeing he told us he was already committed to producing the new Simple Minds album, and that he'd have to back out. Always looking for opportunity in setbacks, we discussed who we'd ideally like to work with, in a blue-sky discussion with Virgin. I was very keen on the producer of Rufus and Chaka Khan's 'Ain't Nobody' and Stephanie Mills's 'The Medicine Song', Hawk Wolinski (cool name). Virgin contacted him, he agreed to do it – then two weeks later his manager called to say that he'd been offered a huge Hollywood soundtrack, and he had to pass. Bugger. I occasionally wondered what *The Luxury Gap* would have sounded like if he'd produced it. I'm still curious now. So, we were back to square one.

During our ongoing search for possible co-producers, Pete Walsh called and suggested his brother Greg, who was very talented and experienced, and had learned his trade with the Beatles/Abbey Road engineer Geoff Emerick. He had also worked with Heatwave, Rod Temperton and a variety of funk and soul acts, and seemed like potentially a good fit. We met and immediately got on like a house on fire, and it rapidly became clear that he could help us to advance our skills, in particular strengthening our vocal arrangement techniques.

From this point, Greg's knowledge and expertise helped us create the 'Heaven 17 sound', which featured complex vocal arrangements, seamlessly integrated electronic and live rock instrumentation, and orchestral colours. This would help lead us to mainstream success, but there would ultimately be a price to pay as this was the start of us losing our laser focus on our original core electronic sound. This ultimately led to the album *Teddy Bear, Duke & Psycho*, where there were hardly any core electronic recordings in evidence.

But at this moment in time, *The Luxury Gap* recording sessions were precisely what working creatively in a studio environment should be about – best staff, best facilities, best atmosphere and best friends. No stone was left unturned in an effort to stun the general public into submission. We were totally focused and determined to succeed this time – we'd had our share of near misses and disappointments, but we'd come through them, toughened up by the buffeting, and still positive and full of righteous energy. Our mindset at the time was something like this – if we only have this chance, we'd better make the most of it or we will probably regret it forever. It's hard to imagine how potentially precarious our situation was, and we were under no illusions – if we didn't make the step up to singles success on this album, it could well be curtains for Heaven 17, and almost certainly BEF.

All the songs and recording sessions are described in detail later, but it was clear when we started to sequence and assemble the album that this group of recordings was probably as good if not better than the *Penthouse and Pavement* sessions, and that we couldn't have done them more justice in terms of arrangement and recording and mix quality. It was as if we'd suddenly been promoted from short-order chef at a funky good-food boutique café to head chef at the Dorchester, and we'd pulled it off. On the first playback of the compiled album there was a stunned silence in the studio. We all knew we'd done ourselves justice. Now, all we had to do was convince the world.

Having finished the album, right from the outset, Glenn, Ian and I wanted to release 'Temptation' as the first single, but Virgin seemed reluctant for some reason. I still regard 'Let Me Go' as the finest song and production that we ever did, and consequently it was agreed with Virgin that this should be the first release. Everybody loved the song, and the video shoot was arranged – we were to film at Marylebone station when it was closed at night, with fifty extras and a huge crew. It was the first time that we worked with Steve Barron, who went on to become a successful Hollywood film director, and who also directed the iconic 'Billie Jean' video for Michael Jackson. In addition to the rail station set, the opening scene location was Threadneedle Street next to the Bank of England in an imagined post-apocalyptic, post-financial crash scenario. On the opening chord in the video, there was even a fake edition of the London *Evening Standard* printed with the headline 'British Electric Foundation Crashes'. Our strong 1950s future-retro styling set the tone for dozens of Heaven 17 photo shoots in the coming months. But, typically, there was a disaster in store. All the beautiful black and white footage of the railway station had been shot on faulty filmstock, and would have to be reshot. Yet another delay, but eventually the single was released in advance of the album, and was enthusiastically reviewed.

We nervously awaited news of midweek chart placings, playlist meetings and *Top of the Pops* scheduling. Midweek placing ahead of the official first week of the charts had the song in the top 40, which would have been good enough to get on *TOTP*, but Radio 1 refused to playlist the song in advance, so it would be touch and go whether it would make the top 40 on the Sunday chart. It didn't. Heartbreakingly, and despite Virgin's best publicity efforts and discounting in chart shops, it had marginally slipped to below the magic 40 mark – *forty-fucking-one* – thereby missing selection for *TOTP*. Once again, both Virgin and we were gutted, even more so because we *knew* this was a near-great record. Would our success ever happen?

Licking our wounds, we decided to redouble our efforts to get 'Temptation' released. The mystery regarding Virgin's reluctance was solved – they were nervous as Carol Kenyon, who provided the guest vocal, was not under contract to Virgin. They didn't want the original mix to be released as a single (nope, I don't understand either), but suggested that it should be remixed in Los Angeles by David Kirschenbaum who had just had a big hit with a remix of 'Different for Girls' by Joe Jackson (which at the time I thought was a little bland). This was the first time that Virgin had shown a lack of faith in our taste, but in retrospect I think it was more about their nervousness to ensure that the next single was to make the grade. We reluctantly agreed, and the remix duly arrived a week later – it was fucking horrible. Bland, disorganised garbage, swimming in delays and reverb, which had lost almost all of its original power and beauty. In a nutshell, it completely missed the point.

'Please, Simon, trust us, just put our version out, it's a hit!' I pleaded at the playback meeting to head of A&R Simon Draper. He half-heartedly agreed, and the single was scheduled for release. This time it was Virgin's turn to eat humble pie.

We shot the video with Page 3 model Gillian De Terville playing the role of Carol Kenyon, who refused to take part unless we paid her a massive fee. Her loss. To this day, many fans believe Gillian is Carol. The video was shot in 1930s German expressionistic style with Glenn, dressed as a preacher, manipulating in Svengali fashion the poor girl in a quite convincing piece of acting, which was not dissimilar to the Joker in *Batman*. Glenn, of course, tried to lure Gillian for real, but I think on this occasion his charismatic wiles failed to pay off. I'm fairly sure that Gillian was rebuffing advances from all and sundry on a regular basis, so for once Glenn had met his match.

The single was released, and this time there was no doubt from the outset: Radio 1 playlisted the song (tick); distribution and advertising was on point (tick); TV promo had already been mooted (tick); in early back-channel discussions, *Top of the Pops*' producers suggested that if the single debuted in the top 30, they would want us to appear (big tick). The proof of the pudding would be in the eating, however, and we nervously awaited news of initial sales.

We called the sales department, headed up by Jon Webster (aka Webbo), on the Tuesday, a day before the official midweek chart. Then we heard the fateful words, 'It's pissing out ...' Webbo elaborated, 'The pressing plants can't keep up with demand, it's selling about 30,000 copies a day.' We were stunned – this was finally the supercharged reaction we had hoped for from the outset. After a few moments, the reality set in – Webbo, in a hushed reverential tone, said, 'If this demand keeps up, next week we have a shot at number one!'

Silence.

Jeezus. Whatever happened from here, this was almost certainly going to be by far our greatest hit, and would ensure excellent sales of the album worldwide also. It was almost like drawing Excalibur from the stone, almost beyond our wildest dreams.

Sure enough two weeks later, the midweek chart was out – it was number 1. Now this was getting real, the tantalising chance of pop immortality. We appeared on *TOTP* on the Thursday, hoping that our exciting performance would seal the deal, and Virgin seemed to be optimistic. 'There's always the possibility that another single comes up on the rails and pips you to the post, but there's no indication that will happen,' enthused the buoyant Webbo.

I'm sure you know the way this was going ... Sunday came along and the news came through that we had been pipped at the last moment by New Edition and 'Candy Girl', an early Jacksons clone/rip-off – fuck, fuck, fuckety fuck. Even worse, we had been beaten by less than 1 per cent of sales. But once the disappointment had died down, it was replaced by pride in our achievement, number 2 is nothing to be sniffed at. We all hoped we had a chance of number 1 the following week, but again we were pipped, this time by Spandau Ballet's 'True'. Bugger.

Undeterred, we soon released 'Come Live with Me', which, thanks to a French love story homage video, achieved big sales, peaking at number 5. Although my favourite song of ours overall is 'Let Me Go', I'm most proud of the classic nature of the lyric writing on 'Come Live with Me'. In an effort to keep hits coming thick and fast, the next release was 'Crushed by the Wheels of Industry', which featured a bizarre video of us living inside a head, the concept stolen from a comic strip called 'The Numskulls' in the UK comic the *Beano*, in which various characters control the thoughts and senses. Their names were Brainy, Blinky, Luggy, Nosey, Alf and Fred if I remember rightly. The video also features an Einstein lookalike, and the three of us in boiler suits as the 'workmen' in the head. Weird but fun. The single peaked at 17. We were doing really well, the album was the seventeenth biggest seller of 1983 in the UK, and we were breaking through to popular acceptance in most of the major international territories world-wide. We were on the biggest roll of our careers . . .

Nineteen eighty-three was also the year of Band Aid. Glenn and I were on a Saturday night session at the Frog and Parrot on Westbourne Grove when a call came in from Midge Ure and Bob Geldof asking if we could take part in recording a charity record (what's a charity record?) with a whole load of other well-known artists, of which he only mentioned a couple. Bob hyperbolically proclaimed that 'We're going to get this fookin' record to number one next week, we've got all the pressing plants on standby – oh, and we're filming the video at the same time tomorrow . . .'

We agreed as we were good friends with Midge and Bob, and it seemed to be a good (if somewhat unfeasible) idea, but the stinger was that we had to be at Sarm West Studios, which was just around the corner, at ten the following morning. Glenn and I reckoned that we should take it easy on the boozing front, but it didn't quite work out that way.

The next morning, drinking pints of milk in a valiant attempt to cure our persistent hangovers, we stumbled towards the studio, only to be confronted by an unimaginable scene. There were multiple TV crews and their remote vans, journalists, artists arriving by the truckload with their entourages, security guards – the lot. Glenn and I had no idea where to go, but we were quickly hustled into the studio away from the crazy hubbub outside where the assembled stars were busy preening and networking (or being aloof, depending on status). People like ourselves, Spandau and Status Quo were just up for a laugh, but many of the solo singers were on high ego alert (Sting and Bono immediately spring to mind). Then it all got real – Glenn was asked to sing one of the verse lead vocal lines, which was a real honour. The solo lines were recorded first, and then the massed choir of artists were coached by Midge and Bob to sing the chorus. I'm known for having a very loud voice (Glenn often says I don't need a microphone), and I'm sure that me belting out 'FEED THE WOO-ORLD' can be heard as a strong flavour in the final mix. The legend of that session is that the 'bad boys', i.e. Spandau, Status Quo and us, were on the hunt for pharmaceutical enhancement, but I can confirm this wasn't the case.

What happened next is well documented: it was a massive success, and it did get to number one, raising a huge amount of money for the African famine, and more importantly raising awareness worldwide.

What a year – peak Heaven 17. For the first time, our songs were included in feature films – *Summer Lovers* ('Play to Win') and a Ron Howard film, *Nightshift* ('Penthouse and Pavement'). As if that wasn't enough, we also released our first VHS video compilation (quite a novel concept at the time) called *Heaven 17's Industrial Revolution*. We were on fire, and it seemed that nothing could stand in our way. Things are never quite that simple . . .

Intermission:

Football and Sheffield Wednesday

I know not everyone is interested in football, or sports in general. For some reason, a lot of people who like electronic music regard it as oafish tribalism – and sport is often the opposite end of the entertainment spectrum for them. Well, I've always quite liked the fact that these apparently incongruous passions exist in my life, both equally important in many ways. The third passion of my triumvirate is food, and I've always said that my dream career (apart from music) would have been to be a food critic, or food futurologist, or restaurateur (but I'd only want the glamorous creative/ maître d'/PR part of it, not the hard slog and financial risk).

Sports are a big part of my life, as a player and as a consumer – growing up I tried out speedway (the Sheffield Tigers, loved it – the smell, the danger), rugby league (when Sheffield got involved with the Eagles), I played tennis with my friends, crown green bowls with my father, saw Garry Sobers of the West Indies play cricket at Bramall Lane, and saw Pelé play at Hillsborough when Santos were on tour (bunked off school for the day). But football is my first and eternal passion . . .

I have loved Wednesday since, as my dad would say, 'my bum was no bigger than a shirt button', but it's not as though we ever had any option, as pretty much all families in Sheffield are exclusively either Owls (Wednesday) or Blades (United). There can be only one loyalty, one religion. Ours derived from my great-grandfather on my dad's side, who was around when the club was established in 1867. Generations of pride and pain, glory and disappointment, and a deeply held antagonism towards the red-and-white-striped side of the Sheffield divide (United fans are known as 'pigs' due to their kit's resemblance to streaky bacon). We were led to believe that Blades were scruffs, inferiors, somehow barely human. This was maybe a tad unfair, but it made for some interesting arguments in the playgrounds, and for the adults the pubs and working men's clubs. It was all very tongue in cheek, part of the playful mythology, a safe outlet which paradoxically helped to glue our community together.

When I was a child, our family had little spare money, and in any case my dad normally worked overtime on Saturdays, so I was indoctrinated way before actually going to see a game at Hillsborough, our home ground. When there was virtually no football on TV, Wednesday reached the FA Cup final in 1966, when I was ten years old. We could actually watch a full game featuring Wednesday for the first time ever! I'd seen a few highlights when I was allowed to stay up to watch *Match of the Day* (rarely), but for Wednesday to reach the Cup final was an incredible achievement, as their last victory had been in 1935. There was absolutely no chance of getting tickets even if we could have afforded them – the whole blue half of Sheffield was decamping to Wembley . . .

So, TV it was. We sat in our new council flat, ready for the big day: full focus on our pay-as-you-go coin-driven TV (sounds unlikely, but it was a way to pay for it over time instead of expensive rental). We put 2 x 50p in the slot, which paid for about eight hours' viewing, as FA Cup final day was an all-day affair in those days. The Wednesday boys looked amazing in their blue tracksuit tops with 'OWLS' across the back, and super-sharp in our all-white change strip. As has almost always been the case for my entire life as a Wednesdayite, everything was hunky-dory until the game started.

But wait! We scored after four minutes, then added a second around fifty-seven minutes: surely not even Wednesday could mess this up. Hold my beer ... two minutes later, Everton pulled one back. I looked at my dad's face, and he was ashen and quiet. Five more minutes, we conceded again – oh God, no ... Clinging on desperately, we fought hard, but a mistake by our ever-reliable captain Gerry Young gifted an easy goal to Derek Temple. There was no coming back. I think it was the first time any team had lost an FA Cup final from a two-goal lead in ninety minutes.

It was the only time I ever saw my father cry (except at my mother's funeral). He was distraught. I was inconsolable. My mother moved into emergency tea and supper mode, but even this couldn't ease the shock and pain. This was soooooo typically Wednesday, as I was to repeatedly discover in the forthcoming decades, but even for them, this was something quite special.

Conversely, my happiest game ever was the first game I attended at Hillsborough – on Saturday 31 August, 1968, when my sister Janet's fiancée Jeff took me to see Wednesday play the European Champions Manchester United. When young Jack Whitham scored a hat-trick and we won, we went completely insane. I was hooked for life, totally and unconditionally Wednesday till I die. How was I to know that this would be the high-water mark of my fandom? What are the chances that I'd never see a game as good as that again, especially where we came out on top?

There have been a few other highlights over the years – in particular our League Cup triumph over, yes, you guessed it, Manchester United in 1991, what a day ... I'd hired a white stretch limo and asked my good friend Malcolm Garrett (graphic design guru) to create a sign for the side of the car, basically the word

OWLSMOBILE and the funky Owl club badge. Pre-match, we celebrated in style with champagne and beer as we headed to Wembley through the crowds, turning heads as we went. There was an incredible feeling in the air that Manchester United might regard this game as a gimme, and we saw many happier Wednesdayites on the way to the ground than the dour and entitled United fans. We out-sang them, the team outfought them, and before we knew it – WE'D ACTUALLY DONE SOMETHING RIGHT! The cup was ours, 1–0, a Johnny Sheridan half-volley in off the post – dink!

Every team has its ups and downs, I know, but being an Owls fan is a hard journey, not for the faint-hearted. I share my love with several well-known Wednesdayites – the Arctic Monkeys, Jon McClure from Reverend and the Makers, Richard Hawley, Jarvis Cocker, artist Pete McKee, Michael Vaughan, David Blunkett, Roy Hattersley, Rivers Cuomo (Weezer), Gary Cahill, Rick Savage (Def Leppard), Jonny Greenwood (Radiohead), Katy Livingston (Olympic athlete), Paul Carrack (Squeeze, Mike and the Mechanics, etc.) – but the very best of all is Jermaine Jackson of the Jacksons (yes, you read that right). He was bored one day off while on tour, holed up in a hotel at Shepherd's Bush, when he was invited to watch Queens Park Rangers play, just up the road. Wednesday were the opponents that day, and against the odds we won. One of our players at the time was Jermaine Johnson (JJ), a Jamaican international who was lightning-fast and unstoppable on his day, which wasn't very often. But this was one of those days. One of the Jacksons fell in love with his namesake and Wednesday that day, and to this day he comments about the Owls in social media from time to time. Let's Get Serious – Shamone!

My ongoing active love affair with my club has created an alternative extended family – I meet the same people at away games, many of whom I know little about, even their names, but the sense of community and 'keeping in touch' with my roots are really important to me. We have a massive shared history of existentially significant experiences – as I always say, going to support your team is cheaper than therapy. You can scream, curse, abuse, transgress (in a playful way), bond, laugh, cry, drink, empathise – all for the price of a match ticket and a couple of pints and a pie. These truths are universal, and I genuinely feel sorry for people who have no faith and community like football, or the church, or smaller-scale community groups or activist political affiliations or ethnic associations, etc. Everyone needs several interlocking communities to provide context and meaning to their lives, and I believe the loosening of these ties is at the heart of the strategies of right-wing governments, often manifest in the increasing isolation of the next generations, which leads to a deep-seated diminution of individuality and identity.

So that's why the culture of live football is so important to me – I played football for the school team, left-wing (one of my friends used to say I had a 'wand of a left foot'), I played left wingback for Lucas Industries (once scored a 'worldie' from 30 yards out on the left, over the goalkeeper's head), and I used to coach football and was chairman of my son's football club Pro Potential Academy, covering the age groups six to eighteen. It was one of the happiest times of my life. Joy and pain are like sunshine and rain, as Frankie Beverly used to say, and participating in the world of football continues to make my life so much richer, and to keep the flame alive. I've passed on my passion to my son Gabriel, who is now similarly blessed/afflicted. My dad would be so proud . . .

1982–4: Tina Turner
and Other Productions

'Times are good or bad, happy or sad ...'

Tina is the living definition of a superstar. I would use the word legend, but this epithet has been so rinsed out that it is now used to describe your mate who is passed out on the sofa after a hard night's binge drinking. Tina Turner a very rare endangered species, of which there are very few left.

She was and is the ultimate professional, motivated, talented, but most of all fully aware of the consequences of not having her shit together at all times. Our discussions were always polite, focused and friendly, almost too businesslike, but softened by her gentle demeanour and generosity of spirit. But ... just beneath the surface, there was a passion for her craft, a life-force that could fill a huge arena, and an intimacy that melted your heart. True stars have a capacity to make you feel like you are the most important person in their world at that moment in time. Tina's is an almost supernatural presence which may be my personal projection, but is more likely to be explained by her aura as a very special person. I am *very* rarely starstruck – I was brought up to feel that I should never believe I was inferior to anyone, but their equal. I always say jokingly that I wouldn't be fazed by meeting the Queen, for instance, and that proved to be the case when I finally did (you'll have to wait until

Volume 2 to hear that story). And I definitely wouldn't accept any kind of establishment honour – not that I'm expecting one any time soon . . . I always somehow felt that I could converse with Tina as an equal, and she graciously allowed me the same status, but Tina is one of very few exceptions to my no-deference rule.

Her performance on 'Ball of Confusion' for BEF was flawless and I was very proud of the final single release, even though it wasn't a hit. So, I wasn't completely surprised when her manager Roger Davies contacted me to ask if I would be interested in contributing to Tina's comeback album. It appears I had made quite an impression (if Tina's autobiography is anything to go by), but Roger's first idea was to ask Heaven 17 to write a couple of new songs for her, rather than produce the record.

I was terrified at the prospect – we'd only ever written songs for our own use, and I was very uncertain whether we could write for another artist, let alone the Queen of Rock and Soul. I discussed it with Glenn and Ian, and we agreed that we were cowards and that we couldn't do it. It just felt like the right decision at the time. Plan B was to suggest a couple of daring and/or unusual songs for her, to be produced with the distinctive BEF sound.

Thank the Lord, Roger and Tina agreed, and I put together a short list of suggestions. If only I had kept a copy of the list, I would present it to you now, but in those pre-laptop days, everything was written in my Filofax, which has disappeared off the planet. I can vaguely remember that there were several classic soul songs (I was an ex-northern soul fan, after all), but the song I really wanted her to perform was the Al Green stone-cold classic, 'Let's Stay Together'. I could visualise Tina delivering the full range of emotions contained in the song – tenderness, honesty, poignancy, vulnerability, passion, certainty, force of will. Tina is as much an actor as she is a singer; her performance is thoroughly considered and delivered with as much depth as the most acclaimed actor performing a Shakespearean soliloquy. She knows how to sell a song, a narrative, an everyday but universal story that people can relate to in their own lives. I was convinced this was the song for her. This was the song to permanently nail her place in the firmament of the greatest soul singers of all time.

Since I'd met Tina, I felt that she'd somehow turned her back on her natural soul genre, and was more determined to become a rock singer, like her new idols Mick Jagger and David Bowie. Well, I wanted people to remember her past, and we could give her a totally contemporary style that would also be electronically soulful.

Also on the list were some more outlandish suggestions, one of which was to cover a Bowie song. She was a self-confessed fan, so I knew this could well appeal, but which song?

Then it hit me. Heaven 17 were the self-fulfilling prophecy of a fictitious group in the film and novel *A Clockwork Orange*. Anthony Burgess wrote it in 1962, and said that the story was set around twenty years in the future, hence we fulfilled the great man's vision by making his imaginary group come to life. We could do something similar with Tina, except this time it would be a reference to the year the record was to be released – '1984', the song from *Diamond Dogs*, itself based on the George Orwell novel, *Nineteen Eighty-four*. This all felt so conceptually connected and neat, and I was determined to do my utmost to persuade Tina of the logic of my reasoning.

I was invited to Tina's rented accommodation in Holland Park to discuss which songs to choose, and as I was let through the enormous gate into the private grounds, I was stunned by the location. There was an enormous walled garden full of roses, there were guards, and at the centre was a beautiful, three-storey Victorian mansion. *All this for one person*, I mused, thinking back to a life spent in tiny council houses. Even my new apartment, nearby in Westbourne Park, would have not qualified as a granny flat in this property. I wasn't really ready for this level of extravagance, but I had to give her credit for her impeccable taste, even if I thought it must have cost a bloody fortune. 'I'd rather have the money,' I mumbled to myself as I approached the front door, accompanied by one of her security guards.

Once inside, Tina informed me that the guards were there because Ike had discovered where she was staying, and she was concerned that he might try to get to see her. She mentioned that he'd already tried to scale the wall but was chased off by the guards. Apparently, he was desperate for money; in his sadly demented mind, he believed that Tina 'owed' him. Ike wrote 1951's 'Rocket 88' – sung by Jackie Brenston (the saxophone player from Turner's backing band The Kings of Rhythm) and recorded by Sam Phillips, who later went on to found Sun records and discover Elvis Presley – which some commentators regard as the first ever rock and roll single. He was an originator, super-talented and motivated, who became a monster. Tina mentioned one day that in the studio, Ike once brought out a huge bag of cocaine, created a white mountain on the table, and announced to everyone, including a young Tina, that 'no one leaves this studio until we've written a hit record'. He then proceeded to lock the door and stow the only key in his pocket. Forty-eight hours later, exhausted, delirious and hungry, one of the band managed to extricate the key from a now unconscious Ike.

What a sad, sad character, an object lesson in not letting fame and drugs and rock and roll control your life. Tina's horrific abuse at the hands of her husband is well documented, but always shocking to recall. She had made a career for herself away from this malignant asshole, and obviously wanted nothing more to do with him, but his various addictions meant that he was clearly convinced that her

independent success was solely down to his delusional and megaloma-
niacal talent. (The battle seemed like it would never end, but twenty-
three years later, on 12 December 2007, Ike Turner died of a cocaine
overdose in his home in San Marcos, California. Contributing conditions to his death included high blood pressure and emphysema.)

Tina's beaming smile put me at ease, and we settled down to a
cup of tea and scones (yes, really). Tina loves being the hostess, and
I find that trait irresistible – warm and caring, not formal at all. I
needn't have worried about my selections. I started going through
my list of about ten songs, and the reasoning for my preferences,
and asked her who her musical heroes were when she was young.

'Sam Cooke, Otis Redding, but I really like Al Green also.'

Alleluia! She loved the idea of 'Let's Stay Together'. The very
notion of having the opportunity to pay tribute to one of her best
friends – who she admired immensely, not just for his songwriting
but his modernity – by performing one of his songs sent her into
giggling fits of laughter. I had clearly hit the sweet spot. What a
relief . . .

We got approval from Roger (who also loved the ideas) for the
budgets, the studios and the dates we wanted to record, and a
couple of weeks later we were in EMI's studio in Fitzrovia, recording the basic backing tracks with our usual crew of musicians.

Work on the backing track proceeded at a feverish pace in anticipation of Tina's arrival. We were working long hours recording at
EMI's studio in Whitfield Street in London's Fitzrovia, Greg Walsh
and I both determined to pour our heart and soul into this production as we sensed this was the break of a lifetime. I worked hard on
the rhythm programming, and felt that I nailed a more contemporary approach, but the magic of that opening chord made the
whole production feel futuristic. (Tech alert: It was achieved by
creating a multi-part vocal harmony and 'freezing' the reverb on a

new outboard studio device called a Quantec Room Simulator. End of message.)

Even though I say so myself, I love the synth string arrangement as it draws out the beauty of the original chords. To be immodest, it's a class piece of work all round – from Gary Barnacle's beautiful baritone sax, to Nick Plytas's amazing middle-eight synth solo, to Glenn and my backing vocals, to the 'sonar' conga sound (à la Marvin Gaye), all beautifully engineered by Greg. But the icing on the instrumental cake was Ray Russell's mind-bendingly perfect electric guitar call-and-response counterpoint to Tina's vocal. This was and still is the single greatest performance in my production career. The entire vocal is one take, no drop-ins, no second takes. Tina had clearly analysed the meaning of the lyrics, decided on her interpretation in an actorly fashion, thereby creating optimum connection with the listener. Purest genius and bulletproof professionalism and technique. It feels like she is pouring out her inner thoughts in a heartbreakingly honest way, and I defy anyone to pick holes in her performance. It is simply perfection. I always use this recording as the gold standard for vocalists when I'm teaching. It still thrills me.

As *Billboard*, which had earlier described the song as featuring 'Turner's extraordinary energy cushioned by Heaven 17-style arrangements', wrote on 24 March 1984 that it was 'the first national No. 1 (maxi single sales) hit of Turner's 24-year chart career. The highest she's ever climbed on the pop chart is number four (with 1971's "Proud Mary"); the highest she's been on the black chart is number two (with 1960's "A Fool In Love" and 1961's "It's Gonna Work Out Fine"). All of these records were duets with Ike Turner, from whom Tina was separated eight years ago.'

I'm very proud to say that 'Let's Stay Together' went on to be the biggest-ever selling 12-inch single in US history, which relaunched her career all over the world. My production reputation was pretty much sealed from this moment on. We got to appear on *The Tube* with Tina performing backing vocals with her two singer/dancers, and she introduced us as her 'producers' – what a buzz . . .

Our recording of Bowie's '1984' was also something that Tina loved, being a big fan and friend of David, and I think we did the song justice. The *Private Dancer* album, which featured the two tracks, went on to sell twenty million copies worldwide, the royalties from which enabled Karen and me to move to a fancy new flat in Notting Hill. For the first time in my life, I was well off, and I made sure that all my friends and family were looked after – I would regularly ask a bunch of mates to join me at some of the best restaurants in London. These were the times of our lives, and I wasn't going to keep all my good fortune to myself – otherwise what would all this success have been for? I went on to produce several more tracks for Tina, which were released as bonus tracks. There was a storming version of 'Take Me to the River', which I still feel should have been a single, and an elegant version of 'A Change Is Gonna Come', which I eventually persuaded Tina to let me use for the next *Music of Quality and Distinction* album.

Tina's resurgence is well documented, as an artist, film star and, most of all, performer, and we've always kept in touch. I was honoured to be asked to take part in her sixtieth birthday documentary, where I was thrilled to see that Al Green himself said he loved our version of 'Let's Stay Together'. What an honour. But the biggest thrill was to be told that I was to be an onstage character for *Tina: The Tina Turner Musical*, which premiered in the West End in 2018 and transferred to New York. What a strange sensation it is to see an actor portraying me – to be honest, it's a caricature (I never wore clothes like that! Or had a 'curtain drape' haircut) but hey, it's a great honour.

I can honestly say I made it to star on Broadway. My mum and dad would have been made up.

1984–5: Heaven 17 – *How Men Are*

'A thirty-day boy in a twenty-day city . . .'

T here seemed to be no limit to what was achievable after the
success of my Tina Turner productions, and all this new attention from international record labels meant bigger and better offers
of work, both financially and in terms of the status of the artists
involved. Suddenly I was on the 'hot list' of producers worldwide,
and I started turning down work for the first time in my career.

The two most notable stars that I figured I didn't want to work
with were Rod Stewart and Bette Midler. I was always a fan of
Rod's voice, in particular on Python Lee Jackson's 'In a Broken
Dream', but I was less enamoured of his laddish persona and top-
of-the-range pub-singer shtick – and I was never really into that
blues-rock thing, which felt lazy and clichéd to me. But the deal-
breaker was his open support of Margaret Thatcher, even to the
extent of extolling her virtues publicly and agreeing to take part in
fundraising events for the Tories, who I have always loathed and
despised (and still do). Also, producing the album would have
meant moving to New York or LA for an extended period, and I
simply didn't want to leave my wife, my friends and my home in
London, especially when we were having such a great time. So, I
turned down the production of an album that would have made
me a multimillionaire, largely on a matter of principle.

Refusing the offer of producing Bette Midler was a different kettle of fish. It also would have entailed a long stint in the US, but the main reason was that I considered it unlikely that she could resurrect her career, even with my help. This, of course, was completely wrong, and it's one of my few regrets that I was stupidly arrogant and dismissive at the time. To prove that, when I'm wrong, I can be very, very wrong, here is a list of her achievements since I turned down the job: 10 Grammy nominations, 2 wins, 10 Emmy nominations, 2 wins, 6 Golden Globe nominations, 2 wins, 10 American Comedy Awards nominations, 6 wins, plus many, many other awards. In other words, since I refused to work with her, she has become an American national treasure.

The thought process behind my big-headed attitude to my career at that time was this … *Now I've 'made it', I can pick and choose when and where I want to work. I don't need a huge amount of money, so if I start running out, I'll just take on more work. The river of money will never stop flowing – happy days* … How stupid and naive this seems now, but it was genuinely thought out at the time, so probably I shouldn't be too harsh on myself.

In any case, the fact that Heaven 17 had a huge worldwide success with *The Luxury Gap* meant that we were under pressure from Virgin to produce the goods for our next album. *The Luxury Gap* album had got Virgin out of a potentially fatal financial hole (as documented in Richard Branson's autobiography), so we were right up there in their onward financial planning – could we repeat this success, and maybe even 'break' America? The usual cliché is 'difficult second album syndrome', but we'd cleared that hurdle with ease. What could possibly go wrong?

We assembled the same team as we used for *The Luxury Gap*: Greg Walsh as engineer/producer, with Aussie Jeremy Allom as assistant engineer, the Phenix Horns were drafted in again, as were the usual session players we used on the last album – this time adding the legendary Mo Foster on fretless bass (I first heard him on Scott Walker's *Nite Flights* album) plus the fantastic Afrodiziak girls, and orchestrations by David Cullen. We booked the same studio, AIR at Oxford Circus, where we would regularly bump into legends like Paul McCartney (and his kids, including Stella, who one day tried to sell us cups of water from the water cooler for 20p – *The apple doesn't fall far from the tree*, I thought), Elton John and George Martin, and Cameo were often hanging out, playing pool. We sneaked into Cameo's studio after they'd left one evening – very naughty, I know – but we just had to see what their secret was and what equipment they were using. It turned out to be nothing more exciting than a bog-standard drum machine and a couple of standard American synths. We fessed up when we bumped into them later that week, and they were so lovely; they freely shared their ideas and geeky tech secrets. We were in awe, but a little disappointed that Larry Blackmon wasn't there, as I'm a big fan of shiny red codpieces. One day ...

We also got talking to Paul McCartney, and we were discussing the history of AIR Studios and some of Paul's favourite artists. We agreed on one in particular – Marc Bolan – and Paul said, 'I've got one of Marc's guitars that he used on *Electric Warrior*. Do you fancy using it on your album?'

Fuck me, I thought. Before he could finish the sentence, I jumped at the chance like a demented puppy. 'Yes please, thank you, thank you ...' Ironic, considering I can't play a note. But we picked it up the next day, and our guitarist proudly tried it out. We were expecting the legendary sound to just emanate from the magical instrument, but disappointingly it sounded nothing like it. Ray Russell explained to us that a guitarist's 'sound' is down to a combination of factors – type of strings, pickups, style of playing, etc., but most importantly the amp and how it was miked up. It all proves how ridiculously naive we were at the time, considering we'd already achieved international success as artists and producers. I can't help thinking that if we had managed to get close to the original Bolan sound and style, *How Men Are* would have been an entirely different album.

Incredibly there was never any discussion about budgets for the album – we could use any resources and musicians that we wanted to. Imagine a blank cheque to create your dream album ... Jesus, what were we and they thinking? We were racking up the bills with absolutely not a care in the world, putting to the back of our minds the fact that all these costs had to be recouped from our future royalties. Stupid, stupid, stupid ... In total, we ended up spending over £300,000 just on recording the album (ouch). Record company theory was to keep the successful artist A) happy, and B) indebted, possibly perpetually. Heaven 17 only recouped album recording costs in the early 2000s. To the uninitiated, that meant that Glenn, Ian and I didn't receive a penny in mechanical royalties (from recordings as opposed to writing royalties) for nigh on twenty-five years. Thank God for publishing royalties and PRS payments.

This was to be our most ambitious project yet, and we were determined to make it a giant success. We would span the whole panoply of our passions – politics ('Five Minutes to Midnight', 'The Fuse'), optimistic, expensive-sounding pop, aimed at the singles charts but tinged with allegory ('This Is Mine', 'Sunset Now'), philosophical 'state-of-the-world' electro-soul declamations ('Shame Is on the Rocks', 'Flamedown'), faux-fusion jazz pastiche with a twist ('Reputation'), and our magnum opus, our ambitious, attempted Beach Boys-inspired episodic masterpiece 'And That's No Lie'. We wrote only the most basic of demos in advance of recording in the studio, and most of the writing, programming and arrangement took place in the studio itself. This is a classic way to burn money, but the record company was letting us do it, so why should we object? The answer is in the paragraph above. The working titles of the demos were (I don't possess a copy of the cassette demos so I'm running on a patchy memory) . . .

TOTGAGDL (which became 'Counterforce'; this didn't make the album but later became a B-side/bonus track)
Jazz Song ('Reputation')
Bloodfeud ('Five Minutes to Midnight')
Starwalk ('Shame Is on the Rocks')
Strange Tales ('And That's No Lie')
Evereddi ('This Is Mine')
Commador ('The Fuse')
Itser ('Sunset Now')
Recharge ('Flamedown')

I'm pretty certain these are correct. What you may have noticed is that 'The Skin I'm In' isn't demoed, and that's because we wrote the track in the studio. After a few weeks of programming and laying down the basic synthetic tracks (programmed via a hardware sequencer called the Roland MC-4 Microcomposer, Ian's Fairlight CMI and my LinnDrum LM-1 programming), we started fleshing out the arrangements. Bear in mind, the last thing that was written on all these tracks was the topline melody, so really we were looking at the backing tracks to inspire the lyric writing and subjects. Some of the songs radically changed in the studio as the ideas developed. A good example of this is 'Five Minutes to Midnight': the central core of the song was arranged, but the weirdness of the structure only organically emerged as the nuclear lyrics were developed. It was obvious we had to make the listener disorientated, and we really went for it as soon as we created the orchestration – it's almost a metaphor for the paranoia that was everywhere at that time.

Greg Walsh encouraged us to experiment, and this taught us a huge amount about multitrack editing and being 'free' and not too attached to demo sounds and structures. Making this album really was a trip, in every sense of the word. Thank the Lord Greg was the grown-up in the room; not only was he very talented and creative, but he was like a brother to us, almost the fourth member of the band. I learned so much from his way of working as a producer – he was a listener, but he had the perfect balance of sensible suggestions and decisiveness, and simply knowing how technically to achieve the many ideas we had at the time. He was pretty much the ideal producer for us, and I recycled much of his wisdom and skills in my future production career. Greg, what a guy . . .

The real crazy motherfucker was Jeremy Allom, our assistant engineer. He was almost like a cartoon Aussie, funny, open, blunt, endlessly positive and knew his job inside out. I agree that doesn't sound particularly mad, but as the album recording wore on into month two, we were starting to become stir crazy. We were drinking and partying too much on our weekends off and would regularly suffer during the early part of the week. We were working very long hours (studios charged per twelve-hour day, therefore we were determined to get our money's worth). At that time, we were not performing live except for TV appearances, and we never mixed live appearance with alcohol or any kind of drugs. But in the studio, I have to confess it occasionally helped. Mind you, at that time Glenn and I both smoked cigarettes – in the studio! – so it was a much less healthy time in general. The house engineers at AIR said that their biggest maintenance problem was clearing the fag ash out from the fader slots – yuk.

Studio recording in those days often required extended periods of boredom as Greg had various technical 'housekeeping' duties to perform – aligning tape machines, compiling and bouncing down tracks to create free tracks to continue recording on to, making vocal comps from highly detailed and colour-coded spreadsheets, even marking individual syllables (green = master quality, amber = adequate, red = rubbish or unusable) – all by hand. Imagine that on the digital audio workstations of today. My students have no idea how lucky they are! Then the final choices have to be stitched together, and this sometimes would take hours. Fun fact: Tina Turner was 100 per cent green (i.e. perfect) on my sheet: she needed no patching-up or comping. She was literally the only artist I ever produced who came close to that kind of talent and professionalism. Young artists, take note. No autotune in those days . . .

The more I demanded of Glenn, the more he rose to the challenge. His is a natural talent, he has great pitching, expression, timbre and a big range. He covers a lot – from baritone to tenor, even falsetto occasionally. Our backing vocal textures relied on our voices' timbres dovetailing perfectly. Although technically I'm quite a good singer with a reasonable range, my voice is much lighter in timbre compared to Glenn's, so the overall texture of our combined voices is both rich and 'shiny', and this was achieved by doing multiple tracks of every harmony. All our signature backing vocal arrangements were equally divided fifty–fifty between Glenn and me – occasionally more of me if required. All the vocal arrangements would be recorded in one specific location on the multitrack – usually on a different tape – and then comped into the track multiple times.

All this took time, which meant that we would regularly get into mischief. After we'd drunk all the tea/coffee, sent out for beers, played pool in the green room (Glenn would cheat at every game we ever played), we'd get bored and start looking for alternative fun. We had to stay in the studio complex as we had no idea how long Greg would be working, so our homemade diversions included buying up multiple chocolate bars in the vending machine and creating Frankenstein combinations (e.g. KitKat and Mars Bar) by putting them in the microwave to fuse them together, and then freezing them. The novelty of this soon wore off, and we would drift back to playing table tennis (I usually lost) or watching telly (boring) or reading magazines or books (deadly boring). Sometimes, Glenn would bring in an acoustic guitar, or we would take a rough mix and write some lyrics, but there was often too much distraction as there were three studios in operation pretty much all the time.

As the cabin fever got worse and we ran out of boredom-busting ideas, we started becoming a little strange. One late night we decided to dress up using anything onsite we could find – carpets, wastepaper bins, cables – you name it, we wore it. This resulted in a photo session on our latest toy, the Polaroid camera. Some of these photos still exist.

One day, I decided to bring in my new purchase, an air rifle. Why? You may well ask . . . Studio One was huge, about 20 metres by 15, designed to accommodate large orchestras. The end of the room was permanently covered by a large thick curtain, which we assumed was were there to dampen down the reverberance of the room. Glenn, Ian and I had a couple of hours to spare in the studio space while Greg was working, so we wheeled three or four acoustic panels in front of the aforementioned curtain. On to the top of the 3-foot-high panels, we placed empty cans (just like a scene in a movie). *Voilà!* We had an impromptu firing range! We spent a happy hour honing our shooting skills, so that by the time we'd grown bored with the idea, we had probably fired two hundred or so metal pellets.

'We'd better pick them up now,' I said, suddenly feeling guilty. 'Let's do it before anyone from the studio notices.'

But we could only find about twenty of them. What the actual fuck was happening? Then Ian noticed a gap in the curtains and pulled them apart to reveal a full-size cinema screen pockmarked with about a hundred or so tiny holes.

'Christ, we'd better scarper,' whispered Glenn, and we quickly shut the curtains, concealing the damage. We never heard from AIR about this, and I'm sure they were completely mystified about the apparently random damage – was it insects? Mice?

Looking back, boredom had also played a role in an incident when we were recording *Penthouse and Pavement* at the Townhouse. We were, as usual, looking for a distraction while our producer Pete Walsh was doing some comping, and we came up with an interesting game, which consisted of batting a plastic skull (one of our mascots, with KEEP MUSIC DEAD written on its forehead) off the top of an acoustic screen with a pool cue – obviously to see how far we could smash it. This proved to be quite amusing as we experimented with several different techniques – taking a run up, changing the angle of attack, etc. We worked out it was better to hit the skull with the thick end of the cue (more weight), so this became the default technique. After a few goes, Ian was winning – he was always surprisingly angry and strong when needed – so I thought I'd give it one extra hard go. As I hit the skull, there was an astonishing crack, almost like a bullet, which surprised us all. I noticed the cue felt different somehow ... then I caught sight of something that horrified me.

'Look!' I gasped in disbelief.

There was a giant crack in the triple-glazed floor-to-ceiling window of the vocal booth, looking for all the world like a bullet had hit it. And then, on the floor beneath, was a piece of metal about 6 inches long, which looked a bit like a thick black pencil. There was a missing rubber stopper on the thick end of the pool cue, which concealed the weight inside – when the cue was swung extra hard, this had obviously shot out (somewhat like a bullet) and created the 3-foot-long cracks in the extremely expensive smoked, reinforced glass. We were mortified. We had no option but to confess to the studio, but as Townhouse was owned by Virgin, I think they just claimed for it on insurance, and we got away scot-free. But no more skull-smashing for us.

Back to AIR Studios: as we were writing and recording 'Five Minutes to Midnight', we were becoming increasingly worried about world news, in particular the UK government's military breast-beating and recommissioning our nuclear deterrent, particularly the cruise missile capability. So, we decided to protest. During one of our crazed periods, we came to the conclusion that we should make a banner and hang it from the top of the AIR building on the corner of Oxford Circus. In our minds, we would definitely make the news as daring activists, all over national or at least London TV, and almost certainly make the national newspapers and magazines (there were lots of anti-nuclear protests happening around that time, it was a very hot topic). So we bought some heavy canvas – about 3 feet x 20 feet – some paints and brushes, and proceeded to use the private en-suite lounge in Studio Two to create the following sign ...

HEAVEN 17 SAY NO CRUISE IS GOOD NEWS

With the addition of the peace symbol, this took almost a full day to finish.

Then, as midnight approached and all was quiet, the next job was to climb on to the roof surrounding the studio, which in turn was bounded by an 18-inch-high ledge which was 3 feet wide. Beyond the ledge was a 70-foot drop to the street below. Not exactly safe, I'd say. At this point, I made it clear that I had no intention of putting my life at risk, but our engineer Jeremy bragged, 'Ah don't be a pussy, it's safe as houses!' Then, by way of proving how safe it was, he proceeded to take his bike out of the window and put it on to the ledge outside!

'What the fuck are you doing? Are you crackers?' I begged him to stop, but he was on a mission.

Despite the obvious existential danger, he got on his bike and rode along the ledge, around the corner of the building and back. I couldn't watch, but he came back into the room triumphant. 'There you go.' He seemed very pleased with himself: adrenaline is a wonderful drug . . .

At this point, I said I wanted no further part in this lunacy, made my apologies, and got out of the building as soon as I could, fully expecting to wake up to some kind of headline like 'Insane pop stars die in bizarre stunt'. Instead, I was woken by Gemma from Virgin.

'You've got to take that sign down right away, or AIR Studios and Top Shop are threatening to sue us – and the police will arrest you.'

Dammit, I thought, *bloody fascist pigs. No way we're taking it down.* But within ten seconds self-preservation kicked in and I rang Glenn.

He picked up the phone and blearily said, 'It looks fucking great, I took some photos.'

'Never mind that, they're going to lock us up. You and Jeremy have got to get down there now and take it down.'

He harumphed, but indignantly agreed.

We got into a lot of trouble for this, but Virgin protected us. We still have the photos, but the stunt never got into the papers or on TV. *Plus ça change* . . .

This period was also wall-to-wall with outside productions – we were commissioned to create songs for the *Electric Dreams* film, including a funky sci-fi-sounding instrumental called 'Chase Runner' (which was probably the best track we made on the Fairlight), but more interestingly we wrote a song called 'Kissing

Time'. The concept was that a sentient computer was trying to write a love song but missing the metaphorical implications and vernacular, resulting in much hilarity. Unfortunately, the film's director didn't agree and it was never used, and I can't find a recording. But I remember one of the lyrics (sung to a simple playground rhyme tune in ¾ time) . . .

In my heart there is a fire, burning very bright
Love is very beautiful, burn yourself tonight

I was also commissioned to produce some tracks on Billy Mackenzie's new album, *Perhaps*, namely 'Those First Impressions' and the title track. Billy was hyperactive at the time, but the end results were excellent. As an example of how unusual working with Billy was, I remember explaining to him in detail and in a friendly way why one of his arrangements was too busy and clashy frequency-wise, and that he'd be wiser to leave some stuff out. He listened patiently to my advice, then clearly stated, 'Ay Martyn, OK then, let's just do it my way then, eh?' in the friendliest tone imaginable. It was impossible not to be charmed by Billy, but he was his own worst enemy much of the time, as he habitually found it hard to accept well-meaning advice.

When we listened to the finished and sequenced *How Men Are* album for the first time, we were overawed. Greg had compiled the album on to a digital-tape format for the first time in our career, which meant unprecedented power and clarity, and near total silence (no background hiss) during fade-outs and gaps between tracks, even when played very loud. In addition, we no longer needed to use Dolby noise suppression – this had always been a trade-off as it would sometimes impair the accuracy of the reproduction of high frequencies. To put it bluntly, the album brought tears of joy to my eyes. It was by far the most beautiful-sounding record I'd ever been involved with. We were all so thrilled with the album, and we left AIR Studios on cloud nine that night. The record company loved the recording and all was set for another triumph. But fate had different plans instore for us . . .

The first single from the album, 'Sunset Now', didn't get on to *TOTP*, so failed to break the top 20. So plans were brought forward to release the second single, 'This Is Mine', which we had huge hopes for. The record company, the pluggers, even Radio 1 play-listers, all heard it and agreed that, given a fair wind and assuming *Top of the Pops* went for it, it should be a top 10 hit. It is still one of my favourite singles we ever made. The melodies, the production, the Phenix Horns, the songwriting, the backing vocals, Glenn's performance, the lyrics, the radio friendliness – all the boxes ticked. This would be a smash. We had even made a fantastic video directed by famous director Stephen Frears, in which Glenn, Ian and I played bank robbers. *Tutto a posto*, as the Italians would say. Virgin made sure there was loads of stock in all the shops, all the (legal) incentives for the retail outlets were in place, and we were coming off the back of a smash hit album. What could possibly go wrong?

The news came excitedly in – *TOTP* were keen, and we were on this week's show, which was filming tomorrow. Yessss . . . Of course, the first thing we needed to do was to go out for a lunch-time beer to celebrate. At that time, Glenn drove a Japanese jeep, which was his pride and joy, but it could be a little tricky to get in and out of due to the height of the doors. Glenn drove us to the local off-licence to get some cans in (pubs closed at 3 p.m. in those days) so we could continue to party. I volunteered to get the beers, but Glenn said, 'I'll just jump out quickly, you stay there.' Glenn leapt from the jeep and immediately collapsed in pain.

'What's up, Glenn, are you OK?'

He looked in excruciating agony. 'I've done something to my knee – it's really painful. I don't think I can get up.'

Oh shit, don't panic, it's just Glenn being melodramatic probably. We tried to help him to his feet but he couldn't face the pain. We found a phone box and rang for an ambulance.

'We'd better get this checked out. We can't miss *TOTP* tomorrow,' I reasoned.

'I suppose so,' Glenn agreed.

Our manager at the time, Keith Bourton, accompanied him to the hospital, while Ian and I nervously awaited any news. The phone rang.

'Not good news, I'm afraid. The doctor has done an X-ray and Glenn's cartilage has ruptured, they're just removing it now. He's on morphine.'

Oh no …

'Will he be OK for the show tomorrow?' I already thought I knew what the answer would be.

'Unlikely, but he says he's willing to give it a shot'.

Good old Glenn, I thought, but I still wasn't convinced.

Keith continued, 'I've spoken to Virgin and *TOTP*'s producer Michael Hurll. I suggested that maybe we could do the following week, but Virgin are concerned that the single will drop if we don't do the show tomorrow. In any case, Hurll refused to accept a change of date, and said we have to come in tomorrow.'

'But what if Glenn can't walk?'

'Hurll said he could sit on a stool.'

I was starting to freak out … 'He'll be on fucking morphine, how is he meant to perform? What kind of monster is this guy?'

The day of the show arrived, and we all went together to the studios for rehearsal. Glenn was in such intense pain that he kept blacking out. Michael Hurll was utterly unsympathetic, and insisted that we went through with rehearsals despite Glenn's obvious disability. After the first camera rehearsal, Glenn had to retire to the dressing room to rest. It was clear he couldn't go on, and that we'd have to pull our appearance on the show. Fevered discussions took place between Keith, a Virgin representative and our plugger, pleading our case for a postponement, or at least to show our expensively made and excellent video (which they would routinely do for non-UK acts). Michael Hurll's response was bluntly to state that if we pulled out of the programme, *TOTP* would never work with Heaven 17 again. What an arsehole. He was a man of his word. We never were allowed to appear on *TOTP* again during his time there, and of course this signalled the beginning of the end for our pop career, as at that time the programme was almost the only game in town. An unmitigated disaster.

The album was still something we were very, very proud of. Thankfully, it reached number 12 in the charts, and was certified silver in October 1984. *How Men Are* is the Heaven 17 album that I'm most proud of. It's closest in originality, themes and songwriting to our vision. It's the best that we could have come up with at the time, and there is one stone-cold classic on there: 'And That's No Lie', all ten minutes of it, featuring the magnificent Afrodiziak. We shall never know what would have happened if Glenn's knee hadn't exploded.

The View Outside: Greg Walsh, co-producer/ engineer, *The Luxury Gap* and *How Men Are*

I have many fond memories of working with Martyn, Ian and Glenn, and also the times Martyn and I spent together co-producing records for Billy Mackenzie and Tina Turner.

I started working in the music industry in the early seventies. My dad was a session musician, one of the finest professional guitarists of his era, and as a kid I often used to accompany him to recording sessions. I studied piano and taught myself how to play drums, and from an early age only ever had the ambition of working in music. I was initially hired as a tape op by Mayfair Sound, a studio which was then situated above a small local pharmacy in London's South Molton Street. It was their signage . . . 'Ear Piercing by Experts' . . . that hung above our door! I left Mayfair Sound to join Audio International Studios as an engineer in the mid-seventies and from there moved to Utopia Studios in 1977.

Throughout this period, there was a finite number of really great studios in London and they were in huge demand. Constantly working in the same room on very different sessions was great experience and allowed me to develop rapidly. It provided an opportunity to experiment with different microphones, placement and general studio setups. Techniques learned on one session were carried forward to the next and, as with most engineers, the more we worked the better we got.

Studio time was very expensive and so had to be used efficiently. A run through for sound then record . . . second takes were frowned upon. So in those days, before going into the studio, a band had to be well rehearsed and ready to record. Alternatively, contracted session musicians would sightread charts written by the artist, a musical arranger or the songwriter. Generally, you'd never go into a studio without a very clear idea of what you were going to come out with.

It had become apparent to me, from very early on in my career, that a great-sounding record was not just down to the sound engineer, great sound had to be nurtured from the ground up, instrumentation and arrangement being key, so becoming a producer and having a voice in every aspect of a recording was ultimately where I knew I needed to be. Perhaps even more importantly, those early stages of my career taught me that the recording studio is a creative tool in itself, a place where great ideas often appeared out of the ether, ideas that needed to be explored and developed, though at that time only a handful of artists were using studios in this way.

By the time I met up with Heaven 17, I had spent virtually every waking hour of my working life in the studio, with great artists, great musicians and great producers. I had learned from them all and been inspired by them. I had also recently returned from the United States working with Pink Floyd on the original live performances of The Wall, *having been invited by my old colleague and friend James Guthrie. James had produced and engineered* The Wall *and asked me to work with him mixing the front-of-house sound. At that time, Floyd were the biggest band in the world. It was an altogether extraordinary experience that I found massively inspiring.*

At that first meeting with Martyn, Ian and Glenn, it was immediately apparent that we had very aligned ambitions as to the kind of record we wanted to make together. I already knew of the band from the work they had done previously with my brother Pete on the Penthouse and Pavement *album. They were undoubtedly talented and had a really great feel for what was happening culturally at that time.*

What first struck me was the total absence of any concrete plan from their side. They were very eager to understand how we could use the latest technology and resources to our maximum advantage to develop a great studio album. How that album could subsequently be performed live was never a consideration. Although I don't remember there being any overriding concept, demos or lyrics, they had a plethora of great ideas that were very liquid and malleable. It became clear that we were going to be working together from a totally blank canvas. Combined with the support and energy of Virgin Records, I was excited at the prospect of working with them; I saw we had an opportunity to make an album the way I believed an album should be made, taking full advantage of the incredible technology that was then beginning to land in the industry. It was a more organic way to make an album, allowing for a much finer level of detail and depth to be built into the structure and arrangement of the recording than was generally happening at that time.

Heaven 17 introduced me to sequencers and modular synthesis. I was familiar with the language of synthesisers and had spent time learning how to get the sounds I wanted from them, although I had generally used them in a supportive role, as a solo colour or an effect within a track. I had also begun experimenting with some early sampling drum machines on the Broken Home and Landscape albums. MIDI was still in development and was not available for The Luxury Gap, so all musical sequencing was done using CV and Gate. Martyn had acquired one of the first LinnDrum LM-1s to arrive in the country and had managed to get it to talk to the Roland MC-4. We just had to figure out how we could synchronise the entire system to tape so we could reliably record and overdub with it; welcome the Friend Chip, an SMPTE to clock convertor, a very scientific-looking piece of kit that would have made a great prop for Stanley Kubrick's Dr Strangelove set!

The technology allowed us to go into the studio and lay backing tracks on our own, entirely electronically, without any musicians or arrangers. I found this aspect really exciting, not because I had an aversion to musicians, far from it, it was the greater flexibility it offered. It allowed us to experiment with the sound, structure, arrangement and tempo, keeping the good ideas and leaving the bad ones behind us along defined reset points. We were organically developing a backing track in the studio, every day building on the previous day's work precisely before adding the live musicians. It allowed us to use the recording studio as an instrument in itself, a creative tool rather than a venue, and gave us total production flexibility right up to the mix.

We began initial production of The Luxury Gap with BLTs for breakfast at the Townhouse Studios in Shepherd's Bush before decamping over to AIR Studios, once the basic tracks had been laid, to complete the overdubs and mix. Recording began most days at eleven and ended when we could

do no more, normally between 2 and 3 a.m. Production of both The
Luxury Gap *and* How Men Are *was undertaken entirely in London
aside from when Martyn and I took a brief foray out to LA to record the
Phenix Horns, the Earth, Wind and Fire horn section. What a sound. We
were both absolutely blown away by the precision with which they played
and what amazing energy.*

*In the formative sessions, tracks were mathematically pieced together
through a huge amount of manually input data ... endless hours of
programming, inputting note values step by step into a Roland MC-4 to
create chords, bass lines and musical sequences, then synching them to the
LinnDrum patterns, which had also been built up measure by measure.
Individual measures were then sequenced into complete songs.*

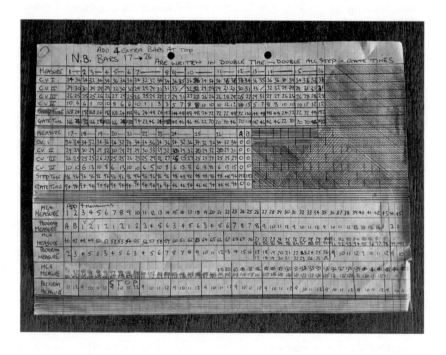

*The attention to detail was phenomenal and the concentration
immense. All the songs had this stuttering birth process and we all spent
many hours with our heads buried in data sheets and manuals to pull it all*

together. *We were pushing the technology all the way, cobbling together bits of gear, trying to get all the electronic components and tape machines to talk to each other in the earliest days of tape synchronisation using SMPTE. On reflection, I find it astonishing, given the immediacy of modern software, the patience we must have had. Today, workstation software provides limitless banks of instruments, tracks, channels and plugins, all talking to one another and immediately accessible beneath our fingertips. Looking back we were producing an album that was as complex as anything that would be produced today, but in a totally analogue domain and without the benefit of an undo button! When you punched record on one of the Studer tape machines, the previous version was gone, forever.*

Eight-track and sixteen-track tape machines had seamlessly morphed into twenty-four-track machines by the time we were putting together Luxury Gap *and some studios had begun using synchronisers to strap two machines together to provide 'forty-eight track' facilities. We figured if you could strap two together, why not three, and by the end of the album we were doing just that.*

By the time we landed in Studio One at AIR we had developed some great basic tracks and continued overdubbing the 'live' elements; guitars, bass, percussion, brass, paving slabs and the signature lead and backing vocal blocks that became a big part of the Heaven 17 sound at that time. Backing vocals were arranged in three- and four-part harmonies, each meticulously tracked in unison six or eight times. It meant endless hours of recording, which was normally done on a secondary reel of tape.

The 'slave' reel usually had a stereo rough mix of the backing track for reference on tracks one and two, taken from the 'master' reel, and an EBU/ SMPTE synchronisation code on track twenty-four. Working on these dedicated slave reels had the added advantage of maintaining the integrity of the original masters until we got to the mix. The constant spooling and playing of tape eventually caused it to degrade and there was no way to come back from this, once it had happened.

THE TOWN HOUSE 150 Goldhawk Road, London W12. Tel: 01-743 9313

TITLE DUB SHEET "LET ME GO" ARTISTE HEAVEN 17 DATE 26/8/82

Sometimes, when the recording was sectional, like the example here for the backing vocal blocks on 'Let Me Go', we simply used another reel of multitrack tape with a reference rough mix. The vocals were recorded and then mixed down to a two-track tape machine so they could be manually transferred back to the master multitrack reels as a stereo pair without SMPTE synchronisation wherever required. This 'on the fly' or 'flying in' technique meant identifying a reference point on the master, usually a snare or bass drum, a couple of seconds before the actual phrase that was to be transferred. A corresponding point on the two-track tape was then marked using a chinagraph pencil, usually a fraction before the reference point to allow the two-track time to spool up. This mark was then aligned with a fixed point on the machine deck. Pushing 'play' manually on the two-track when the reference point was reached on the master then allowed the phrase to be transferred. It was incredible how fast and accurate this technique became. Its advantage was that we could use variations of the same 'bounced' section throughout a song, which made the whole process more efficient, but nothing like the simplicity of modern software-based sample and

206

structure techniques. This technique was developed for the album and was quickly adopted by others.

We were working mostly to a forty-eight-track master format; however, a few of the more complex songs ended up in a seventy-two-track format over three machines but mixing was a nightmare. 'Temptation' was one of these. Whenever a song was started midpoint, to adjust for example a small drum fill or a phrase of lead vocal, it sounded like the gates of hell were opening as three machines all sped up and slowed down to chase sync. The cacophony of sound was at times accompanied by shouts from the sofa . . . 'That sounded fuckin' amazing!'

We were pushing the technology to its absolute limits and usually found ourselves at the end of every mix on The Luxury Gap using every available track of the tape machine, every available channel and bus on the console, and always running out of patch chords. The patch bay itself was almost invisible by the end of a mix. I have many fond memories of the four of us sitting at the desk (pre automation!), trying to control the beast, riding faders, opening and closing sends, panning, spinning. It was extraordinary. The guys were great. They had boundless energy and patience, and never tired of chasing perfection.

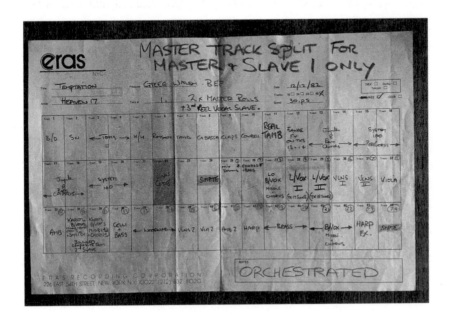

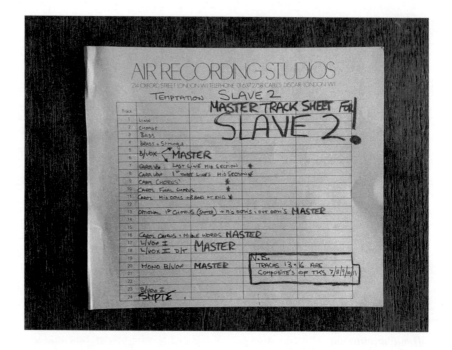

But for every three hours recording there was at least the same amount of time spent again in tape preparation, aligning machines, preparing backing tracks and then mixing down the newly recorded material to get the performances back to the master reels. Often the down time left the guys free to roam Oxford Street and more often than not they would return to the studio with a new surprise! Silly hats, sunglasses, strange gizmos, a billiard table, lethal crossbows and BB guns, footballs, tennis rackets, to name just a few, all of which were immediately set up in the studio play areas.

George Martin owned AIR Studios. I knew him from my days at Audio International and one morning he strolled into the control room of AIR Studio One for a chat. He was absolutely astonished by the amount of equipment we had in the control room. Beyond the plethora of in-house equipment that the studio had provided; the three twenty-four-track tape machines and one of the largest Neve recording consoles of the time, we had also hired additional racks of digital delays, reverbs, noise gates, compressors and other outboard FX. George said he had never seen anything like it *and, to be honest, neither had I ... He was perhaps even more astonished to find that the large recording area of Studio One had been converted into a leisure centre! We had built our own full-size squash court, made from acoustic separation screens and gaffer tape, installed a half-size billiard table and a firing range! In a corner lay a couple of paving slabs that had been brought up from Oxford Circus and used as an effect for 'Crushed by the Wheels of Industry'. Every available glass surface and door was plastered with track sheets, lyrics, doodles, magazine cuttings and never-ending to-do lists. Guest musicians would sporadically appear, although I remember we had to sadly break down the squash court to make room for the orchestra. Studio One always looked more like a kids' playroom than one of the best recording spaces in London.*

There were absolutely no rules. If we wanted to try something we did it, regardless of the cost, effort or time it would take. Creatively we all bounced off one another and, for the larger part of the sessions, at the end of a studio day we had something great to show for it and carry forward into the next. It was a great creative environment. We had a load of fun and knew we were making some great music.

1986–8: *Pleasure One, Teddy Bear* and the Long Goodbye

'We've won, we've lost, we've counted up the cost ...'

Despite the problems with *How Men Are*'s singles, we were still in good heart, and looking forward to writing our new album with full support from Virgin. There was a change of direction creatively – somehow, along the way, we'd been gradually losing faith in the original purity of the electronic vision, and felt that we'd tried the electronic route and we owed it to ourselves to be a 'real' (i.e. rock format) band, like the idols of our youth. We had acquired a house band of musicians, all of whom were excellent and great friends, and we were inexplicably devolving responsibility more and more to them regarding parts and arrangements. The net effect of this was that our 'brand' (which at the time we thought was evolving and improving) was becoming less daring and more mainstream. We wanted to be more mainstream, and certainly Virgin did too. Also, we became more obsessed with creating an authentic soul-funk feel, which was much easier to achieve with excellent real musicians. I'm afraid, in retrospect, it was just not as interesting or innovative ...

But, but, but ... there are some tracks on *Pleasure One* that would make my top twenty songs we ever wrote – 'Contenders', for instance, a genuinely funky, strange and exciting song with lyrics based around global power struggles, is up there with our best. We performed the track live (first TV appearance with a fully live band) on *The Tube*, with whom we'd had an amazing relationship ever since Glenn and I had appeared on their first programme as backing singers for Tina Turner singing 'Let's Stay Together'. 'Contenders' got a great reaction, but pluggers couldn't persuade Radio 1 to playlist the song, and *Top of the Pops* had fallen out with us since Glenn's 'This Is Mine' injury no-show during the last album promo cycle. The writing started to appear on the wall.

'Trouble' was the most 'Heaven 17' pop song on the album – uptempo, sequenced synths, memorable melodies and chorus – but this also raised little interest as a single. It made the top 20 in Germany, but the UK had lost interest in us. It was the last single to be released off the album. 'Red' was written under commission for a French sci-fi film called *L'Unique* starring crossover opera/pop/ film star Julia Migenes-Johnson. We were to be handsomely paid – we recorded the basic tracks in London, then we were to finish in the presence of the film's producers in Paris. There, all seemed to be going well until our manager Keith Bourton announced one day that he was concerned that the first 50 per cent of the fee agreed still hadn't reached our bank account. Thinking about it, we were a little uneasy that the producers were not completely enthusiastic about 'Red', and had suggested that they bring in the famous film song composer Michel Legrand (or Big Mick as we liked to call him) to 'write some melodies' that we could work on. This made no sense to us, but we let them know that we were willing to collaborate. We still didn't feel comfortable.

To cut a long story short, Keith also stumbled across a loaded gun in a producer's car glove compartment, which didn't fill us full of confidence. On the plus side, we were staying at a five-star hotel on the Champs-Élysées with an unlimited expense account, which we could use in the three restaurants and four bars – their willingness to pay these bills surely meant that they must be on the level? So, when the film producers reneged on paying the advance for the third time, and our time in Paris was down to one night, Glenn, Ian and I decided that if we were not to get paid, at least we'd go out with a bang. That evening, we ate at all three restaurants and ended the night at their jazz bar, which specialised in very rare whiskies. While Dizzy Gillespie was performing, we looked at the drinks list. There was a 1940 bottle of Glenmorangie, which was priced at £100 a shot, or £4,000 for the bottle. 'Give us the bottle,' I casually exclaimed. 'Mais oui, monsieur!' responded the somewhat surprised head barman, who proceeded to invite us behind the bar to get the best view of the legendary trumpeter.

What a night that was. Tasting note: the Scotch was very smooth and flavoursome, but I wouldn't be in a rush to spend my own money on it. I reckon we racked up a bill of around £12,000 that night – get in. Nobody fucks with Heaven 17. Except they did – the next morning, Keith insisted on accompanying the film company's financial controller to their bank to ensure she paid the advance into our account. She paid the cheque in, and we left for the airport feeling smug. By the time we landed, she had cancelled the cheque, and we never received any money from them. *C'est la vie* . . .

Simon Mayo interviewed me about *Pleasure One* and the move away from our electronic sound at the time, and I told him, 'I realised that while it was taking me two days to programme a machine to play a few bars, a good musician could do it in thirty minutes and probably with more feeling. The public won't stand for intellectual twaddle any more. They want instant satisfaction. I think we have come up with a very good intelligent pop LP.'

True. Our method was well-meaning but really a misjudgement by us, covering up an ebbing of confidence in our identity. Glenn and Ian were in full agreement with the approach at the time, so I can't take all the blame. Another factor was that the definition of 'electronic pop' was becoming more and more vague and ill-defined – wasn't almost every pop record in the charts 'electronic' to some extent? Samplers were ubiquitous, so in the grand tradition of zigging where others zag, we decided to go 'fuck you' in an attempt to bolshily buck the current trend. Another misjudgement – ouch. Bolshy contrarianism doesn't always pay off.

Aaron Badgley from AllMusic later wrote, 'Heaven 17 attempt to make a danceable political album, and on some levels they are successful. The groove and strong melodies are present, as is Gregory's usual stunning, deadpan vocals. Some of the songs are among their best, including "Trouble" and "Contenders". But other songs are overambitious and tedious. The ideas are there, but the songs are not executed to their fullest.'

Hmm … not sure I agree. 'Overambitious' – good: 'not executed to their fullest' – cheeky fucker. We were always trying as hard as we could. Virgin had a soft spot for us, and to be fair supported our independence and provided us with resources without question, but an anonymous comment on Discogs sums up the problems with the album: 'Brave to evolve but too bad it didn't keep the synthetic edge of the group's previous albums and explore it further. With "Pleasure One", Heaven 17 deliver a decent adult pop album of the year 1986, but you can cut ambition with a knife here – the rich arrangements are at the same time the album's highest point and its worst enemy.'

We had drafted in our good friend Brian Tench, a youngish engineer/producer who would become hot property when he produced the Bee Gees comeback record 'You Win Again' in 1987. His sound was more contemporary and less traditional – lots of drum squashing (compression) to create a massive backbeat, usually fed through a new device called a Quantec Room Simulator, which did precisely what it said on the tin – it made the drums sound like they were in a real room, creating a solidity and force which was manipulable. He also liked to pump mixes through expensive compressors *for the sound of it*, not just to keep levels under control; in other words, using compressors almost like a guitar pedal to mutate the overall sound. Add into all this his preference for a louder, more 'middly' mix, and you had the Tenchy sound. This worked well with the live players from the album, and we certainly threw the kitchen sink at it . . . Tim Cansfield, Preston Heyman (ex-Kate Bush), Phil Spalding (loads of credits, but best known for Mike Oldfield) and Nick Plytas formed the core band, but we also drafted other top musicians and backing vocalists including, after patching up some old differences, the magnificent Carol Kenyon ('Temptation').

The title of the album, in case you're wondering, was intended to re-emphasise the human/sensual connection (à la Human League) as a counterbalance to the perceived austerity of electronic sounds and processing – hence the Malcolm Garrett-designed sleeve, created to our brief, featuring a computer-style 8-bit background, with cut-out lettering spelling out 'Pleasure One' and revealing a sweating, non-gender-specific naked body. He did a great job, as always.

We have always been proud of our songwriting, and I still believe that this is the strong point of the album. Unfortunately, the overall feel of the album was uncomfortably 'try-hard' and a little overblown. Throw in a little, indefinable old-fashionedness (not helped by loads of rock musicians and less programming) and you have enough to tip the balance towards the wrong answers to the questions 'Have Heaven 17 lost their edge?' and even 'Has Heaven 17's time passed?' We didn't want to acknowledge this, of course, but subconsciously it was a concern. I suppose I was thinking, *I'm a world-famous successful producer, how could I possibly get it wrong for my 'passion project' Heaven 17?*

Well, I did – we did. Or maybe it was just the natural life-cycle of an, albeit credible, pop/rock band?

Meanwhile, during the recording of the album, there was a subplot developing. Virgin felt that the best chance of making money from Heaven 17 was to sell the concept and this new, more rock-friendly album to the American market. We had no idea at the time, but an alliance was forming with Arista Records, and their legendary head of A&R Clive Davis (responsible for signing Aretha Franklin, Patti Smith, Dionne Warwick, Ace of Base, Alicia Keys, Ray Parker Jr, etc.). When Virgin told us of his interest, we snootily said the equivalent of, 'OK, cool, let us know when the deal is done,' thinking this would be a payday for us (or at least help to pay off our unrecouped balance with Virgin).

One day, we were under time pressure to deliver the final tracks on the album, and we received a call from Gemma at Virgin. 'Clive Davis is in town and he'd like to take you to lunch.'

'When?' I said.

'Now, today, in an hour.'

'Tell him thanks for the offer, but we have to finish this track today, we're really up against it.'

Gemma coolly replied, 'I don't think you understand – this is CLIVE DAVIS.'

'We don't have time to be schmoozing today. Can't he come here to the Townhouse?'

'IT'S CLIVE FUCKING DAVIS, MARTYN!'

'Tell him sorry, we can't,' I said, and put the phone down.

Yet another open goal missed. God what an arrogant, stupid prick I could be ...

It didn't stop Arista signing Heaven 17 for the US, but we were told later that this severely undermined our barely started

215

relationship, and we never saw or heard from Clive Davis again. No one turns down Clive fucking Davis . . .

Not only that, but I think this was the start of the breakdown of our relationship with Virgin. We delivered the album, and a few days later Keith called us. He told us Virgin had licensed the album to Arista.

'Great news!' I enthused.

'It's not quite that simple,' Keith explained. 'They have licensed the rights to *Pleasure One* for the US for 750,000 dollars.'

'Woohoo!' I exploded. *Our ship has come in.* I thought.

Then the killer blow: 'I'm afraid that all goes into Virgin's pocket, you're not entitled to any of it . . .'

A long pause . . . I couldn't believe it . . .

'Have you asked Brian Carr [our lawyer] to check this?'

Keith replied, 'Yes, they have the right to do this – any money they receive from another territory as an advance is theirs. Not only that, they have done this in return for a reduced royalty rate [so we would get *less* money], and added a clause that Heaven 17 have to pay 50 per cent of any video costs, and that you don't have any approval on budgets.'

I was gobsmacked. They get $750,000 and we don't get a cent of it. We had been sold down the river . . . The reality sank in. Oh. My. God. We'd been shafted. Shafted by the same record company who we'd had a fantastic relationship with, and who we trusted.

Keith stormed into Simon Draper's office at Virgin, and screamed and argued but to no avail.

'It's just business,' he said.

Devastated, we realised this was the beginning of the end. Virgin could no longer be trusted. It's only business, after all . . .

Pleasure One was released to lukewarm reviews in November 1986, and peaked at a wounding 77 in the UK album chart. Not good news at all.

Despite the series of disappointments, we ploughed on with our next album. Bear in mind we received increasing advances for every album we were commissioned to record by Virgin, but we were unsure what our creative direction should be, given the lukewarm critical and commercial success of *Pleasure One*. During this period, I was heavily distracted by my growing reputation and success as a producer, and it's quite possible that I took my eye off the ball regarding Heaven 17. Maybe subconsciously I'd already decided that production was an easier way to make a living – *If I need more money, I can just pluck it off the trees* was my naive thought. It seemed like the good times would never end. But all empires fall, and this mini-empire of Heaven 17 was crumbling at the edges, if not yet fully disintegrating.

Meanwhile, in an effort to keep the Heaven 17 ball rolling, we released a cassette-only 12-inch mix compilation called *Endless*, which was well received, but regarding the main event – the new album – *Teddy Bear, Duke & Psycho* was our last throw of the dice. To put it bluntly, we blew it.

There were some half-decent moments – 'Train of Love in Motion' (Motown again), 'Responsibility' (Philly homage) and 'Big Square People' (half-baked Cameo attempt) – though the rest is well-meaning but unfocused and frankly tired-sounding. One thing I'm very proud of from around this time, however, is our collaboration with Jimmy Ruffin, 'The Foolish Thing to Do', which we co-wrote with Nick Plytas. Again, it was supported on TV by our friends at *The Tube*. The single featured a Luther Vandross cover version, 'My Sensitivity', on the B-side, and both performances by Jimmy were exemplary. This almost felt like a eulogy to our pop career, though, compared with the carefree, experimental, daring nature of our earlier work. Maybe Heaven 17 had simply run its course – it felt like we'd had a good innings compared to most bands. But it's hard to let go.

None of this affected our love of partying. The World Cup of 1986 was a good example. Karen and I organised a World Cup final party, which rapidly descended into a Bacchanalian orgy of tequila and enhancements, resulting in the second half of the final being watched only by myself. Everyone else was attempting to drink tequila while standing on their head. Happy, crackers times ...

It was around this time that Red Bus Studios became my go-to studio, and would remain so for many years to come. It was old-school but professional, reasonably priced and central, just off Edgware Road near Paddington. I also started working with Graham Bonnett, Red Bus's house engineer, who was both very talented and great fun. We continued to work together until the mid-1990s, and we made some really fantastic records, including volume two of BEF's *Music of Quality and Distinction* ... the start of the early nineties BEF and Heaven 17 renaissance ...

The View Outside: Tim Cansfield, BEF guitarist, 1986–94

I met Martyn Ware and the Heaven 17 crew in 1986. I was contacted by Preston Heyman (a larger-than-life character and session drummer) and was asked to contribute to a Jimmy Ruffin single to be produced by Martyn and H17 as a BEF project, almost certainly as a result of the successful resurgence of Tina Turner's career, facilitated by Martyn himself. I dutifully turned up at Swanyard Studios on the day, at the appointed hour.

We cut two tracks: 'Foolish Thing to Do' and 'My Sensitivity', a Luther Vandross composition. To my recollection the band consisted of Nick Plytas on keys, Camelle Hinds on bass, Preston on drums and yours truly on guitar. We all got on like a house on fire and, to cut a long story short, not too long after the successful conclusion of that project, H17, who had been contemplating a new album, put some demos together and let Preston have a copy. He invited me over and asked if I might like to contribute to the tracks.

On the fateful day Preston invited me around to listen to the H17 demos, he produced his 'pipe of peace'. I partook enthusiastically, then he played the music . . . I was horrified, accustomed as I was to chords, vocals, etc. There was only a very rudimentary drum pattern and monophonic synth lines, and I was not helped by the onset of the effects of the 'pipe of peace'. I couldn't figure out what my role would be in such an alien sound-scape, so much so that I seriously considered telling him it wasn't my kind of thing and stepping away. I will always be eternally grateful to him for his encouragement. Nothing fazed him at all: 'We'll get down there, plug in and figure it out.' I have to say I left there with my head full of doubt and herb.

We turned up at Red Bus Studios, H17, Preston on drums, Phil Spalding on bass, myself and an Emulator 2 (one of the newest synths then) ably marshalled by the eccentric Ian Craig Marsh, and began what became the album Pleasure One. *I think the first track we cut was 'Contenders' and that was it – I LOVED the way these guys went about their business. They were creative and of course, as a consequence, subversive. They seemed to bypass the whole of Virgin A&R, Simon Draper included, whether by design or not. They got on with their work, delivered it and then moved on. All had their parts to play, Glenn, Ian and Martyn, distinctly different individuals who appeared conjoined in this brave new world of monophony and imagination.*

For my own part, I loved all the records we made, the subsequent BEF projects. The only downside I can think of was, maybe as a consequence of their subversive nature, the Virgin promotions department, whether on instruction from the powers above or not, missed out, in my opinion, on some of the finest pop music hybrids made at that time. Both albums, Pleasure One *and* Teddy Bear, Duke & Psycho, *are a testament to that, so many great tunes that never seemed to see the light of day.*

The only addendum I'd like make to this is that having been an avid

Sheffield Wednesday watcher since the late seventies, I had unintentionally but thankfully walked into a veritable cauldron of Wednesday support!

The View Outside: Nick Plytas, Heaven 17/BEF keyboards, 1981–8

Although I met Martyn as a hired musician to work on the first BEF and the second Heaven 17 albums, we quickly became friends and I was accepted into the extended family of Sheffield mates that he had around him. My time with Martyn was always accompanied by a party. I worked on so many records where there was always some other activity going on in the studio. I remember we were waiting for Jimmy Ruffin to arrive at Swanyard Studios. It was pretty late at night and we started developing a devil-themed fancy-dress party. I had found an old red velvet curtain as a cloak and was just applying the final touches to my burnt-cork fake moustache when the doorbell rang. It was Jimmy coming straight from the airport. On seeing the first of many spooky characters, he said, 'Ah, Halloween,' and just carried on as if it was perfectly normal.

The mixture between the Sheffield culture and international musical icons seemed very natural. Established American singers were genuinely grateful to be making another record and, of course, we all felt totally privileged to be in their company and helping to make something happen. On meeting Tina Turner around the time we cut 'Let's Stay Together', I remembered so clearly seeing her perform with Ike in 1974 at what was then Hammersmith Odeon . . . just about ten years before. Such a wild and vibrant performer. Seeing her now, she was so calm and humble. I think she called Heaven 17 the new Beatles. She was really enjoying the next adventure in music with a very different approach from her previous stuff.

Martyn had a great energy in the studio, as most good producers do. It was always fun with Martyn doing fantastic Barry Gibb impressions. For me personally, I was always given a lot of creative space on all the records that I contributed to. It is the best way to get a result.

1987–8: A New Direction – Sananda Maitreya and Other Productions

'Erotic images flow through my head . . .'

The year 1988 was not exactly vintage. My marriage to Karen had been on the rocks for quite a while. She was spending more and more time away from home with her new band Kiss That, who had recently been signed to Chrysalis Records. They were pretty good, and persuaded Mick Ronson (one of my all-time heroes) to produce their album. He did a good job, but on the only occasion I met him it seemed clear he was somewhat star-spangled. We know now that at that time he was fighting hard against alcoholism and substance abuse, but nevertheless he was as charming and lovely as you could possibly imagine. He was a fellow northerner from Hull, as is fellow Spider from Mars Woody Woodmansey, with whom I have since become friends, thanks to Tony Visconti's Holy Holy employing Glenn to brilliantly perform Bowie's early albums – but that's for Volume 2 . . .

I confess that I was so wrapped up in my own woes with Heaven 17 that I paid not enough attention to Karen's practical and emotional needs, and this was almost certainly a big reason for our divorce. It's also uncomfortable to admit, but I believe Karen wanted children, and I didn't feel ready for that, given the time my burgeoning production career was taking up (i.e. most of it), and the nagging tick-tick-tick of the timebomb that was my failing Heaven 17 career. I was self-centred, as I was acclimatised to success and things going my way almost all the time, and it is still a source of deep regret for me that I could have been so inconsiderate. I was also drinking and indulging too much, which no doubt distorted my perception of the reality of the situation. We parted with many issues unresolved, and this all upset and shocked our mutual friends as Karen was and is a well-loved and popular person. I always think of the soul standard 'Didn't We Almost Make It' when I think of our marriage – they were great years but, in the words of another, very poignant song, 'Everything Must Change'. Our lives had drifted into unhappiness, based on our lack of mutual support, and the party was over. The divorce process was a very hard and sometimes depressing period of my life. But we have since made up and we have a lot of very happy memories . . .

As often happens, another unexpected disaster lay in wait. One day in late spring, a letter dropped through the letterbox from Virgin Records' legal department. Assuming it was some technical legal request or suchlike, I nonchalantly opened it while eating breakfast. I couldn't believe my eyes – at first sight it looked like Virgin had simply stated that they were not going to be paying the advance for the next album, but then the reality hit me: our ten-year association with Virgin Records had been ended by letter, not a meeting or even a phone call. A letter, which in tone resembled a final gas bill demand. How could they?

I immediately called Glenn and Ian, and they confirmed the dreaded truth. Heaven 17 were finished. Or were we? As was often our way, we immediately tried to find some kind of positive opportunity from adversity. Fuck Virgin, we're free! Surely there'll be another label who would want to sign us? Right? Right? We convinced ourselves this was the case, and immediately started putting the word out.

Within a week, EMI had shown interest but, more interestingly, Trevor Horn's relatively new ZTT label (who we admired greatly) were interested. Even better, our old friend Paul Morley was now head of A&R – it seemed too good to be true. ZTT owned Sarm West Studios just down the road in Notting Hill, five minutes' walk from my apartment, and it was one of the best studios in the UK.

The three of us soon feverishly hunkered down to try and recapture the songwriting spirit of the early post-split *Penthouse and Pavement* sessions, and we were enjoying the process. We quickly wrote two brand-new songs, both aiming for single status: one full of righteous anger about the state of the world (going back to our core values) called 'The Age of Disgrace' – a sample-driven production, which we thought was the best we'd written in a while – and 'Baby Giant', for which I had dreamt the chorus, an ironic take on love and relationships. I've looked high and low for these recordings, but they are lost, I fear, in the great 2004 hard-drive catastrophe (we've all had one, right?) where many obscure experiments and rarities went to digital heaven, beyond the cloud . . .

We presented these to ZTT, expecting a few notes and suggestions, but we were stunned when they notified us that they wouldn't be proceeding. Not even a suggestion? No feedback? Wow, they must have thought our direction was, to put it bluntly, not interesting enough or maybe, criminally in the world of pop, too old-fashioned. Now *this* was a blow and was independent verification that our time was up. We had one more throw of the dice with EMI, but their opinion was the same: more rejection without justification. It's a shit business as League of Gentlemen's Les McQueen would say.

These two hammer blows destroyed our confidence. We had no live work as we didn't play live, so there was nothing else for it. We issued a statement saying that Heaven 17 would be taking a break for an indeterminate time, but that we weren't splitting up, and we would continue on our own projects. Glenn enigmatically had the last word, 'It's not over yet.' How prescient that defiant statement was to be . . .

The ramifications took a while to sink in, and once they did, I was determined not to let them discourage me. I'd already survived and thrived through the Human League split, but there was something more deeply disturbing about not having that bedrock of working with my best buddies most of the time. It was almost like reaching the end of a professional footballer's career, and having to find an alternative path. Fortunately I was already reskilled in full effect as a record producer, and I threw myself into almost everything that was offered to me. Dan Hartman (producer, writer and performer of the smash hit 'Instant Replay') contacted me to see if I would be interested in producing *him*! I couldn't imagine why, but he said, 'I really want your European urban sound.'

What the fuck is that? I asked myself, but as I was a big admirer of his work, I listened to his demos, agreed terms, and he flew over. We were to record in Swanyard in Islington, and my engineer and I waited for his taxi to arrive from the airport. He bubbled into the room, a bit jetlagged, and immediately launched into preparations for the next day's recording sessions.

'Where's the band? Where are all your synths and keyboards?' he demanded in a jittery manner (he was a renowned keyboardist). I was pretty laid-back as I'd had no advanced demands from him or his management.

'Well, let's discuss what you'd like,' I calmly responded.

He became more agitated as it became apparent that he or his people had fucked up. 'I need lots of keyboards – how do you get your sound? Where is your band?'

I felt guilty, but I shouldn't have done: a simple preproduction phone call would have sufficed. 'Don't worry, Dan, we'll sort it in the morning. All will be well.'

'It better had be,' he grumped.

The next day, I brought in all my equipment, hired some extra outboard gear, and got all the session players down – I was taking no chances, I didn't want him jumping back on a plane to the US. Of course, it was all fine, and we soon got down to recording, but I still think he found it a bit of a shock that I wasn't a virtuoso keyboardist, which was almost a prerequisite for US-based producers. Anyway, I knew the European Urban Sound™ ... He was a typical brash, gay American who was a lot of fun, but who simply *loved* the sound of his own voice.

One day, the band and I decided to take him down a few notches. We were deciding on what takeaway food to order in, and Dan proudly stated that he loved Indian food and that no curry was too hot for him. Now I've spent time in LA (where he lived), and I can tell you their version of Indian food contains hardly any heat at all. Or any Indian influence, or sub-continental influence, apart from the names of the dishes. At a restaurant I went to, even the waiters were usually out-of-work white actors with huge moustaches and turbans – you would have to see it to believe it. It was like an Indian-themed Village People gig.

So here was our chance. I discreetly ordered the hottest curry on the local Indian takeaway menu – a Phal – and explained that my friend wanted it to be (wink, wink) extra hot.

'No problem, sir,' the waiter responded.

'Oh, and by the way, could you give me a big portion of your hottest lime pickle please?'

The order arrived, Dan was crazy with hunger and anticipation, desperate to show us his proud spice-consumption skills. I'd asked the assistant to plate up the food in the kitchen and to hide the lime pickle under the rice as a special surprise. The food was presented, and we all carried on as normal. After about two minutes, Dan fell silent, as his face was becoming redder and redder.

'How's the curry? Hot enough?' I innocently asked.

'Yeah, it's definitely hot.' He could barely speak, and we were struggling to keep a straight face. Dan wouldn't let on that he was in intense pain – what a weirdo – and it was only the following day when he was suffering a degree of gastric discomfort that we admitted to him our prank. He took it in good humour, and he never shot his mouth off again.

Sarah Jane Morris is a very good friend of mine (she was in The Communards with Jimmy Somerville, and they had a huge UK hit with 'Don't Leave Me This Way'), and her smoky jazz-inflected mezzo-soprano voice is instantly recognisable. Post-Communards, she had forged a growing reputation in Italy, where her flaming-red hair, winning smile and unique performances had propelled her into mainstream success. She approached me to produce her new album for Virgin Italy called *Heaven*, and I was thrilled to oblige. The musicality and authenticity of her approach and her musicians made for a fantastic studio experience. The album was well received in Italy, and did good business across Europe.

I seemed to be high on the priority list for major UK record companies regarding their female artists, probably due to my success helping to relaunch Tina Turner's career. In this period, I worked with Deni Hines (Australian soul singer and theatrical star) and Pauline Henry (ex-Chimes rock and soul singer), both prodigiously talented but trying to make that elusive mainstream break-through, and I suppose I was flagged up as having that capacity in my wheelhouse, as they say. But it's never that simple. Despite making two of my favourite recordings, neither was a big hit. It just goes to show, so many elements have to be in alignment for the magic to happen, or else everyone would be doing it.

Jill Jones was the stunningly beautiful girlfriend of Prince, one in a long line of backing vocalists to become the consort of the diminutive singer. I have always been an enormous fan of Prince, right from his first album, and the chance to work for his record label Paisley Park was a once-in-a-lifetime opportunity. Jill and I got on very well, both as friends and professionally, but I found her innate sensuality and beauty almost too much of a distraction. She was simply the hottest woman I'd ever met, and I include Tina. Even though I was newly on the market, she was way out of my league. Of the three songs we recorded, my favourite was a song that Prince had written for her called '4 Lust', which consisted of her listing a whole bunch of stuff she would do to you if she was in the right mood. This was painful, and I mean that in a good way. I was gutted when our tracks never got released, and the album never made the grade – who knows why they didn't use it? They are really, really good songs.

More female artists came and went – Deepika, Hannah Jones, Annabella Lwin. In Hannah's case, she had been signed to a vanity label run by the unfeasibly rich son of a Lebanese fruit magnate (you couldn't make this shit up). Of course, the fees were great and Hannah was a genuine talent in the disco-diva mould, but however much money you have, acceptance within the industry is needed in order to promote and succeed with a new artist. Some of that can be bought, but not all. Hannah's label even managed to get an original Diane Warren song for her to sing (God knows how much that must have cost – Diane has been nominated for a total of twenty-seven Oscars, Grammys and

Golden Globes). We also recorded a version of 'Gimme Shelter' with her and Heaven 17 for the homeless charity Shelter.

But these were only sideshows – the undercard, if you like, to the main event: the godlike genius of Terence Trent D'Arby (or Sananda Maitreya as he now prefers to be known. I shall use his preferred name Sananda from now on in this story). In the wake of the disappointment of getting dropped by Virgin, I was taking on a lot of production work, some of it not of the highest quality. In 1986, the year before I broke up with Karen, I'd agreed to produce an artist for EMI, who paid well, but the artist concerned was not on my wish list, shall we say, when I received an urgent call from an enthusiastic young A&R guy called Lincoln Elias at Sony Records. He said he'd been working on developing a young black American soul singer-songwriter and he felt I would be the right producer for his debut album. When I asked why, he said that he'd always been a fan of my work, and that at school, he had done his final A-level Music project on my first BEF album! I was massively flattered, and he sent the cassette over.

The songs I heard blew my mind – not only were they diamonds in the rough, but Sananda's *voice*! It was like a hybrid of Otis Redding, Sam Cooke and Stevie Wonder with an indefinable grit which was all his own, and the songs displayed an uncanny maturity. It was abundantly obvious even at this early stage that he was potentially a great recording artist, but I needed to see what his image was. I needn't have worried. The enclosed photos showed him as a stylishly slinky, tall dude with great fashion sense (biker chic) and a mesmerisingly, androgynously beautiful face, which was a mixture of what looked like black and American First Nation – high cheekbones, paler skin but with dreads. Fuckin' 'ell, he was the complete package, and I knew this instantaneously.

I excitedly called Lincoln immediately to set up a meeting the next day. Sananda was even more impressive in the flesh – a flashing smile, graceful demeanour, and enough charisma for ten pop stars. The women in reception at the record company were almost swooning. We were going to win, provided Sananda agreed. Thank the Lord we got on really well, and soon became good buddies, together with the engineer that Lincoln recommended, Phil Legg. Phil and I went on to work together for years afterwards, and he is still one of my closest friends.

Sananda was a dream to work with in the studio – focused, motivated, intelligent, talented (obviously), willing to listen to good advice even about his own vocal performance, but most of all mischievous and fun. More importantly, he didn't drink or take drugs of any description. It was as if he was in exactly the right place at the right time, full of confidence and youthful certainty. He was also full of sexuality and desire, and there seemed to be no shortage of suitors willing to join him on his sensual journey. I remember one day, walking with him down Dean Street in London's Soho, and girls walking past and turning their heads – he was so striking. I used to joke that I might as well have been invisible, or that I was simply regarded as an obstacle to their ogling. No one at that time could have competed with his magnetism though. Various women would be invited to the studio, many of whom were well-known personalities. Paula Yates certainly took a shine to the young Adonis, as did Patsy Kensit. But one notable story features someone who I can't name ...

One day, Sananda and his latest consort arrived at Battery Studios in Willesden. It had an unusual structure, as the control room was on the floor above the recording area. We'd just been recording 'Dance Little Sister' with the live band, so it was all set up with mikes, but the lights were very dim, almost off. Sananda led his partner directly into the studio, without checking whether anyone was in the control room, but Phil and I had unexpectedly arrived back early from lunch. The control room monitors were dimmed, but the mikes were still on, and we could here whispering and rustling. We immediately became curious and turned the volume up to see if we could hear what was happening. Then the killer idea ... we should record this! Oh my God, too good to be true ... Of course, the small talk was only going to lead in one direction and, sure enough, within minutes, there was a perfect recording of the sounds of lovemaking. We sneaked a peek into the near darkness, and the deed was actually taking place on the Steinway grand piano.

This is so Sananda, I thought to myself. *He is his own personal mythmaker.*

We never told Sananda, and we felt so guilty that we erased the tape. What a rock star does in his own time is his business.

On another occasion, Paula and he were looking for a place to hide from the eternal paparazzi jackals. He called me at 2 a.m. and asked if they could stay on the couch at my flat in Notting Hill, and I said yes. No big deal, but six months later it became front-page news in the *News of the World*. How? Here is an insight into how low these people will go ... The *NOTW* paparazzi had followed Sananda and Paula that night to my house, but obviously that wasn't a big story. Months later, I was in Sheffield, hanging out with the Sheffield Wednesday players and staying at Lee Chapman's house, when I received a phone call.

'Is that Martyn Ware? This is the *Mail on Sunday*. Would you like to make a response to tomorrow's *News of the World* front-page story? We'll pay you. You can set the record straight ...'

'What the fuck? What story?' I said and put the phone down.

Oh my God, what is the content? I immediately rang my lawyer Brian Carr, who strongly advised me not to make any comment to anyone until I'd seen what had been published. Someone faxed me a copy of the front-page early edition – the story was about Sananda and Paula's drug-crazed 'romp', including an implication that I was supplying them with cocaine, and that a young, named female student witnessed everything from the balcony bedroom overlooking my lounge!

Several points here . . .

1 WHAT THE FUCK IS THIS SHIT!?!?
2 Who is this person who claims to have been there that night?
3 As she wasn't there, how did she know the details and layout of my flat?
4 How can they get away with such lies?

It transpired that *News of the World* needed more information about the interior of the flat, and a 'witness' would make their fictitious story details sound real. So, incredibly, the scum employed a young student to befriend *my wife* and her band, who would regularly go to our flat for band meetings while I was in the studio working. The *NOTW* ringer then reported back authentic details of the flat (including photos). *Et voilà!* They had themselves a largely fictitious but seemingly true front-page story. Motherfuckers.

I wanted to sue for libel, but as my lawyer said, 'Do you want to be doorstepped for the next twelve to eighteen months? It's hard, but remember it's tomorrow's fish and chip paper . . .'

I was incandescent, but I had to admit his advice made sense. So, I swallowed my pride, explained the truth to my horrified family and friends, and told Karen *never ever* to let strangers into our home without asking me first.

The album's standout tracks seemed to be 'Wishing Well' and 'If You All Get to Heaven' from the outset, but one that surprised us at the mix stage was 'Sign Your Name'. I'd had the idea of starting the arrangement with synthetic strings (futuristic), and slowly changing to a real string section (warm, human, familiar) in the middle eight, and this worked beautifully. I still reckon that this recording was the easiest mix I have ever had to do – it almost mixed itself, and took only half a day, as opposed to one to two days for all the other tracks.

As we were on the final stretch of the album, there was enormous pressure from the record company to finish mixing and mastering within a week. So, we worked ourselves into the ground, finishing the mix at 7 a.m. on the final studio day, two hours before we were due to master the album. (The intro to 'If You All Get to Heaven' took hours to get right that night.) We were exhausted and half asleep as the mastering engineer did his stuff. I didn't know what Phil and Sananda were thinking, but I thought the whole album sounded limp and lifeless – really disappointing – but I didn't want to let on.

As we left the studio and blinked into the blinding sunshine, we stumbled into a black cab, and no one spoke. We'd fucked it – what a waste of time and effort. It was more than a week before I could bring myself to listen to it at home on my personal lacquer (vinyl test cut). This time it sounded awesome! I realised that it was just the combination of weird monitoring and total exhaustion that had pushed us into despair. What a relief!

In anticipation of the release of the album, Sananda started to perform live, and his debut gig at Heaven in Charing Cross with his live band was one of the most exciting events I've ever witnessed. Not only were the band slick, and Sananda sang like a possessed angel, but his *dancing*! Holy shit, he was phenomenal, it was like Mr James Brown at his peak combined with Otis Redding. Talk about a star is born ... everything exploded from that point. The next thing I knew, he was on the front page of *Rolling Stone* with the hyperbolic headline I AM A GENIUS!, and incredibly people seemed to agree.

Introducing the Hardline According to Terence Trent D'Arby was number 1 in the US and the UK, and top 5 in almost every other territory, and sold around 12 million copies worldwide. I was on 3 per cent of retail for nine of the eleven tracks … not too shabby, but there was one thing that irked me. Although in my contract I was entitled to credit on all artwork as producer, the only credit shown was this: 'The Hardline was hardened by Martyn "Teddy Bear" Ware' (Sananda's nickname for me). Now, everyone in the business knew the truth, but the public would have no idea what that meant.

'Wishing Well' was my first American number 1 as producer in the Billboard Hot 100 charts, and it seemed that we, the team, had cracked it – we had won the lottery. Money was flooding in and Sananda was almost as famous as Prince. In fact, he and Prince saw each other as rivals. At one point during recording the album, Prince contacted Sananda and asked if he would send him some of his demos! Cheeky bastard! Sananda was a big fan, but realised this would be suicidal, and from that point, the rivalry commenced. He was determined to prove he could surpass his nemesis.

The initial furore had settled down into a continuous stream of triumph. The further singles and touring were all stratospherically successful, and the money started *really* flooding in. Excited preparatory conversations were taking place between myself, Phil and the record company to capitalise on the world-beating triumph of *Introducing the Hardline* … Sananda had gone off radar, but that was OK, as the record company told us he was deep into writing mode. Then a letter arrived. I can't remember the exact words, but I will paraphrase …

Dear Martyn,

I hope this letter finds you well. This has been an exciting time for me, and I have some news. I feel it is time for me to fulfil my potential, and I intend to write, perform, mix and produce my next album on my own. I am very grateful for your excellent work so far, but this is my time.

Much love, Sananda

Stunned, I called Phil, and he'd received a similar missive. I called the record company and Lincoln, who was horrified and promised to try and persuade Sananda to reconsider, but no luck. Why would he break up such a winning team? To compete with Prince? That was my only rational thought. The letter had an effect on me similar to the classic 'Dear John' letters that soldiers in Vietnam received from sweethearts who could wait no longer. It also brought back resentful feelings from the split with the Human League, and in particular Phil's betrayal.

Neither Fish nor Flesh was the next album's title – a double album of patchy brilliance. His voice was still there, but the mixes were a little vague to say the least, and lyrically and sonically obtuse. I could hear no singles (except maybe 'Billy Don't Fall', which was never released). The ideas were there but they just didn't gel. And that's what a good producer (or sub-editor, if you like) is for. It was only later that I heard on the grapevine a claim that Sananda had mixed most of the album on psychedelics – probably not the best idea. I still love a lot of his work as Sananda Maitreya to this day; his voice is more glorious than ever.

The View Outside: Sarah Jane Morris, singer and songwriter

I had just won the San Remo Song Festival in Italy, with a song written in Italian, by Riccardo Cocciante and Mogol, and in English by myself and Cheryl Moskowitz. Riccardo, who was already a huge Italian star, was signed to Virgin Records and shortly after the festival I was approached by Virgin to make an album for them. I was talking to many top producers about this album, but was drawn to Martyn Ware, who I'd originally met in Stratford-upon-Avon in 1978, as one of his best friends, Ian Reddington, shared a flat with my then boyfriend, Bill. Martyn had not only been a member of Heaven 17, a pivotal group in the 1980s, but had also produced Sananda's incredibly successful album and had helped relaunch Tina Turner's career. At this point Tim Cansfield was one of Martyn's right-hand men and I took an instant liking to his laid-back manner. Martyn invited me to the Town and Country Club to hear Tower of Power with them both, and that just about clinched the deal.

Martyn managed to negotiate a good deal at Red Bus Studios, a small complex off the Edgware Road. We needed a studio large enough to record the band together. I brought to the project my main guitarist Matt Backer, and my rhythm guitarist John Marshall (with whom I'd written most of the songs), and Alastair Gavin on keyboards. Martyn provided the rest of the musicians, who all had a musical history with him. There was Chuck Sabo on drums, Randy Hope-Taylor on bass and Jeff Scantlebury on percussion, Tim Cansfield on guitar and friends of ours, The Kick Horns, on brass with lush string arrangements by Nick Ingham. The backing vocals were usually sung by myself and John Marshall, but for a couple of tracks we were joined by friends and mega vocalists Glenn Gregory, Helen Terry, Ian Shaw and Mitch Hiller to make the sound of a gospel choir on 'Heart to Heart' and 'Heaven', the title track of the album. As I remember, we had Graham 'Fingers' Bonnett as engineer, who worked extremely well with

Martyn. The recording process totally agreed with me and we would all meet to record every day at about 10 a.m. and carry on into the evening when needed.

We mixed the album at The Strong Room and I remember having to leave one of the mixes late at night to go to the Labour Party headquarters, where Matt and I had already set up earlier in the day, as we were going to be performing as the results came in for Neil Kinnock, who we had imagined was going to be the next prime minister. In the early hours of the morning it became apparent that this was not going to be the case and I remember arriving back at the studio at about 4 a.m. for the end of the mix, feeling very deflated.

Virgin and I were delighted with Heaven *and it went on to have a couple of hits in Italy, Greece and Germany. Alas the album never got a UK release as EMI had just taken over Virgin, and it was one of those albums that had been released in Europe first and got shelved while the takeover was happening. Very frustrating for all concerned.*

I got married to David Coulter in May, shortly after the album was recorded, and Martyn and Landsley's wedding present to us was the use of their wonderful Venice apartment for our honeymoon. I sang in the church for Martyn and Landsley when they were married that year, singing 'The First Time Ever I Saw Your Face'.

A beautiful man, and a great friend.

Intermission:

Venice

My autobiography would be incomplete without describing my life-changing, visceral and profound love of the most beautiful city on earth – Venice, *La Serenissima*, the location of the Most Serene Republic, whose empire lasted almost a millennium. It is the world's best example of the resourcefulness of humankind, and how to take the most unpromising of locations and curate it over centuries into a miracle of city planning and environment adaptation. An entire city built on mud, using stakes piledriven 30 feet into the unstable, swampy gloop, Venice stands on ten million ancient, petrified tree trunks sitting on a firm bed of clay.

OK, so that's enough of the facts. I fell in love with Venice immediately and permanently at the termination of my honeymoon trip on the Orient Express with Karen in 1982. She had been encouraging me to go, as she had fallen in love with the city when she was a cruise-ship dancer, docking every Saturday for months on end. The Orient Express was ridiculously glamorous, and we made the effort to do the whole 1930s costume thing – we looked the business. Despite being the youngest couple on the train by about twenty-five years, we had a ball, and by the time we pulled into the gorgeous deco-esque Venezia train station and emerged straight on to the Grand Canal, I was hooked. As a surprise, I had booked one of the most glamorous and historically famous hotels, the Danieli (originally the fourteenth-century home of the blind Doge Enrico Dandolo), which was definitely hard to beat from a romantic point of view.

From this trip onwards, Venice felt like home, even to the extent of feeling I'd lived there in a previous life. My good friends Marcus Vere and Tich Critchlow from Living in a Box have given me the nickname Il Cardinale or Cards for short. I spent a lot of time there with friends in the eighties, and then when I divorced Karen it became my second home. It was guaranteed that any girlfriend I asked out would never turn down the opportunity of a flying visit to the most romantic city on earth. It wasn't cheap but it was an impressive thing to do.

One day, my lawyer Brian Carr called to tell me in his usual understated manner that I might be quite impressed with the royalty cheque I had received for the first six months of sales of the Sananda album. I was stunned. I was rich beyond any reasonable expectations of a poor working-class boy from the Socialist Republic of South Yorkshire, and my first reaction was, *If I could buy anything, what would I really want?* I *needed* nothing – I had enough money to put a good sum away for my pension (thank God I did that) and still have money to spare. I didn't drive (still don't), didn't need or want a bigger house, wasn't into 'big boys' toys' – boats, helicopters, etc.

Then it struck me . . . I'd been spending huge amounts of money on five-star hotels in Venice. Instead, I could buy an apartment and rent it out when I wasn't using it. Even better, it transpired that property prices were much lower than in London. So, after a lot of viewings, I bought an apartment on La Giudecca (the long, thin, curved island at the bottom of the Venice city map) and my friends Carlo and Caterina Cattaneo-Valmassoi helped me furnish it. This was my bolthole for twenty-seven years from 1989 until 2016, and I used to joke that this place had literally saved me thousands of pounds on therapy.

Visiting kept me grounded and sane, provided a modest income, and enabled me to bring up my children Elena and Gabriel with my second wife Landsley in the heart of a caring and empathetic environment full of culture, beauty and sensory immersion.

As I speak, I'm about to buy another apartment there, and spend an increasing amount of time with the Italian people that I love. I honestly believe that my creative energy, determination and artistic explorations have largely derived from my time in Venice. I have been to every Art and Architecture Biennale (alternate years) since 1984, and this relentless exposure to the best and most innovative creativity (together with occasional pretentious garbage) has given me an inexhaustible and unique wellspring of ideas, which crosses over into every creative area of my life – music, immersive design, architecture and innovation.

Venice is not only my love, it is my inspiration, and I feel an almost human emotional connection to every street, alleyway, square, campanile, canal and building from the eighth century to the twenty-first. I love the people's playfulness and dignity, and their love of festivals, art, exhibitions, learning and history. There's a sense of poignant wistfulness about the loss of their republic to Napoleon and subsequently their dislike of their Austrian oppressors, and there is massive pride in their naval history as evidenced by the flowing of many tears joining the waters during the touching spectacle of the Regata Storica every year, when historical boats restored to their former glory are once again rowed proudly along the Grand Canal, saluting the visitors and their fellow citizens with the shout of 'Alta remi!' (high oars) – the symbolic encapsulation of the melancholic loss of their loved city's naval power. During the late thirteenth century, Venice was the most prosperous city in all of Europe. At the peak of its power and wealth, the city had 36,000 sailors operating 3300 ships, and it dominated Mediterranean and

Silk Road commerce. It once commanded an area covering almost half of the Holy Roman Empire. All down to the stoic nature, intelligence and resourcefulness of people from a maverick city that triumphed over adversity to create greatness.

If I lived to be a thousand years old, I could never tire of the pleasure that Venice has given me, or exhaust its mysteries, so I want to take this opportunity to thank Venice for all it continues to nurture in me – namely my endless love for immersive beauty and knowledge.

The legendary sign we risked life and limb to hang above Topshop on Oxford Circus. We were very, very close to being arrested . . . *(Courtesy of author)*

(above) Anton Corbijn took this in more Air Studios Oxford Circus roof hijinks. I love my Simple Minds T-shirt . . . *(Courtesy of author)*

(right) This is just at the start of Heaven 17 – not really sorted out our style yet . . . *(Courtesy of author)*

The 'I'm Your Money' photo session on London's South Bank, 1981. Ian looking especially stylish.
(Virginia Turbett)

Bucolic and vintage – interesting combination of styles . . . retro futurism anyone? *(Steve Rapport/Getty Images)*

Not sure who's idea this was, but I really like it! *(Virginia Turbett/Getty Images)*

This was the most exciting TV appearance and most nervous I've ever been – real show business on live national TV . . .
(ITV/Shutterstock)

I loved my Johnsons of Kings Road suit, and what lovely and talented people Sandie Shaw and Paul Jones are. This was at the BEF *Music of Quality and Distinction Vol 1* launch party.
(Virginia Turbett/Getty Images)

I love this photo. We're definitely working the boots angle . . . *(Gered Mankowitz/Iconic Images)*

Another early H17 session in 1981.
(Courtesy of author)

Happy days as we were ascending the slippery ladder to success . . .
(Ilpo Musto/Shutterstock)

We did a PA tour in nightclubs to promote *Penthouse and Pavement*. This was in Liverpool.
(Courtesy of author)

A contact sheet from personal shots in 1981. *(Glenn Gregory)*

This was around the time of our mid–nineties album, *Bigger Than America*. *(Courtesy of author)*

Backstage shot from our live British Electric Foundation show in 2016. Left to right: Glenn, Glen Matlock, Owen Paul, Kim Appleby, Rozalla and yours truly. *(Lorne Thomson / Getty Images)*

In Scotland with Gary Kerr and friends. *(Courtesy of author)*

Yet another live show in 2018 featuring Berenice Scott on keyboards, and Kelly Barnes and Rachel Meadows on vocals. *(Trevor Benbrook/Alamy Stock Photo)*

Still rocking the house in 2022 . . .
(Lorne Thomson/Getty Images)

1988–91: BEF – *Music of Quality and Distinction Volume 2*

'A change is gonna come ...'

In 1989, in the wake of the stellar success of *Introducing the Hardline According to ...*, I was hot property once more. I was soon headhunted by several agents who saw potential for amplifying my success as a producer, and I was introduced to a man who was to become a close friend and ultimately Heaven 17 manager, Stephen Budd. For now, he wanted to act as my manager for production work, and he obviously knew many, many people and was super-connected, so I was happy to agree. I'm glad to say this approach quickly paid dividends. Soon Steve was putting the word out internationally about my availability, and the offers started flooding in.

First out of the traps was a young artist called Tashan. He'd just been signed to Russell Simmons's new label Def Jam, and he was being groomed to be the new Alexander O'Neal. We recorded some amazing tracks featuring an orchestra and the best session players I could muster (most of whom went on to form the core BEF band).

Tashan surrounded himself with some questionable characters. One particular assistant seemed to have no identifiable provenance or previous experience in music, but for some reason Tashan had taken him on. I always wondered if he was part of some dodgy underworld thang. He certainly looked and talked the part – he rarely smiled, wore pitch-black glasses all the time, and cultivated a menacing attempt at passive domination. But none of that bullshit impressed me at all. I come from the wrong side of the tracks, and I've seen many, many things – intimidation doesn't work on me.

As I was working on the album, which was going very well indeed, I had met the love of my life, Landsley, through a blind date following a brief encounter at my birthday party (when I was blind drunk). We had almost immediately fallen in love, and I had arranged to take Landsley to Venice so I could propose to her, only a month after we met. I'd arranged the time off a few weeks in advance, and cleared it with the record company and Tashan, and the fateful weekend arrived. I was a few hours from popping the question, when I received a phone call.

'You must return immediately to the studio, or you will be fired,' threatened the unconvincing assistant.

'Fuck off, that's not going to happen. You've no chance. I'm here for a purpose.'

He carried on threatening me for a while, eventually got bored and hung up.

When I returned to the studio, newly affianced on the Monday, Tashan's goon was there, refusing to speak but trying to stare me out (or at least I think he was), but Tashan and I just cracked up. He was a busted flush. Moral of the story: don't let anyone bully you. As the 1990s approached, the giant cheques kept rolling in from the *Introducing the Hardline . . .* album, and the money was burning a hole in my pocket. No one in my family or even extended family had ever owned a business, was wealthy or had ever inherited any money to speak of. Born, school, work, marry, work, kids, work till you drop, retire, die. That was my preordained path, together with almost everyone I knew in Sheffield. But I wasn't in Sheffield any more. All this money felt inherently wrong to me – my father had slaved away and died with £3000 in the bank, and virtually no assets. And he would have had less had I not helped to support my mum and dad. Although I have talent, worked hard, had the breaks and made the most of them, I didn't feel I deserved what I felt was largely unearned filthy lucre. Of course, I never admitted this to anyone at the time, and I enjoyed the freedom it gave me (buying my apartment in Venice was a dream), but something inside me needed to put the money to good use.

I'd never had an entrepreneurial spirit, and I don't like taking financial risks – I don't gamble unless the odds are in my favour. In fact, I enjoy being an amateur bookie for my friends for that very reason – all the financial quizzes I take put me on the 'cautious' end of the scale. So, I put a fair amount away as a pension, spent huge amounts on travel, fine dining and potential future long-term partners, and still felt there was something missing ...

I was looking for another major project to get my teeth stuck into when the thought hit me. How about volume two of *Music of Quality and Distinction*? Of course, it made perfect sense! This time, I could start recording by financing it myself, at my home studio Red Bus, and I was pretty sure I could find a record company to buy the rights and help me promote it. But, for once, I'd be in complete control of the recordings, no more 'he who pays the piper calls the tune'. Excited, I started planning – what would be the central premise this time? Which artists should I approach? I knew that I had built up a worldwide reputation for highly profitable productions, in particular with electronic soul arrangements, and usually with female singers. That was it! I determined to record a make-or-break, daring, international record, with not only famous UK singers, but legends of soul. It felt so right, and what was the worst that could happen? At least it would put me back in the fore-front of record companies' minds for future work, even if the record itself wasn't a stone-cold hit.

As soon as I mentioned my plans to my good friend Mick Clarke (who had started his own sub-label 10 Records as part of Virgin), he wanted in. Mick was just as much of a soulboy as I was growing up. He discovered and signed the likes of Soul II Soul, Leftfield, Maxi Priest, Loose Ends and Grooverider during a career which included stints at Columbia Records, Virgin Records, 10 Records and Higher Ground, where he was managing director. He was one of the few A&R people in town who lived for music, knew the scene inside out, and was loved for his charismatic and generous personality. We quickly agreed the deal, and my recording costs were covered. More importantly, Mick knew every major record company exec in the US soul and R&B scene, and could make introductions for me.

I started making a wish list of artists to approach, and we had some early successes by signing up Sananda (on one condition, that he could do a Bob Dylan cover!), the magnificent Billy Mackenzie, Tashan (whom I'd just finished recording), and Green Gartside of Scritti Politti.

The key to pushing this further would be to persuade some famous American singers, so I was thrilled when Tina Turner agreed to take part. (I think she felt it was payback for *Music of Quality and Distinction*'s role in her early eighties comeback). Now the doors started opening – Chaka Khan, Mavis Staples, Billy Preston and the young Lalah Hathaway, daughter of my favourite soul singer of all time, Donny Hathaway. My old friend from Living in a Box, Richard Darbyshire (who I'd always thought was criminally underrated as a singer) and a new Portuguese artist called Ghida De Palma completed the very strong lineup. Just to balance this out a bit, there were almost as many people who turned me down. David Bowie, Errol Brown (both for the second time), Peter Gabriel, Kate Bush (who almost agreed but kindly explained that she 'wasn't quite ready'), Aretha Franklin, Alexander O'Neal, Maurice White, Isaac Hayes and Barry White. But the one that really got away was George Michael, who I'd been an acquaintance with on various activist projects. We spent a long time on the phone, but the timing wasn't right for him. I think George also was used to running his own show, both as an artist and producer, and was too polite to say he didn't want to relinquish that. What a pity. I asked him again later for *Volume 3* in 2007, but no go. Ah well . . .

There were some other abortive attempts to record artists for the album. I'd put together an electro-reggae-flavoured arrangement for Maxi Priest, who had agreed to take part, but he never turned up at the arranged time at the studio and never apologised. Arsehole. But by far the funniest story of failure on the album involved John Lydon. John and I had become good friends since appearing together on *The Tube*, so I asked him if he'd consider taking part in the project. He agreed, and we travelled together to a country retreat studio near Munich recommended by my good friend Dirk Hohmeyer (ex-head of A&R at Virgin Germany). John is a huge reggae fan, and I suggested that we do a couple of electro-reggae arrangements for the songs he chose. He picked two songs, one of which I can't recall, but the other was a rare recording called 'No One Shall Escape the Punishment of Jah'. Of course, John changed the lyric to (you guessed it) 'No one shall escape the punishment of John'. Very droll. We settled into recording the vocal, and as luck would have it, John had a chest infection, so insisted on having a bucket as a spittoon next to him as he sang. The tape rolled, and John started . . . 'NO ONE SHALL ESCAAYEEAAAPE THE PUNISHMENT-AH OF JOHN-AH . . .' What a racket, but a brilliant racket. He continued, 'YER MUMMY AND YER DADDY SAAAAY-AH, YER CARN'T CUM AHHHHT TER PLAAAAY-AH ...' followed by a giant hoiking sound of phlegm being launched into the spittoon/bucket with a resounding splat. Priceless, if only we'd filmed it.

The songs turned out really well, but when I came to compile the album, they just didn't fit with the vibe, so they didn't make the cut. I still have the recordings, and I asked John if he'd allow me to put them on a retrospective boxed set we put out in 2011, but he refused. What's the bloody point, John? Onwards and sideways ...

Before we get into the descriptions of the recordings themselves, we need to talk about the BEF band – heroes the lot of them. I shall pay special tribute to Ian Craig Marsh towards the end of the book. Suffice to say, we were joined at the hip for decades. I miss him so much. Randy Hope-Taylor was the key man for this album. Not only was he schooled as part of the Incognito band, he was a great bass player and all-round musician and arranger. The album could not have been made without his programming brilliance on many of the tracks, the finest examples being 'Someday We'll All Be Free' with Chaka Khan and 'Free' with Billy Mackenzie. He was always a great ally and friend, and I miss his company.

Tim Cansfield is a legend in his own right. Born in Trinidad and a self-taught musician, this enigmatic and self-effacing genius has been the first choice of many recording artists, including the Bee Gees, Steve Winwood, Elton John, Heaven 17, Billy Preston, Chaka Khan, Tina Turner, Whitney Houston, Seal and many more. He is also one of the nicest guys in the business, just as happy playing calypso for nothing in the Trinidad carnival as he is touring the world with major artists. His relaxed and funky style helped define the sound of this album and several Heaven 17 recordings. And

I've converted him to being a Sheffield Wednesday fan! We are still great friends.

Phil Spalding ... I've always secretly wanted to be a bass player, and they don't come much better than Phil. He's played and appeared with Mick Jagger, Seal, Orchestral Manoeuvres in the Dark, Elton John and Randy Crawford and, of course, Heaven 17. Phil was a madman, full of talent and enthusiasm; he was a cheeky cockney who could play just about anything. But at times his personal indulgences got the better of him. I once performed with him on a German TV show, and the record company took us to dinner afterwards. This normally entailed an open tab for as many drinks as you liked but, on this occasion, there was also additional entertainment, if you catch my drift. Never one to shy away from getting out of it, Phil proceeded to take the brakes off in spectacular fashion, leading to his disappearance into the night as we all headed for bed (early flight tomorrow). The following morning, Phil was in an incomprehensible state – he could barely walk or talk, and his skin had a greenish tinge. We managed to get his shit together for him, checked out and arrived at the airport. Phil unfortunately was finding walking difficult, so we decided to pour him on to a baggage trolley and wheel him to check-in. Astonishingly, the staff allowed him to board and we took our seats, which were scattered around the aircraft. After take-off, and as soon as seatbelt signs went off, one of the stewardesses came up to me and said, 'Is you friend OK? It's just that I've been working for British Airways for forty years, and I've never seen anyone that colour.' 'Oh don't concern yourself,' I replied, 'he does this sort of thing all the time.' Phil cleaned up his act years later, and his talent is now shining through again. God bless you, Phil.

Chuck Sabo completed the band. He was a rock-solid drummer of considerable power, just the way I like them – solid, no-frills. He is also a songwriter, producer and musical director.

So, each of the band members had multiple skills and appreciated each other's contribution to the whole. I only have one rule for collaborative working – no assholes. This simple epithet has saved me a huge amount of time and energy in my career. All of the band were great musicians, but also good, creative and open-minded people, and all of us understood that we were greater than the sum of our parts.

The under-credited 'sixth man' of the band was Graham Bonnett of Red Bus Studios, a self-effacing, elite sound engineer with great sensitivity and taste in musical arrangement. We used to call him 'The Ghost' due to his almost translucently white skin, reminding me of the methodology used for creating white asparagus, which is grown away from the light to maintain its whiteness. I believe Frank Zappa called it a 'studio tan', as he himself spent most of his life in the studio. Graham's effortless excellence and relentless dedication to the cause made the difference between a good recording session and a timeless one.

A special word for Glenn here. I tend to take him a little for granted, as I'm sure he does with me, but despite the fact that he was not on this BEF album, he would freely give up his time and expertise in the studio sessions just for the fun of being around. Glenn is my brother. I love his talent, relentless generosity and goodwill. There is no situation in which Glenn does not make what's happening better. We will be the best of friends until the day we die. Love you, Glenn.

The album was finished, and I don't think I've ever been so excited. Videos were planned, the record company were enthusiastic, we appeared on *Wogan* on BBC One with Lalah Hathaway and our excellent (even though I say so myself) version of 'Family Affair', which was our first single. The album was released all over Europe to moderate success and good reviews, but none of the singles made much of an impact. All was not yet lost: our masterplan was to crack the top 100 albums in the Billboard charts in the US.

Although BEF's *Music of Quality and Distinction Volume 2* was a creative triumph, commercial success depended on the American market, and the record was enthusiastically scheduled as a top-priority release by Virgin America (making it virtually a certainty to succeed). But then it was unexpectedly brutally axed from their release schedule at the behest of the head of their 'urban' department (which services the black radio stations), who refused to work on the record when she realised that I was a white producer of what she had assumed was a 'black' record. It sounds unlikely now but it was true – something about the two Donny Hathaway tunes 'Someday We'll All Be Free' and 'Song for You' seemed to smack of cultural appropriation to her, despite being sung by two of the world's most famous black female singers, Chaka Khan and Mavis Staples. This was an enormous setback, and despite pleading with our record company, they couldn't or wouldn't change their minds. All that hard work and effort down the pan with an arbitrary, racially motivated decision.

I'm still proud of this album, which I believe has stood the test of time – check it out . . .

The View Outside: Sandie Shaw, legendary vocalist, BEF albums 1 and 3

Martyn is most definitely a legend in his own mind. And what a mind! Always brimming with ideas, always off the wall and left of centre. I met him in the eighties when he was part of Heaven 17. A friend's son played me Penthouse and Pavement *and I was won over. I became part of an extraordinary BEF album by singing his electronic version of 'Anyone Who*

Had a Heart'. There was a beautiful soprano sax solo. Hank Marvin of The Shadows flew all the way from Australia to add a Fender guitar solo which didn't make the mix. I would love to hear the outtakes.

Some years later I found myself DJing in a dingy basement disco in Barcelona with Martyn — don't ask! His mop of hair and waistline had disappeared and he had morphed into an extraordinary image of a kind of Italian film noir director, pointing out the scenic beauty of the city at night. He has a great eye as well as a cool ear.

Soon after that I joined him in another studio production singing 'Just Walk in My Shoes'. A few weeks later I suddenly found myself barefoot sharing the Roundhouse stage with Martyn and being introduced by Boy George, who insisted on chanting the Buddhist invocation of 'Nam Myōhō Renge Kyō' with me before I started singing.

Martyn (over)paid me for my efforts with the most wonderful present of staying in his fabulous flat in Venice. I remember pinching some china from the teashop in St Mark's Square. It's all always fun working with Martyn.

1990–2: The Fall and Rise of Heaven 17

'Adorable creatures with unacceptable features ...'

The years 1990–2 saw much more production work generated by Stephen Budd's office. I was honoured to be offered the chance to work with Green Gartside from Scritti Politti as I was a great fan, and it was agreed to record a couple of cover version collaborations with Shabba Ranks and Sweetie Irie. Green was a massive reggae and toasting fan, and was thrilled to get the super-hot Shabba Ranks on board, and Sweetie was, as you'd expect, a sweetie. Firstly, we decided to work on an electro-reggae-flavoured version of The Beatles' 'She's a Woman', and Shabba's management seemed happy with the prospect.

When Shabba arrived at the studio, he turned up with a posse of twelve dreadlocked dudes. He firstly insisted on being paid in cash (literally a brown paper bag), and then decided that each of the assembled multitude needed a copy of the contract to read. This took about half an hour of copying, and when we eventually gave them the documents, only about three of them showed any interest at all. This was just a power trip. Then his manager, who had arrived late, introduced himself as 'The Specialist'. He stood at around 5 foot 1 inch, short and wiry, which looked ridiculous compared to the stacked and muscular Shabba, bedecked in gold jewellery like a fucking Christmas tree, who stood at around 6 feet 6 inches. The two of them reminded me very much of Dustin Hoffman and Jon Voight in *Midnight Cowboy*.

It became obvious immediately that A) Shabba had never heard the backing track before, and B) he didn't know or recognise Green, and therefore ignored him, even though Green enthusiastically introduced himself (being an enormous reggae/dancehall fan). The Specialist insisted on being in the recording booth next to Shabba as he sang every word – he would literally suggest his 'improvised toasting' as he was listening to the backing track, with no obvious attention to timing. Obviously this led to a shambles, so we spent a huge amount of time shuffling his, admittedly charismatic, rapping around until it somehow made sense in the final arrangement. The end product worked, and was a fun and unusual top 20 hit, although the Sweetie Irie follow-up, 'Take Me in Your Arms and Love Me', didn't fare so well.

Another fascinating experience, probably a year or two later in 1993, was working with Urban Cookie Collective, who had just had an enormous worldwide dance hit with 'The Key the Secret'. They were lovely people, and we tried hard to replicate that mysterious pop formula with some new material they'd been working on, but there was something indefinable missing. We tried a few things, but then we were talking one day and realised we were all Parliament/ Funkadelic fans, and I had an idea that we should get Bootsy Collins (who I knew was in London) to come in – not to play bass, but to capture his instantly identifiable voice and get him to rap the middle eight. Everybody loved the idea, calls were made, and Bootsy was booked for the next day. I assumed that Bootsy would have been relaxed and 'off duty', but when he entered the room, he was wearing full Bootsy regalia – cowboy hat and boots, medallions, tight white jeans, the works. Not only that, he was carrying a swag-bag of stuff, which turned out to be his own Bootsy merchandise, which he proceeded to flog to us. His voice was like a cartoon character, swooping up and down in pitch, exactly like on the records . . . 'Heeey there, Martyn, how you doin', the name is Bootsy!' Like I didn't know who he was. 'Would you like to buy some stuff?'. He laid out cassettes (handprinted), medallions, stickers, T-shirts and other paraphernalia, but what caught my eye was the clearly handprinted 'BOOTSY' trucker's caps, with sixties hippie typeface in badly stencilled gold ink. Two minutes into our first meeting, I was hooked.

'Er – how much are these?' I said, pointing to the caps.

'Well, Marty, they're ten pounds each, but I can let you have three for twenty-five pounds.'

I didn't really want or need three, but I bought them anyway.

He was charming and hilarious as he recounted tales from life on the road with George Clinton and the band, and we got a great series of takes out of him. They sounded so good that we loaded some of the best bits into my sample for future use as seasoning on other dance tracks.

In the late summer of 1992, all was ticking along nicely when I received a life-changing phone call from my old friend and colleague Rob Manley, who was now working with Mick Clark at 10 Records. He'd just returned from a rave-filled holiday in Ibiza and he sounded as though he might be still feeling the effects.

'Martyn, there's a white label mix of "Temptation" being played in just about every club. It's by Brothers in Rhythm [super-hot remix team]. The kids can't get enough of it! I reckon if we release it, it would do really well!'

'Calm down, Rob.' I tried to pull him back to reality. 'What does it sound like?'

'It's Balearic beat, you know, some Spanish guitar samples, mainly electronic, chopped-up girl vocal intro stuff – very spacy and atmospheric. It's a fucking epic! It's about seven minutes long!'

I asked him to get us a cassette or white label, and we'd make a decision.

'To be honest, Mart, we don't really need your permission, we own the rights, but you'd be crazy not to approve it.'

OK, I thought, *touché* . . .

The track was every bit as awesome as Rob described. The intro mysteriously pulsated, leading to a thrilling drop into Glenn's commanding baritone, 'I've never been closer, I've tried to understand' (crowd goes wild) and the excitement continues to build and build relentlessly until the final orgasmic release of the 'happy ending' (crowd lights a fag in the afterglow).

Virgin quickly snapped up the release slot in late autumn, and early indications from retailers were stunning. As Rob had said, this was not only heading to be a top 10 hit, but might even have a shot at top 5. This was completely beyond our expectations, and Virgin rapidly put together plans for a 'Best of Heaven 17' compilation to follow it up. It was all kicking off, and sure enough, we got a slot on *Top of the Pops* (no doubt courtesy of the fact that Michael Hurll was no longer working on the programme), the Radio 1 A-list and the playlist on almost every commercial radio station in the land. We even kissed and made up with Carol Kenyon, whose performance on *TOTP* once again blew everyone away. It was fucking crazy, nearly ten years after the original hit! We joked that all we had to do was release a new version every ten years and that would be our pension sorted.

The song reached an astounding number 4 in the singles charts, and number 1 in the dance charts. What's more, it had sold almost as many copies as the original single! The compilation album called *Higher and Higher* reached 31 in the album charts, and featured the

Brothers in Rhythm remix, together with several other dance remixes, including the Rapino Brothers banging, brand-new Italian house version of '(We Don't Need This) Fascist Groove Thang'. The Rapinos were great guys, and were massive fans of Heaven 17 from way back, and had just broken through with their gargantuan breakthrough number 1 mix of 'Could It Be Magic' for Take That, which launched their career.

Suddenly Heaven 17 were back in the public consciousness. Glenn and Ian had been working on their own projects in the last few years, I'd been wall-to-wall producing, and now we were all 'back in the room' – and it felt good and right. Sometimes the good guys can win, and we were determined to capitalise on our reanimation from the pop grave. We started writing new material together, which we hoped would lead to a new album, being signed either to Virgin again or someone else: in other words, proving to the world and ourselves that we weren't just washed-up has-beens. A bit hard on ourselves perhaps, but there was definitely an undercurrent of pride that we'd not fallen apart, and that when the opportunity arrived (if it ever was to arrive) we'd be ready, willing and able to fight the good fight once more. Let's face it, I like being part of a team. I can and do work alone, and am self-motivated, but I love that collaborative feeling. There's nothing quite as fulfilling as creating something that each individual would never have been able to do alone. Little did I know that the second act of my career was to be even more successful than the first . . .

The year 1993 changed everything, as you will find out in Volume 2 . . .

Analogue Epilogue

A tribute to the brilliance and mystery of Ian Craig Marsh and the artist Ray Smith.

The first time I met Ian was at Meatwhistle; he was ostensibly a slightly nondescript character, dressed in schoolish dark grey trousers, a white shirt and a grey V-neck pullover. He was quietly spoken, appeared to be shy but polite – all in all nothing to write home about. My initial impressions proved to be entirely wrong. Within weeks it became increasingly evident that this particular patch of still water ran very deep indeed.

Mark Civico (who was also at Meatwhistle) was his closest friend, and a more diametrically opposed character could barely be imagined. Mark, who sadly passed away a few years ago, was a brash, open, fun, extrovert character who was the main instigator and lead singer of Musical Vomit. 'Tache, muscles, hairy chest, the lot – but a thoroughly lovely and reliable guy. Ian and he were inseparable at school (in much the same way as Phil Oakey and me), but there were dark rumours that something had happened between them at school which had temporarily driven them apart. What had happened? I dug a little further and Glenn spilt the beans.

He told me that Ian and Mark were the school 'renegades', and that they were often chastised for various pranks, usually targeted

at teachers they had little time for. This resulted in the usual deten-
tions (and hero worship from most of their classmates), but there
was nothing particularly unusual about that. Until, one day, Mark
and Ian had an idea, which they proceeded, foolishly, to commit to
paper. They planned a nefarious attack on the headmaster, based
on an idea to drop a plugged-in electric heater into his bath,
thereby electrocuting him. This was clearly a mad, unrealistic
fantasy, and never going to happen, but unfortunately the written
evidence was found by a teacher and presented to the headmaster.

Now, as far as I'm concerned, a simple dressing-down and
temporary suspension would have sufficed, but it appears that the
headmaster was in no mood for understanding and compromise, so
the two boys were frog-marched to his office. When asked who
was responsible, Mark (terrified as he realised they'd gone too far)
said he had nothing to do with it – thereby landing Ian in the
proverbial shit. It was true that the plan was written in Ian's
hand. The quiet but unpredictable Ian was instantly expelled for
being an undesirable subversive element. Ridiculous. But obviously Ian and Mark had kissed and made up, as all seemed to be
back on track between them.

This story shows the dichotomy at the heart of Ian's personality.
He was a brilliant and super-intelligent lateral thinker, maximally
creative, who always thought 'outside the box'. I can honestly say,
hand on heart, that The Future, The Human League, British Electric
Foundation and Heaven 17 could never have existed without his
genius. Ian, Adi Newton and I were totally on the same wavelength,
and it was a frictionless, gliding path of outrageous inventiveness,
originality and imagination, which was a tap that only needed to be
turned on – and a large part of that was down to Ian. The Future
was really 'out there', but Ian enabled us to pick and choose from a
myriad original ideas, which he was more than happy to let the

group sculpt into any shape we wanted. His generosity of collaborative spirit was, and still is, an inspiration.

Of course, it was Ian's last-minute decision to join me in a new venture after The Human League split that changed the course of my musical career, and for that I am eternally grateful. I will never forget the sheer excitement as Glenn, Ian and I spent many happy hours at his parents' house in Sheffield, experimenting with video, photography and ideas, all while being fed and watered by his lovely family. These were the happiest of times, and possibly the most fruitful exploration of Ian's seemingly fathomless talent. Most of the early artworks for The Human League and Heaven 17 were created there.

Ian has always been a gentle, enigmatic soul, and it was only later that we realised he suffered from depression and was undergoing therapy (which continued for decades). People really didn't talk about such things at that time in Sheffield – it was very much a 'buck your ideas up, pull yourself together' kind of environment, like most industrial cities in the UK. I feel bad now that we didn't understand the depth of his issues, or help in more proactive ways, but Glenn and I simply didn't understand at the time. At his happiest, possibly manic, Ian would be the most amazing company, hilarious, and frankly he could have been an alternative comedian in the Eddie Izzard stream-of-consciousness vein. Other times, he would retreat into himself, apparently lacking the confidence to contribute fully.

On our various jaunts to TV shows in the UK and abroad, enigmatically he seemed more at ease. His fashion sense was original and impeccable, and we always looked forward to his outfits. Ian also had a predilection for extremely beautiful and unusual girlfriends. They seemed attracted to his gaunt good looks and mysterious but friendly personality. Again, it only became apparent later that his compliant nature meant he was to be cruelly exploited by several of these girlfriends – without wishing to go into detail, he has had a very tough time, especially regarding finances.

Another intriguing issue was Ian's fascination with credit and investment, which was to become a problem he later fixed. He would enthuse about getting as many credit cards as possible to build up a credit score, then using the low transfer rates to reduce overall interest. Hmm . . . I also fell for it for a while, but it seemed very dangerous to me, as it was predicated on an endless earning capacity.

Ian was the main conceptual driving force of the *Penthouse and Pavement* album, and he brought in the album artwork we were to pastiche with the help of Ray Smith. I mean, who else would subscribe to *Newsweek*, *National Geographic* and *Time* magazine? I only ever saw those in dentists' waiting rooms! Ian was a conceptual artist, a situationist and an early example of a meta-modernist. He was also responsible for a large proportion of the most interesting lyrical ideas on *Penthouse and Pavement*, particularly 'Let's All Make a Bomb' and 'Geisha Boys and Temple Girls' – and he was at least a 33 per cent contributor to all the tracks.

His programming and sound design skills on the System 100, and later System 100M and Fairlight, were second to none. His rhythmic command of the 100's sequencers still thrills musicians I talk to today, who find it hard to believe that every rhythm track was created from scratch in a bespoke manner – even live! Can you imagine the faff of resetting knobs and sliders and replugging between songs? Ian even built his own Perspex 'cage' to house his precious equipment for the various Human League tours in 1978–80 (his dad was a builder, and Ian has always loved getting his hands dirty).

As we became more famous, Ian started to go back into his shell a little. We had released *Music of Quality and Distinction* as BEF in

1982 as a production team, but as soon as it looked like we were about to implement the BEF production working methodology (possibly six albums/six group identities per year), Ian decided he didn't want to be part of BEF any more. I tried to dissuade him, but he was adamant. I still to this day don't understand his decision, as we were about to embark on our first third-party production for Hot Gossip on the DinDisc label (a sub-label of Virgin). I was gutted, but my instinct was to make the best of a setback, so I asked Glenn if he'd like to join BEF as an equal partner, and that I'd train him up to be a producer (at that time, Ian and I produced Heaven 17). Glenn's response was roughly 'thanks for the offer, but I can't be arsed – all that hanging around in studios'. *Oh well, I suppose BEF will be just me then from now on.* I didn't make any announcement at the time, as I couldn't understand Ian's decision, so I thought it was best to let it lie in the realm of the evolving BEF/Heaven 17 myth/conceptual art project.

Ironically, shortly afterwards, I was approached by Tina Turner, so neither Ian nor Glenn benefitted financially from the great run of success that followed.

There were still moments of crazed insanity featuring Ian. During promotion for the release of *Penthouse and Pavement*, Heaven 17 were flown out to Hamburg to continue our successful UK PA tour (the three of us singing to backing track). The venues were usually smallish nightclubs, as we wanted to be as close as possible to our audience. On this particular occasion, there was a lot of hanging around; we were bored between the soundcheck at 6 p.m. and when we were due to perform at midnight. Glenn (the usual mischief maker) suggested we had a few drinks to pass the time away, which was a big mistake ... unbeknown to us it was a Kahlúa (very sweet alcoholic Mexican coffee liqueur) promotion night. We embarked on a mission of Kahlúa mixed with Coca-Cola (yuk), and by the time we reached midnight, we were smashed. Since that day, we only allow ourselves minimal alcohol before performing.

The gig was OK, but for some reason we decided to carry on afterwards, probably due to a sense of relief that we'd not passed out on stage. Another mistake. It's worth mentioning that Ian rarely drank, but when he did it was usually eventful. The night progressed, and Glenn and I realised we were among the last in the club at around 3 a.m. Our hotel was only half a mile away, but while we'd been in the club, there had been a major snowstorm and the streets were now 9 inches deep in snow. We looked around the club for Ian, but couldn't find him, and we assumed that he'd bailed out earlier to go back to the hotel. Glenn and I trudged through the snow and made it back to the hotel, and we gratefully slumped into the warmth of our respective rooms.

The following morning, Ian came down to breakfast (early start to catch the flight home), and he literally looked like death warmed up. It transpired that the previous evening, a totally trashed Ian went to the toilet to throw up, which he did, but then he fell asleep slumped in the cubicle. When he blearily regained consciousness, he was in total darkness. The club was closed down and all the lights were off. He blindly and drunkenly staggered around, trying to recreate the structure of the club in his mind so he could find an exit, which after half an hour or so he did. This, however, was just the start of his troubles – he couldn't remember where the hotel was, and by this time there was no one to ask and the temperature had dropped to sub-zero. Still toxically inebriated, exhausted and frozen, miraculously he eventually happened upon the hotel. He meandered to his room with chattering teeth, and suspected he might have hypothermia, so he ran a hot bath. He eased himself into the water, and almost immediately passed out, only to be awakened by a drowning sensation – he was in fact drowning, it wasn't a dream, as he had slipped under water in his unconscious state. Terrified, he eventually slid into bed at around 5 a.m., to be awoken two hours later as we had an early flight home. Glenn and I had a serious hangover, but we can only imagine the full horror of what he felt at the time, poor bastard. I think that experience put him off drinking for several years.

With the benefit of hindsight, it was from the point of leaving BEF that Ian's confidence seemed to start declining. We still had great times making the Heaven 17 albums *Luxury Gap* and *How Men Are*, and Ian's contribution was just as critical, but something wasn't right. The periods of carefree fun seemed to be rarer, and Ian became quieter and more thoughtful. The wellspring of ideas had started to dry up from all of us, but most missed was Ian's sparkle and 'special sauce'. *Pleasure One* and *Teddy Bear, Duke & Psycho* (our nicknames, with a somewhat awkward and inappropriate attempt to make light of Ian's increasingly withdrawn personality) were both relatively uninspired lyrically (except 'Contenders', which Ian contributed majorly to).

The record company axe fell in 1988, and we were all upset, but determined to forge on. We created some demos for ZTT and EMI ('Baby Giant', 'The Age of Disgrace'), but they both passed. Glenn announced in the press 'this isn't over'. But, for now it was. Ian had just been working programming with Right Said Fred on their smash hit 'I'm Too Sexy', and was working on his own solo project entitled 'The Forward Forties', which didn't make an impact. Meanwhile, Glenn had formed a band called Ugly, and I was having huge success with various productions, including Sananda's first album. So Ian lived a quiet life until the early nineties …

We were all thrilled at the unexpected success of the Brothers in Rhythm remix of 'Temptation', which unexpectedly relaunched our career as Heaven 17 in 1992, reaching number 4 in the UK charts. This resurgence post-1993 will be documented in Volume 2 of this autobiography, but it was great to see Ian back on track and on TV with us. We have always had the greatest respect for him as a brother and as an artist, and this seemed like justice.

Ian, you are always with Glenn and me in everything we do. We love you.

Tragically and unexpectedly, one of our best friends and the artist responsible for Heaven 17's most iconic sleeves, Ray Smith, passed away aged sixty-nine in 2018 from dementia – typical of the man, he kept his condition secret from the world until his death.

But I'd prefer to remember Ray as a shining light as part of all the happy times that we shared. Ray was introduced to us by head of A&R at Virgin Simon Draper – his artworks had been featured on various Virgin album covers, and when we mentioned we were considering a stylistic pastiche of an illustrative advertisement, Simon reckoned Ray was the man for the job. His work on *Penthouse and Pavement* was exemplary, and we quickly became friends for life. Ray embodied everything in the art sphere that we wished we could be – he was funny, ironic, irreverent, a master craftsman and, above all, a great and original thinker who was happy to collaborate and work to brief. His demeanour reminded me of Kenneth Williams, not the voice, but he could do a mean impression. The *Penthouse and Pavement* artwork made such an impact that we were determined that he should create the cover for our next two albums, *The Luxury Gap* and *How Men Are*, both of which are exceptional pieces of work. My fondest memories relate to a mail-based remote conceptual art collaboration between us. We were amused by one of Ray's playful and funny concepts, which we bought into – Ray had an alter ego called Tony Garzone, who ran an imaginary art sales company called 'Qwality Rubber

Art Goods Ltd'. One day, Glenn suggested that we should send 'Tony' a conceptual art creation of our own, which Glenn named Bag-'O'-Men, primarily because we wanted to send him a padded bag full of plastic soldiers, and a threatening note in badly written and ineptly spelt handwriting (like some kind of psychotic ransom note), which said something like . . .

Der Tony,

Weer not scared of you or your rubber company. We're watching you and yours and weer not scared. Qwality Rubber Art Goods will nevver win – Our Bag-'O'-Men™ (enclosed) will see to that. Don't even try to stop us cos we cannot be stopped. Let this be an end to it.

Yours not scared

Bag-'O'-Men™ (Worldwide)

The package contained a handful of the smallest and cheapest green plastic US toy soldiers in a display of utterly non-scary strength.

Ray's response was similarly strange . . .

Dear Bag of men or whatever . . .

You have no idea what has been unleashed. Your men are lying at the bottom of the ocean, and parts of them are enclosed to prove that I'm not joking or scared. Your tactics of intimidation are frankly pathetic, and Qwality Rubber Art Goods will never be defeated. Never, never, never. So put that in you pipe and smoke it. Never. Never.

Yours unimpressed

Qwality Rubber Art Goods Inc. (Universe-wide)

PS Leave my family out of this

The package arrived with this note, addressed to 'Bag Of Men (losers)', and contained a small, mysterious box (which clearly previously housed cufflinks). The gold embossed lettering on the suedette case had been scribbled out, and replaced scruffily with a felt-tip handwritten 'Qwality Leather Art Goods'. When I opened the box, there was a crumpled grey satinette insert, into which the severed heads of several of the plastic soldiers had been place, complete with delicately painted blood on the necks. I still have this, and I look at it every day on my bookshelf at home. This exchange of stuff went on for a couple of years intermittently, and I have at home several other artefacts that Ray kindly sent us.

I also have the original artwork for the first three albums, together with studies for several albums that never reached the light of day. I became a patron of Ray's work – in fact, I bought an incredible 8-foot-high plywood reproduction of a Letraset figure (a worried boss smoking) which is still in my front room. He is called Derek. Maybe Derek *was* Ray ... He was a man of many talents – sculptural, figurative, technical, playful and he deserves much more attention and kudos for his life's work.

Der Ray, we will always luv you – yours, Bag-'O'-Men™.

Coda – The View from Now . . .

When I was planning this book, it became quickly apparent that I seemed to have two distinct 'Acts' in the narrative of my life. The period covered by this book, up to 1992, when I was thirty-six, felt like the natural span of Volume 1. In the late eighties, it seemed that my career was on a pretty traditional storyline – main career (Heaven 17) all but over, enough work from my production career to carry on until I decided enough was enough, no wife or children responsibilities, and enough cash in the bank to keep me going for quite a while. I could have easily settled for that – but . . .

Something inside me told me a couple of things. Firstly, I still felt as creative as ever, and wanted to carry on developing my own creativity and future-facing ideas. Secondly, I didn't want to do this on my own. I had finally reached the point where I was ready to settle down and raise a family – in fact, I craved it. I knew in my heart that I needed that stability and support and *significance* in my life. I had certainly covered quite a lot in my lotus-eating decades, and it had started to become tiresome to keep chasing the distractions of girlfriends, clubbing and indulgence. I don't regret any of it, it was just time for a change of direction. So, I married the love of my life Landsley in 1992 after a whirlwind romance, and we're still together. Her support and encouragement have enabled me to relaunch my career with Heaven 17, both live and in the studio, and we have two grown-up children, Elena and Gabriel, who are the centre of our lives. I never wanted to be the kind of dad who was always missing from home and their development, so I moved my studio to a spare room in my new house in Primrose Hill, so I could be with them almost every day. And they would benefit too, meeting artists, hearing music in development, being treated as intelligent, creative little humans, not trophy toys for absent parents. But all that's to come in Volume 2 . . .

The year 1993 saw me meet Vince Clarke and Andy Bell for the first time, which was a life-changing event, and my stories of working with them will heavily feature in the next tome. But the part of the story that is most interesting is the randomness of the resurrection of Heaven 17. No one could have predicted that incredible turn of events, but I have to say that the famous phrase 'Opportunity has to find you prepared' is most certainly appropriate. If I have one talent that has served me best, it is that I've always had a capacity to see *a little* into the future. Not Nostradamus, just a few moves ahead, and I am not always right, but it keeps me moving forward. I read and absorb knowledge voraciously (always have done), I am still a sponge after all these years . . . I have learnt way more in the second act of my journey so far than all the experiences I crammed into the first.

Volume 2, 1993–2021 (or Act Two if you prefer) will cover . . .

- The rebirth of Heaven 17
- My times with Vince Clarke and Andy Bell
- More Heaven 17 and BEF albums (some unreleased)
- Heaven 17 performing live and touring for the first time
- Forming Illustrious Co. Ltd. with Vince Clarke – 3D immersive soundscapes worldwide
- Worldwide activism and education
- More outrageous stories of famous artists

Music, creativity, friendship, travel, humour, love, sport, socialism, nature, exploration, philosophy and many other subjects – despite all the setbacks that come along, they always refill my soul with joy in a never-ending abundance, and nothing gives me more happiness than to share my good fortune with others. This essentially sums up my attitude towards life – I am a humanist, I have faith in the innate goodness of my fellow residents of earth, and I will help fight against injustices of extreme wealth, violence, discrimination, and to advocate for the underprivileged and under-represented all over the world. If this sounds pious (or a term I hate, 'virtue-signalling') then this is more of an indication of your state of mind than mine. I am unrepentant. But I believe if you've got this far into the book, you'll probably understand or even agree with my point of view. More to the point, I hope you've enjoyed this book as much as I've enjoyed writing it. I have learned a lot from this process, and I thanks all the contributors, characters and most of all my family and friends for all their help and advice, I couldn't have done it without you all. It's been quite a journey . . .

Until next time, I am, and will always be,

Electronically Yours

Martyn Ware

Appendix 1:

Track by Track

The Future and very early Human League, 1977–8

'Looking for the Black Haired Girls'

One of the original four tracks recorded as The Future at Ken Patten's studio in Sheffield. We wanted the intro to evoke a terrifying sense of dread, which I think we achieved after sourcing foghorns and a woman screaming from some BBC sound library records, combined with a funereal and psychotic death march and minor-key echoed blipscape. We were writing soundtracks for films that only existed in our warped minds ... in this case the subject matter that was obsessing us was the Son of Sam murders, which for some reason was of particular fascination to Ian (which was a tad worrying). Between the summers of 1976 and 1977, David Berkowitz, aka 'Son of Sam', terrorised New York as he gunned down innocent young people in their cars. He claimed that Satan had possessed his neighbour Sam's dog, which then sent him messages to kill. We were hoping Ian wasn't inspired by this (he was expelled from school for plotting – jokingly – to electrocute the headmaster). Yes, Ian was a sweetheart but definitely had an edge. The rest of the 'song' consisted of the three of us solemnly and scarily reciting CARLOS-generated lyrics like 'the total modern murder' and 'the talking cool Jesus', like an undiscovered Samuel Beckett play as performed by Jim Morrison. One can only imagine the response of the straight-laced A&R executives when listening to this surprisingly impactful slice of horror. Let's just say that I don't think the cash registers were exactly tinkling in their imagination.

'Blank Clocks'

'I stand alone on Westminster Bridge, amid acoustic distortion. I turn towards Big Ben ... there is no time. The face across the street is blank – blank clocks, blank clocks, blank clocks, blank clocks'. Another CARLOS-driven piece of abstract electronic expressionism that must have caused despair during the A&R meetings when we presented these in London. More gibberish sound poetry – 'Your face ... the clock ... my mind ... blank heart ... you're fine ... the pain ...' The pain, indeed. If we'd have tried to compose a piece to ensure a lack of commercial interest, this must have been pretty close to perfect. The charmingly tuneful arpeggiated style was not dissimilar to early Kraftwerk, but in hindsight it feels very slight and timid. Not one of my favourites.

'Cairo'

Another early piece inspired by film and literature – in this instance, I reckon it was a scene from J. G. Ballard's *The Atrocity Exhibition* set in a non-specific desert. At that time, I had no experience of desert apart from the film *Lawrence of Arabia* (or possibly *Carry On Follow that Camel*), but I reckon I made a pretty good stab at evoking a timeless, epic sand-dune scenario thanks to the Roland System 100 'Resonant Wind' patch and some fifths on my Korg 700S sounding like all we were short of was Wilson, Keppel and Betty sand-dancing (look it up). Adi Newton's recital at the end of the track is as though J. G. Ballard himself had been possessed by a steelworker's son.

Dada Dada Duchamp Vortex

The title was inspired by one of Adi's creative outbursts, seeking to conflate the art movements of Dadaism and Vorticism. We couldn't imagine anything more hilarious and pretentious – in fact, this seems to be a theme of our work at the time, the more irritatingly pretentious the better, as we regarded contrarianism as a badge of honour. The instrumental itself has aged well, and it is mysterious and evocative, maybe even a little moving. It features a beautiful piece of analogue synth programming by Ian with some less-focused noodling added by my good self on the Korg 700S. Overall, a piece to be proud of.

'Daz'

At the time of this bonkers experiment, we were heavily influenced by various reggae dub plate white labels that were being passed around our group of friends. We had also recently acquired a much-desired Watkins Copicat, a device featuring a tape loop that could create beautiful and creative tape echoes which could be fed back on itself in a blizzard of noise degradation. It was also much used by reggae deep-dub pioneers like King Tubby, Lee 'Scratch' Perry and The Mad Professor. At the time I lived in a council estate next to a run-down area of town called Broomhall, which was largely populated by people of Afro-Caribbean descent. I would occasionally visit one of the several 'blues clubs' – not really a club, but a cellar knocked through between two terraced houses, big enough for about ten to fifteen people, with a bass-heavy sound system big enough to rock the street. Entry to the 'club' was via a normal terraced house front door, requiring a special knock, 'ba-de-ba-de-ba-de-ba-bap' – it had a speakeasy vibe – and entrance was £5. In return you received a pre-rolled joint. I think you can imagine what a hot, sweaty, pungent smoke-filled room with no air-conditioning must have felt like for a relatively naive twenty-one-year-old white guy from the estates. It was completely, intoxicatingly forbidden and fantastically naughty. Talk about epiphany. I've been obsessed with authentic dub-style reggae ever since – it was the finest education money could buy. Our risible effort to emulate the dub greats on 'Daz' is nevertheless charmingly weird and hilarious, and features our great friend and bass player Jud, who tragically lost his life after injecting heroin cut with rat poison. It was the first drug-related death of a close friend in my life. It wouldn't be the last. I believe at that age we all have a sense of immortality until the first bomb drops. As Bowie said, 'It's No Game'. I have never touched heroin, opium or any opiates. There is simply nothing 'cool' or 'hip' about them. They destroy lives.

'Future Religion'

Yep – this must really have sealed the deal in those A&R meetings. Even for my admittedly super-eclectic tastes, this is a hard listen. Another sci-fi horror film study in random atonality and timbre. In its own way, it demonstrates our freewheeling sense of playful doom, but I can't honestly say I like it in any way, apart from its 'fuck you, we'll do whatever we like' dauntless audacity.

'Pulse Lovers'

The most poppy of the four tracks from the original recording sessions. A jaunty, insistent attempt at some form of dance track, I suppose. Our attitude was to aim for something we liked but had little to no knowledge or skill in recreating, then hope that something interesting would spontaneously emerge. It usually did – for example 'Being Boiled' was my attempt at sounding like Bernie Worrell, the synth player for Parliament/Funkadelic – aim for that, miss by a mile, get something interesting and bizarre out of the Dadaist sausage machine. Once again, some CARLOS-created gems on this, together with some early backing vocals from myself, finding confidence that I could actually hold a tune. This would become a feature of forthcoming recordings, but I never had the desire or confidence to take a lead role (except for 'You've Lost That Loving Feeling', and even that was after plucking up the courage to perform the duet live with Phil). But I quite like my clear and wobbly voice on this.

The Human League (pre-Virgin experiments), 1978–9

'Dance Like a Star'

One of our favourite disco tracks, which seemed to embody the lyrical futility and meaninglessness of the hedonistic glamour of the time, was 'Let's All Chant' by The Michael Zager Band, featuring the timeless stanza 'Your body, my body, everybody move your body'. Flawless, crystalline, pure euro-inanity. Nevertheless, a great, pompous, electro-orchestral magnum opus of a dancefloor filler. As disco was almost totally reviled by the *NME*-reading press, we, of course, adopted our usual contrarian position and declared that we would always love all things disco, especially electronic disco. Our attempt at creating a similarly inane song was 'Dance Like a Star' – 'Dance like a Star, be who you are, hear the guitar [please note – there was no guitar], dance like a star, dance, dance, dance, dance, da-ance'. The arrangement was clearly and deliberately inspired by Giorgio Moroder's classics from that period, including his magnificent work with Donna Summer, and his own Munich Machine albums like $E=MC^2$. We thought this was all hilarious, but simultaneously we loved the provocative nature of it too.

'4JG'

For J. G. Ballard – our literary inspiration and future dystopian – also a sly nod to '2HB' (to Humphrey Bogart), a track on the first Roxy Music album.

'Dominion Jingle'

A faux sci-fi future advertisement inspired by Michael Moorcock's Jerry Cornelius novels, read by Phil in a transatlantic voice, imploring the buyer to try 'Pulcinello Labs' new anti-depressant Dominion – safe when used as directed'. Later, I discovered that the American composer Raymond Scott (band leader, pianist, record producer and inventor of electronic instruments) had made a career out of similarly bizarre and futuristic soundscape advertising for his company Manhattan Research Inc., but in his case they were for real products, for which he was paid handsomely.

'Disco Disaster'

A very strange track indeed – mechanistic ramblings evolving into a sub-early Ultravox robotic chant – 'Running with the endless beat (running), looking at the teenage heat (looking), waiting for a future night (waiting all night), looking for a senseless fight (looking for you), moving in a machine daze', etc. This could have been the final appearance of the CARLOS lyric system. Half satire, half electro–punk.

'Interface'

Now this is more like it . . . a genuinely exciting, driving electronic composition with Ian's System 100 programming at its stratospheric best. Possibly our most effectively futuristic composition from that period, and even featuring a beautiful rallentando at the end.

'The Circus of Dr Lao'

This is a unique and disturbing composition. Phil composed this with Ian, and without my help, as an experiment. It also features a frankly bizarre interlude with Phil appearing to be speaking to the fictitious Dr Lao in a one-sided telephone conversation.

'Reach Out (I'll Be There)'

I've always adored this song from my childhood, and I was keen to create a new version using our strange, impressionistic palette of squawks and crashes. Unfortunately, Phil refused to sing on this, which I still think is a real pity as the end result would have been fascinating and, who knows, maybe even controversial and commercial. Or not.

'New Pink Floyd'

Here's another experiment by Phil and Ian, less successful I think – wasn't really sure what to make of it. Still not sure.

'Once Upon a Time in the West' (Funeral March Mix 1)

Another part of my ongoing experimentation with different genres – this time Ennio Morricone's masterpiece, inspired by my recent purchase of the Roland Jupiter-4. The sparkling arpeggiation introduced in the middle section wasn't previously possible with our equipment (this technique of 'super-fast arpeggiation as texture' was also used to great effect on the track 'WXJL Tonight' on the *Travelogue* album). Considering the limited amount of synthesiser resources at our disposal, I'm very proud of the epic-sounding nature of this recording (pats self on back).

'Overkill Disaster Crash'

The intro features distorted dialogue from the sci-fi dark comedy *Dark Star*, John Carpenter's first film. More genius electronic sound creation from Ian; a galloping, neurotic rhythm anchors the composition, overlaid with an imaginary film scene of increasing panic.

'Year of the Jet Packs'

More film references – this time our favourite-ever film musical *West Side Story*. Creating the electronic finger clicks was a complex but rewarding challenge. The source idea was to create an imaginary soundtrack for a world where we would all be flying around strapped to jet packs. The wheezy sequencing and the insistent and hypnotic eight-note sequence changing key constantly create a pretty impressive if simplistic scene.

'C'est Grave' (feat. Tim Pearce)

Tim was our sound engineer, a friend of Bob Last's, who also helped us set up our first electronic studio in Sheffield. He was somewhat eccentric as is evidenced by this strangely unattractive composition. He persuaded us to make this on a couple of Sundays off. We indulged his eccentricity, and this is the mutant outcome. I suppose it has a certain charm ...

'King of Kings'

I'm not really sure what the noise-based intro was all about, but I do believe that this interpretation of Miklós Rózsa's biblical epic soundtrack is a success. The most challenging aspect was the timpani, but we nailed it.

'Last Man on Earth'

We were all obsessed with the 1964 post-apocalyptic science-fiction horror film *Last Man on Earth*, based on the 1954 novel *I Am Legend* (rebooted with Will Smith). This version starred

Vincent Price as literally the last man on earth, after a plague had wiped out the rest of humanity, except for the inevitable zombies. I'm very proud to have composed this with Ian, as a powerful evocation of strangeness, pathos and loneliness. The correct version is nine minutes forty-five seconds long.

Track by Track ... *Reproduction* by The Human League (1979)

'Almost Medieval'

This song was one of the very first we started working on when Phil joined The Human League. From the moment he first performed the lyrics of 'Being Boiled' for us, it was glaringly obvious that we were dealing with a very unusual talent with a unique perspective on what constituted the notion of a pop song lyric, or even entertainment as a concept. Ian and I were so thrilled to have Phil on board, as he seemed to give zero fucks about tradition or rules – he was the renegade master that we'd been looking for (we didn't have to look very hard: he was there all along). But I have to give myself credit for spotting his yet-to-be-revealed talent. I mean, I never saw any evidence that he had any compositional ability – no poems, no singing, no prose, no inkling of anything apart from his wild, untamed eclecticism, his irrational total self-belief and his unwillingness to compromise his worldview (which would unpredictably change from day to day like underwear). Admittedly, I was pretty similar in many respects, which would prove to be a major problem later ... The song itself was inspired by the Philip K. Dick 1967 novel *Counter-Clock World*, which describes a future in which time has started to move in reverse, resulting in the dead being reborn in their own graves, living their lives in reverse, and eventually returning to the womb where they split into an egg and a sperm during copulation between a recipient woman and a man. Not exactly a traditional subject matter for a pop song, but nevertheless it fulfilled the intended purpose of shocking the audience with intelligence and edgy mystery, starting a thread of intentional obfuscation, which would lead devoted fans to ruminate for decades about the metaphorical meaning of various lyrics. We wanted to be intellectually pretentious, and we certainly succeeded. Strange, considering none of us went to university, or even art college. Hence the 'moving backwards in time' premise for the song. This song was also the opening salvo in our live sets, and it was definitely impactful. I'm quite proud of the electronic sackbut sound on the intro, by the way.

'Circus of Death'

The original B-side of the first Fast single. It starts with a continuity announcer and a kind of futuristic TV station ident. We are then transported to an airport via jet sound effects and PA announcements. The lyrics are inspired by the spooky fantasy film *The Circus of Dr Lao*, including the intention to tap into the common fear of clowns (coulrophobia). Really this was a way of creating a theme tune to an imaginary film – that was the inspiration. The monologue in the middle eight of the song refers to the fictitious drug Dominion, which I believe was referring to a similar narcotic mentioned in Michael Moorcock's Jerry Cornelius novels (which we were all obsessed with at the time). I still perform this song live with Heaven 17 and it is a showstopper (unfortunate, as it's at the start of the show).

'The Path of Least Resistance'

More 'Devil's Mode' fifths throughout. Our attempt at a mutant electro-punk, this sounded much tougher live; in fact this is one of the several songs that suffered from an evisceration at the hands of our engineer/co-producer Colin Thurston. This was not entirely his fault as we were very inexperienced and more than a little in awe of reputations and big studios at the time. There were very few engineers who knew how to deal with pure electronic music at the time. This is one of the lyrics I wrote alone on the album.

'Blind Youth'

Very punky song, which again worked much better live than on record. I wrote these lyrics – quite proud of the Richard III reference. The theme of the song was a rallying call for optimism in the face of the late 1970s economic gloom. We would spend several weekends visiting Manchester to attend gigs, and the prevalent zeitgeist there was disaffection and ennui, often for effect. We hated this; it was the opposite of the mental toughness required to withstand a life of drudgery in Sheffield, and we regarded it as self-indulgence. There was even an early version of our song 'Austerity' called 'Depression Is a Fashion' (a little harsh, but it was really a call to positive action). I wouldn't subscribe to that view now, but I was naive.

'The Word Before Last'

Starting with a speech by James Callaghan (ex-Labour leader) and ending with a reference to Margaret Thatcher from a news bulletin, this is our first venture into the world of politics. This version is quite weak in comparison to the live version we performed around that time. Even Phil's performance sounds unconvincing and polite. Virgin insisted that we recorded everything from scratch in the Townhouse Studios, which we found quite daunting. In reality, we hadn't really found our feet in this world – we felt like imposters, so we didn't feel in any position to argue with production decisions made on our behalf by our co-producer. Later, we determined never to make that mistake again. The theme of the song is paranoia and depression.

'Empire State Human'

Our demented attempt to create a chart-storming single, based around a childlike chant that surely anyone would find irresistibly hooky and commercial. That wasn't the case. Virgin released the single to almost unanimous indifference (except for the trendy music press). This was to be a continual theme in our increasingly desperate attempt to 'cross over'. I'm very proud of my Eno-esque, Roxy Music-style solo in the middle eight though ...

'Morale / You've Lost That Loving Feeling'

One of the few songs on the album that actually benefitted from the relentless polishing of Colin Thurston's production techniques. I was completely, hopelessly besotted with the Roland Jupiter-4 synth, the arpeggiations of which work perfectly as a counterpoint to Phil's beautifully emotive rendition of the 'Morale' section ... chilling and thrilling. The transition to the Righteous Brothers' magnum opus is still luscious, and I'm very, very proud of our work on this – a genuinely innovative interpretation of the desolation inherent in the lyrics. And it's my recording debut as co-lead vocalist! It is still one of our most popular songs performed live with Glenn for Heaven 17 – when we get it right, it brings the house down. A big shout out to Ian's sublime System 100 sound design on the warbling, ring-modulated, sequenced textures.

'Austerity / Girl One'

This insistent, sequencer-driven monster of a track has more of a 'showtune' feel to it with changes of mood and time signature. More eccentric storytelling from the inspired pen of Philip, this song features the killer couplet, 'When the best of men take bribes, isn't it the fool who doesn't?' The first part is almost like a commentary on the narrative to come, and the middle section refers to the confusion of teenage angst (I think – I never asked him!). Other subjects covered are problematical parental relationships, self-obsession and psychological insecurities. 'The Oracle' – what the fuck is that? 'Prediction and ambiguity go hand in glove' – an inner dialogue of near madness, reverting to the faux-commentary of the intro . . . philosophically obscure but fascinating.

'Zero as a Limit'

It was my idea to create a song that accelerated exponentially tempo-wise, which would induce increasing excitement and even panic in the audience. The intention was for this to be the final song of the live set – ending with a giant thrash-electro-metal explosion of excitement. The subject matter is directly inspired by the J. G. Ballard novel *Crash*, which features the psychosexual aspects of car crashes and random contemporary violence as portrayed vividly by Andy Warhol and his car crash series – real-life police photographs of the gory results of major car crashes. Warhol's work had much influence on our attitude towards art in general (viz. 'Overkill Disaster Crash').

Bonus tracks:

'Introducing'

This instrumental was occasionally used as an introduction to our early Human League live shows. Sometimes known as the afore-mentioned 'Overkill Disaster Crash'. Tension-inducing nightmare scenario.

The Dignity of Labour (Parts 1–4)

In April 1979, we released our first EP on the Fast Product label entitled *The Dignity of Labour*, which contained four experimental instrumentals. The title was appropriated from a mural depicted in the flat block of the droogs in *A Clockwork Orange* (in both Anthony Burgess's novel and Stanley Kubrick's film). This was our deter-mined effort to show our loyal fans that we had no intention of 'selling out'. The title rang true as part of my upbringing as the son of a steelworker/toolmaker, and as a devout socialist there was always the mystique of the Russian space effort and the conceptual power of the first man in space – Yuri Gagarin. Ian and I created a four-part electro-industrial soundscape inspired by the sounds of industry and the glamour and promise of the space race, featuring no vocals at all! To Phil's credit, I don't recall anything other than support for the idea at the time. I blame Bowie for releasing *Low* and *Heroes*, two albums that blew our minds, both featuring highly atmospheric and futuristic instrumentals – we aspired to that aesthetic. This was us as 'serious composers', and I don't have any regrets regarding trying to establish our creative credentials at the time. The compositions are by turn playful, futuristic, industrial, optimistic and finally depressing – hardly top 10 stuff. Despite the record's sales being disappointing, the original and daring approach, combined with the increasing popularity of our live shows, meant that more and more interest was being shown by the major record companies. Behind the scenes, Bob Last was working hard to find a label that would match our ambitions and, more importantly, move us on to a bigger and more commercially-minded audience.

'Flexi Disc'

The most 'meta' release ever. As a bonus artefact included in the *Dignity of Labour* 12-inch sleeve, this features the band plus Bob Last (our manager) discussing whether or not to do a flexi-disc commentary on whether or not to release a flexi-disc as part of the package. A perfect example of our desire to out-pretentious ANYONE. Subjects covered include Yuri Gagarin and his metaphorical significance, drinking tea in Russia, how much time should be on the flexi-disc, etc. Some of Phil's quotes are pure gold: 'not simple, not complex, it's multiplex', 'no matter how big you are, you're gonna be dead soon'. Ladies and gentlemen, I present Philip Oakey, the Brian Clough of experimental electro-pop . . .

Track by Track ... *Travelogue* by The Human League (1980)

'The Black Hit of Space'

After the disappointing and thin production and sound of *Reproduction*, which we felt didn't represent our real sound and the dynamism of our live act, we put our foot down with Virgin and told them we wanted to record our own songs using our newly equipped studio in Sheffield, the ironically titled Monumental Studios. 'The Black Hit of Space' was designed to shock in its rawness and power, and the sound of this recording became a template for the attitude we wanted to portray to the listening public. More distortion, more pedals, more 'live' sounding ... Once again, the subject matter returns to the bizarre world of cutting-edge black-hole physics, and James Burke, the TV science expert, even gets a mention! We always conspired to undermine our chances of mainstream success – this time with a bizarre monologue in the middle eight which was more like an extract from a Philip K. Dick novel than a top 10 hit. In a strange way, this lyric could be perceived as a prediction of the forthcoming collapse of the music industry, so much so that one fan referred to us as the 'Nostradamus of Electronic Music'. I hate to disappoint everyone, but this wasn't the intention. We just wanted to make a catchy pop song, hence the childlike simplicity of the chorus melody.

'Only After Dark'

This is an early example of us trying to appeal to a mass market, while in reality maintaining an insistent experimental edge. Covering famous songs also helped to provide a counterbalance against accusations of intellectual elitism. We were all massive fans of Bowie and anything associated, so when Mick Ronson released a solo album, we were of course all over it. In the early 1970s we habituated a nightclub in Sheffield called the Penthouse, which was essentially a glam-rock night. Mick Ronson was a god to us. As well as his exquisite guitar playing and his wild strawberry-blonde hair, he was Bowie's best mate, and he was, like Woody Woodmansey, from Hull (at that time part of Yorkshire), so we felt a kinship of sorts. 'Only After Dark' was a staple on the playlist at the Penthouse Club in Sheffield where we danced to all the glam hits, and this particular song was exactly the right tempo to fill the floor with teenagers doing 'the futurist sway' – hard to describe but suffice to say that our good friend Midge Ure used to dance that way on *Top of the Pops*. It was a safe and easy dance to master – important if you didn't want to look like a complete tit on the dancefloor.

'Life Kills'

This is probably my least favourite song on the album – it's a bit of a conceptual hangover from our electropunk support-act days. It's a rant against conformity, but I never really thought it worked properly – the lyrics are trite and haven't aged well. It's a bit too trad construction-wise, a bit too try-hard. Quite like the Boys of Buddha horns though ...

'Dreams of Leaving'

This song is a work of beauty, even though I say so myself. That intro with the bubbling Jupiter-4 arpeggiator rudely and shockingly interrupted by the 'metal-machine-music' buzzsaw chord, which just as unexpectedly disappears, is something I still find thrilling. It is a melodic song, full of drama, unexpected twists and turns, and probably owes a great deal to Van der Graaf Generator's Peter Hammill in terms of Phil's delivery. There are several analyses of this song online, and there are no right or wrong interpretations, and I never asked Phil to nail down the meaning: it would have taken the magic away, so I didn't want to know. All I do know is that this is his finest lyric writing during our version of The League. I presume the song is about refugees, longing for home, but also needing and wanting to be elsewhere. From an early stage of conceptualising this song, we determined to make it a portmanteau or episodic piece – apportioning equal importance to music and lyric, not paying any heed to convention or length. Time signature changes, great sonic design by Ian and me, weird random interstitial noises ... and section three (before the reintroduction to the more conventional song-like final section) is curious. I am struck now by the influence of the sound collage techniques of Frank Zappa, of whom we were all massive fans. The end section is truly heart-rending, and one day I'd love to hear it performed using giant orchestral forces. That would be something else.

'Toyota City'

It's obvious to see the influence of Bowie and Eno's instrumentals from the album *Low* on our work. Also, we were fond of the musical approach of the band Japan (our labelmates), for whom we had great respect. The synthetic sound colours of this composition are reminiscent of very early Future work, which may have sounded like this had we used a proper studio and engineer. Our synthesiser patch design on this track is close to the peak of what we could achieve using our (deliberately) limited tools. The idea for the title came from another news article, this time about a city built specifically for the workers at the giant Toyota factory in central Japan.

'Crow and a Baby'

Ian and I had an idea to create a sort of menacing, dancey, marchy track with a hint of a military feel, and we completed this before we handed it over to Phil to weave his lyrical magic. By this time, Phil's storytelling was growing in confidence, and he knew he had to up his game every time if he wanted to impress us and himself. When he first sang the words 'A crow and a baby had an affair' I was sold, not dissimilar to the feeling I had listening to 'Being Boiled' for the first time. At that time, consciously or not, it seemed that Phil's metaphorical efforts were driven by issues with his father and his family life. I never broached the subject, but the Roald Dahl-like, black fairy-tale quality is utterly unique in this context, enhanced by the nightmarish chant of the chorus. I even had the idea to highlight the word 'father' every time it was sung in the verses using a pitch-changer and sped-up horror vocals. I love doing this live with Heaven 17, as do the girls, who for some reason particularly relate to it. Who knows? What is your interpretation? It's just as valid as mine . . .

'The Touchables'

Another attempt at writing a commercial pop song, and apart from the fact that the constituent sounds are largely bonkers, it's quite a charming piece of writing. This time, the lyrics were mainly written by me so I can speak with a little more confidence about the meaning. It's about sexual insecurity, and the feelings of vulnerability towards our sexual partners (a hot topic for us at that point). The chorus is very catchy, I think, and I love the line 'then panic occurs, no seeds to spill'. Performance anxiety is an interesting subject for a pop song. I also love the fact that that the song finishes unexpectedly and abruptly during the final pre-chorus. My favourite paradigm, the meaningful denial of expectation ...

'Gordon's Gin'

We always loved the original of this advertisement when shown at cinemas, and thought it would be amusing to pay it justice as an epic, bombastic synth piece. It also reminds me a little of Wendy Carlos. I find the intro, in particular, hilariously sad. I was lucky enough to meet Jeff Wayne recently, who complimented me on my arrangement, which was gratifying.

'Being Boiled' (new version)

Ever since version one of the song, we were determined to clarify how we originally wanted the arrangement to sound. We were stymied by the recording limitations at the time, and even though the original recording has a certain 'period charm' it still left me feeling the subject was unresolved. We wanted it to sound more like the epic, exciting final number of a Parliament/Funkadelic concert (you know, spaceship leaving the planet), and it needed to be *funky*. Right from the start, the intro is already a fucking winner, and as the opening salvo blasts out, we've got them hooked, baby! Ian pulled out all the stops and created a fantastic soundscape of rhythm 'n' bleep, and my arrangement of Boys of Buddha synthetic varispeed horns is as funky as I could ever muster – I was hoping it would be reminiscent of Curtis Mayfield or Tower of Power on Mars, even down to duelling horn sections in the middle sixteen. Playing it live it stuns the audience and we still perform this on most Heaven 17 gigs as a special encore. I thought Bootsy and George Clinton would like it, and that was confirmed when I worked with Bootsy in 1993.

'WXJL Tonight'

A curious squelchy rhythm track, an atmospheric and melodic chorus, and varispeed simulation of a 'rhythm guitar', the superfast Jupiter-4 arpeggiation – all innovative and interesting, but the real killer here is Phil's thrilling vocal performance, sounding very close indeed to one of his idols, Neil Diamond. The lyric and arrangement were my creation, inspired by the criminally underrated Harry Chapin and his paean to jobbing radio DJs and their flawed lives, the magnificent, psycho-dramatic 'W.O.L.D.', which documents the poignant story of the divorced, ageing DJ, told in flashback, the chorus ironically impersonating the radio jingles of the time. 'There's a tyre round my gut from sitting on my butt, but it's never gonna go away', and 'Sometimes I get this crazy dream that I just take off in my car, but you can travel on 10,000 miles and still stay where you are'. Lyrical and conceptual genius, one of my favourite records of all time. All our lyrics here are delivered from the point of view of a robotic DJ who (like Hal 3000 from the film *2001*) pleads not to be switched off. The 'tonight' harmony jingle on the outro took me and Phil a full day in the studio to make sound convincing, but it was definitely worth it.

Bonus tracks:

'Marianne'

We were 100 per cent convinced that this song would launch us into the charts and popular consciousness, and I still think this is early Human League's finest songwriting and vocal arrangement moment. It even features my voice as a co-lead for the first time on an original composition. It is only now I realise that the world wasn't quite ready for such a radical soundscape backing arrangement. It's still a great song, with really engaging lyrics written largely by Phil, and even featuring three-part counterpoint – fucking hell, we were turning into Puccini!

'Rock 'n' Roll/Nightclubbing'

The lead track from the *Holiday '80* gatefold double EP, our final big push towards chart success. We loved the Glitter sound, and 'Rock 'n' Roll Parts 1 and 2' was seminal for us: this had all the major food groups – heavy double-tracked 'tribal' drums, that mono electric guitar sound, and chants – hook after hook after hook. Later, when I recorded with The Glitter Band, they told me the secret of the guitar sound – all the strings were tuned to E at different octaves, so all they had to do was bar the frets up and down. Mike Leander's creativity was legendary. We all thought that if we couldn't get into the charts with this, we were in trouble. Phil sounded totally authentic, my backing vocals and harmonies were powerful, and the icing on the cake was the segue into a braggadocio-filled, strutting version of the Iggy Pop tune 'Nightclubbing' – come on, what's not to like? This was our first appearance on *Top of the Pops* – little were we to know this was also the last appearance on TV of The Human League Mk 1. Kudos also to the great production skills of John Leckie, who helped us realise our vision to its fullest extent.

Track by Track ... *Music for Stowaways* by BEF (1981)

Cassette Side 1 (Uptown)

'The Optimum Chant'

This is a weird and I think very interesting hybrid of dub-reggae, funk and experimental electronics courtesy of Roland System 100's hardware sequencer techniques, as brilliantly programmed by Ian Craig Marsh – also featuring extensive use of feedback tape delay. It's pretty funky ...

'Uptown Apocalypse'

This was a jam with Adi Newton and Jud on bass as an attempt to make something danceable – I'm not sure if we achieved that, but a lot of the guitar and synth feedback stuff is pure Cabaret Voltaire.

'Wipe the Board Clean'

This was created as a potential backing track for a later topline vocal, but we decided it worked so well as an instrumental that we'd better not ruin it. I remember feeling at the time that this was an attempt at electro-punk, and that it encapsulated the 'anger-converted-to-creative-energy' after the split from The Human

League. Features our first attempt at using pre-amps on our new mixing desk to overload and distort the synths – beautiful. We should perform this live one day.

'Groove Thang'

All I have to say is drop to your knees and pay homage to the genius of teenage prodigy John Wilson, lord of all he surveys. Of course, this is the instrumental of 'Fascist Groove Thang', but it's incredible to be able to hear John's work with obstruction on this; both bass and rhythm guitar are magnificent and still give me shivers.

Side two (Downtown)

'Music to Kill Your Parents By'

I was hoping (and still do) that we would get some commissions as film soundtrack producers, and this was our 'pitch' for a horror film. The rhythm track is as close to Wendy Carlos's 'Timesteps' as we could get.

'The Old at Rest'

Always looking for an unusual subject matter, we felt this languid and beautiful instrumental, derived from our version of 'Wichita Lineman', deserved its own space. The semi-improvised topline synth was part played by me and part randomly arpeggiated by Ian's System 100. I also particularly love my use of downward arpeggiation on this track – I was utterly in love with my new Jupiter-4, and I still am. My favourite synthesiser of all time – warm, luscious and excitingly quirky . . .

'Rise of the East'

Another piece of awesome patch design by Ian, beautifully simulating the tonalities of tablas, while the chirruping was triggering another unit of the System 100. The change of time signature was achieved by switching timing options on the sequencer, all fed through the Watkins Copicat.

'Decline of the West'

Ian's design of the introductory (and coda) electronic rainstorm is a thing of immense beauty, and the overall rhythmic soundscape is highly evocative. And the weird alien monster roars ... wow, among Ian's finest work. I must confess to a little self-aggrandisement as I'm very proud of the musical composition. (One day, I'd love this to be played by a Mahler-scale orchestra – I've always loved Mahler's symphonies and their heart-wrenching power.) Despite my lack of musical training, I feel I nailed a poignant sense of loss and yearning. And, yes, the West has declined, and the East has risen – call us the Nostradamus of electronic music ...

Track by Track ... *Music for Listening To* by BEF (1981)

Side one (Penthouse Side)

'Groove Thang'

'The Optimum Chant'

'Uptown Apocalypse'

'BEF Ident'

One of the two tracks that weren't on the *Music for Stowaways* cassette. Designed as a marketing ident, as a piece of sonic branding – this was commissioned by us and composed by Mal Veale (aka Captain Zap), an old mate from Meatwhistle. We still use it as walk-on music for our live shows.

Side two (Pavement Side)

'A Baby Called Billy'

This sounds surprisingly current, featuring electro-jungly rhythm, extensive use of varispeed squeaks, and even the syndrum fills were played at half speed. Those drugs were quite something . . .

'Rise of the East'

'Music to Kill Your Parents By'

Track by Track ... *Penthouse and Pavement* by Heaven 17 (1981)

'(We Don't Need This) Fascist Groove Thang'

The excitement of starting a brand-new venture with my best and oldest friends was almost too much to contemplate. This was to be the first song we wrote, but where to start? We already knew that we wanted to create an electrifying (natch) new direction, but amid all the energy, resentment, confusion and, frankly, a desire for revenge, it was hard to pin down exactly how to start. In the studio, as always, we began working together on designing a rhythm pattern on the Roland System 100, tweaking the gnarly, white-noise-based filtered sounds until something interesting emerged. This was a very organic process, pretty much hit and miss, and the way that 'Fascist Groove Thang' emerged was based around letting the ideas flow without criticism or interruption. We used to jokingly say to our friends that Glenn, Ian and I were not just like brothers, but 'three heads on one body' – in other words, we were so close that we would literally finish off each other's sentences in that particularly cliquey and in-crowdy way of twentysomethings completely immersed in a whirlwind of creativity. For some long-forgotten reason, it was decided that this song should have a very fast tempo – I think it's around 158 beats per minute – which, of course, is ludicrously rapid, even for punks to flail around to. We regarded 'Fascist Groove Thang' as a sort of hybrid electro-punk-funk, and we didn't really care what people thought about it, we were on an innovation mission, and we loved the direction that was emerging accidentally. The liberation that Ian and I felt after slavishly following the self-imposed, buttoned-down rulebook of The Human League was tangible, and the

296

charisma and energy of Glenn added the missing devil-may-care ingredient to the mix. Phil was a very talented friend with a unique and angular approach to his craft, but Glenn was an entirely different kind of super-extrovert, the kind of person who lit up a room and everyone wanted to be in his company. We'd laid down a rough rhythm track, some chords and a loose structure, and it felt like something experimental and daring was emerging. Then, a lightbulb moment ... I'd always been influenced by Parliament/Funkadelic and Bernie Worrell's funky and simplistic synth bass riffs, but I suddenly realised we were no longer restricted to using synths. I blurted out, 'What would it sound like with a real bass in the middle eight? Do we know any funky bass players?' At this point, we didn't really mix with musicians as we felt a bit self-conscious about our total lack of musical training – that and the fact that most of them were a bit 'white bread' for our taste. We were more likely to hang out with artists, photographers, graphic designers, poets, actors ... creative mavericks of any other sort. Glenn (who was working as a stagehand at the Sheffield Crucible theatre at the time) responded, 'I could always ask in the staff room, they might know someone.'

He dashed down to the theatre's green room, asked the question, and a single hand was raised – a seventeen-year-old quiet guy called John Wilson said, 'I play a bit of bass.'

'Can you come down to our studio and have a go?' Glenn asked.

John replied, 'I have to pick up the bass from home first. I just bought it in a car-boot sale for £20, the strings might be too old.'

'We can buy you some strings,' Glenn replied.

'Nah, it's OK, let's try it first – by the way, I've never played bass before.'

Oooookaaaay, thought Glenn, *but hey, what did we have to lose?*

Two hours later, we welcomed John to Monumental Studios (the inappropriate name for a semi-derelict ex-veterinary surgery on West Bar in Sheffield). The aforementioned bass was unwrapped from its blanket. It looked pretty beaten up: £20 sounded about right. We played the backing track once to John while he sussed out the chords and the root notes, and we sorted out the recording and compression settings, then asked him whether he'd like to hear it again before having a go at the middle eight. John nonchalantly said, 'I think I've got it,' which to be honest surprised us a little. We briefly discussed our love of funk and soul, and told him this was the rough direction we'd like to aim at – Bootsy Collins, Larry Graham, Bernard Edwards kinda vibe . . . The pre-roll timing was agreed – four bars – and we pressed play . . .

It is no exaggeration to say that what John Wilson played for those ten seconds changed the course of our musical development forever. It was beyond anything we could have imagined or hoped for. A stunning explosion of technique and feel that attracts admiring comments from famous bass players around the world to this day.

Ba-dap, bap-bap-bap-bap ba-da . . . babadabadap, babadabadap badap, bap bap bap babada . . . Jeezus, it gives me chills just thinking about it.

We stopped the tape and looked at each other, slack-jawed with awe. What had we just witnessed? I gathered my composure and blurted out, 'Would you mind having a go at the rest of the track from that point?'

John humbly agreed, and then proceeded to astonish us with a kind of bass playing that none of us had ever heard before – it was kind of half funk slap/pick bass evolving into half bass-as-rhythm-guitar – crazily exciting and box fresh.

'Can you play another track of the same thing? It doesn't have to be exactly the same. In fact, it would sound great extreme left and right in the mix' – as always, I was busking my thoughts and instructions on instinct and feel. Once again, the man of few words and astonishing talent obliged – incredible … The two tracks are intact on the final version of the song – no 'drop-ins' or repairs – all first take. Then another thought occurred – we'd accidently stumbled across a fucking genius, and we didn't want this session to end: could this guy play anything else?

John casually and quietly dropped the bomb: 'To be honest, I'm really a rhythm guitar player.'

Glenn said, 'Do you have a rhythm guitar? And can you play like Nile Rodgers?'

'Yes, it's at home, and yes I could have a go at that style.'

Ian chipped in, 'Who's your favourite bass player?'

John replied, 'Bach.'

What the fuck? That explained a lot, but raised the question – what kind of musician do we have here?

'Oh, and I'm learning violin at the moment,' he nonchalantly threw in, with not a hint of conceit or arrogance.

We had struck gold, no wait … diamonds, uranium. We genuinely could not believe our good fortune.

Glenn hailed a taxi and rushed John home and back within an hour. To say that John nailed the Chic vibe is an understatement. As far as we were concerned, we had almost instantly solved the problems we'd always had with The Human League's lack of commercial success – this was going to be a smash and, even better, we were going to beat the new Human League to the punch and release our single first! Little did we know what was to come …

'Penthouse and Pavement'

In the white-hot, febrile excitement of the first few weeks of Heaven 17's existence, ideas were exploding like fireworks everywhere and anywhere – some good, some bad, some epiphanic. The day that Ian walked into the studio with a copy of *Newsweek* was another day that defined our style and significance. (Sidenote: which hip rock musician of that time would have been reading such magazines? Ian was a very bright and maverick talent, and the wide and unexpectedly lateral influences he brought to the table were a large part of what made us unique.) He opened the magazine to a bookmarked page – it was an advert for Toshiba Corporation, a highly stylised, illustration-painted montage about the most generic kind of business activities, you know the kind of thing – handshakes, secretaries, meetings, skyscrapers, meaningless slogans, etc. Glenn and I immediately understood the ironic humour in this, and it sparked a blaze of thoughts regarding whether we could present Heaven 17 in a similar manner as a form of satire. I have always been a big admirer of the alternative comedy scene, which was a burgeoning movement at the time – particularly in protest against Thatcher, Reagan, globalisation, global warming, nuclear war and so on. I often bumped into various comedic luminaries from that time (Rik Mayall, Alexei Sayle, Lise Mayer, Ade Edmundson – we were huge fans of *The Young Ones* and *The Comic Strip Presents . . .*) in pubs in Notting Hill and nightclubs in the West End, in particular Soho, where I regularly frequented seminal hangouts like the Wag Club. I always seemed to be drawn towards trying out different creative enterprises, even if I had no prior knowledge or aptitude. It's that continuing theme – shoot first and ask questions later, or 'Have a go, what do you have to lose?' We had been mulling over and discussing ideas regarding inequality, and trying to find a way to incorporate this into a central premise or preferably a pithy title for a song and/or album, and Ian had come up with the answer in shining, crystalline form.

'How about "Penthouse and Pavement"?' Ian sounded a little hesitant; as usual his quiet demeanour belied his inner brilliance.

'That's such a deep idea,' I said, somewhat gauchely, but nevertheless it was true.

Everything we wanted to hang our ideas on was there in just three words – the haves and have-nots, the have-nots looking up from the gutter towards the stars, the haves not giving two hoots in their luxury penthouses. The phrase even subtly alluded to the elusive aspirational 'guilt' of our own circumstance (as in 'What would happen if we were rich? Would we become assholes overnight?'). This would become a continuing theme for the rest of the decade. So many people misunderstood the ironic nature of the very powerful *Penthouse and Pavement* album artwork (brilliantly realised by Ray Smith) that we spent many interviews correcting the misinterpretation that we were all really yuppies at heart, and that potentially we were even aiding and abetting the yuppie culture as powerfully exemplified in the film *Wall Street* by Michael Douglas as Gordon Gecko – the mantra 'greed is good' became a bellwether for the times. Of course, we didn't want any part of that nonsense. I mean, how could anybody take the banal faux-corporate slogan 'OPENING DOORS ALL OVER THE WORLD' seriously? We assumed that everybody realised we were taking the piss, but maybe we mixed the cocktail a little too dry. In retrospect, it's open to interpretation, as a lot of the best provocative art tends to be.

At this time, Simon Draper (a good friend and head of A&R at Virgin Records) was enthusing over our work and offering great support and guidance. We lived near to Virgin Records' old offices in Vernon Yard just off Portobello market, and spent a lot of time informally popping in and out in our usual friendly manner. We didn't have a day-to-day manager (although Bob Last and our lawyer Brian Carr would help us from a business perspective), so it was down to us to make things happen. I genuinely believe that our face-to-face presence at Virgin was a big reason why we were so popular with all the staff – we made a point of fussing over them, and they in return put themselves out for us. A lesson for young aspiring artists. One day Simon saw us entering the building and raced up to us. 'I've got something in my office you have to see.' Curious, we followed him and there it was in all its glory on his desk – the LinnDrum, the world's first drum machine featuring real drum samples that were triggerable by touch pads, individually tuneable, and programmable using bar-length patterns chained together. All this was unique enough, but most exciting was that each drum element could be output separately into a mixing desk, and therefore could be shaped and manipulated into something resembling real drums for the first time. It's hard to overestimate the important leap forward this was in composition and recording possibilities – we were immediately freed from the shackles of expensive and time-consuming studio recording of drum kits and percussion – bear in mind, studios and tape were expensive commodities then, even assuming the drummer could keep time accurately! Of course, we grew up with a love of rock-solid machine timing (Kraftwerk were our gods) and now we could have that *and* what we thought was a real-sounding kit. Bye-bye drummers – yay – for now at least … Of course, it didn't quite work out that way, it was even better. I took it upon myself to become Heaven 17's LinnDrum expert and for the first time I could create patterns that no drummer on earth could play. Several of the drummers I talked to felt threatened for the first time by the LinnDrum, and they would say of my programming, 'But that's not realistic, no drummer would play that,' and I would reply, 'THAT'S THE POINT!'

So, 'Penthouse and Pavement' became the first song that we recorded using the LinnDrum, and from that day (for a few years at least) it became an integral and identifiably important part of the Heaven 17 sound. Re the lyrics, once again we used our William Burroughs cut-up technique, this time with a focus on the theme of the working man/woman, their lives and recreation, inspired by the Giorgio Moroder/Donna Summer song 'Working the Midnight Shift' from the *Once Upon a Time* album. The idea of combining innovation, glamour and the workers was such a juicy prospect, and the song was a breeze to put together – it almost wrote itself. As on 'Fascist Groove Thang', John Wilson's bass and rhythm guitar provided the perfect counterpoint to the simplistic and robotic rhythm track – genius. All topped off with wailing sax from Ian Craig Marsh!

'Play to Win'

Our first appearance on *Top of the Pops*. By the time we were writing this song, we were fully in the swing of our production and sonic palette – LinnDrum, basic synth chord structures, some System 100 percussion/hooks, John Wilson's exemplary rhythm and bass work, and last but not least Glenn's unique youthful baritone and our backing vocals. This was different again and was authentically funky and fresh, syncopated and swingy; good Lord, how the hell were we now creating the kind of tracks that we actually listened to in our nightclubbing lives? I blame John Wilson for making us believe it was possible – just being in the same studio and listening to him play was an unbelievable honour. The tracks in general were sounding lean, spacious and eminently danceable, but this one was even more in the pocket. We were on top form, and it sounded like the living embodiment of braggadocio – the jaunty rhythm of the vocals, backwards recording(!), the whistled hook (idea nicked from Peter Gabriel's 'Games Without Frontiers'), the handclaps (borrowed from any number of disco tracks), the chant (I loved chants in choruses – listen to 'Let's All Chant' by The Michael Zager Band). We used to laugh hard as we wound up our more serious musician friends who regarded disco as beneath them – we would tell them these lyrics are all you need. The double speed recording of the Bernie Worrell-inspired synth hook, and the *pièce de résistance*, the double speed 'Boys of Buddha' horns in the middle eight (proud of that), and lest we forget, the brilliant electro-marimba-ish sixteen's pattern – all topped off with the sound of a party scene of hooting and hollering, recorded at the Townhouse. Five tracks of me, Ian and Glenn as party people, and we smashed a few glasses in the process ...

'Soul Warfare'

I love this groove – this is my first blossom of drum-programming creativity. Listening back to it now, I love the funky sparseness, just piano, LinnDrum, bass, synth hooks (courtesy of Ian), and Glenn and I on chorus vocals. Once again, John's middle sixteen solo is exemplary – fluid and supple, like some kind of graceful animal. Literally the only brief we had to give was an artistic reference and John Wilson would do the rest. At this point, we were not really comfortable with writing straight-up love songs, so here is a perfect example of our thought processes around that period. The guiding principle was this ... what kind of twist or angle could we use to avoid the obvious? Could we talk about love gone wrong? Or alternatively, the psychological complexities of human relationships? To be honest, anything that would save us from appearing to 'sell out', which, believe it or not, was still an important notion to us.

This song was the last to be written on the album, composed at Townhouse Studios in Goldhawk Road, Shepherd's Bush, London, where we were recording and mixing the whole album with Pete Walsh (who was an enormously influential part of the team, as well as being an inspired young up-and-coming engineer). We had one day left booked in the studio, and we still hadn't got a title or theme for the song – just this funky, city-like soundscape, in my mind redolent of striding down the mean streets in the edgier parts of Lower Manhattan. I came up with a title featuring two words that seemed incongruent, 'Soul' and 'Warfare', embodying the nature of a broken and decaying emotional landscape. It was 2 p.m., and we decided to get out of the studio to clear our minds and head for the roof to brainstorm the lyrics. Two hours later, we descended, pleased with the outcome, and we headed straight into the recording area to perform the freshly minted opus. One interesting point I've realised while performing this thirty-five years after it was written, is that when we were writing these songs we never intended for them to be performed live. We regarded ourselves as sort of a neo-Steely Dan without the pretention – super-focused on studio recording, but no live work except TV and videos created mainly for use on the newly launched MTV channel. Glenn always complains, while explaining to the audience about this song, 'If we'd have known I was going to be singing this thirty-five years later live, we wouldn't have written so many bloody lyrics!' Glenn also pointed out many years later the studio performances were literally the only time he sang these songs

– there were no demos or rehearsals, just written and recorded simultaneously with no time for reflection, just do it! This was so Heaven 17. Performing this with a full live band for our thirtieth and thirty-fifth anniversary shows (Al Anderson on electric drums, the magnificent Julian Crampton on bass, Asa Bennett on rhythm and lead guitar, Berenice Scott on synths and, of course, the girls –any two from Kelly Barnes, Billie Godfrey, Rachel Meadows, Hayley Williams) was a joy, particularly Julian's uncannily accurate replication of John Wilson's fluid funk gymnastics.

'Geisha Boys and Temple Girls'

There was something always niggling in the back of my mind at this time. I wasn't quite ready to abandon the experimental side that was so much part of the early Human League's work, so I was intent on weaving this into a more direct 'commercial' approach. This was not just bolshy bloody-mindedness – I felt sure that the creative friction between the two styles would surprise and delight our followers, and hopefully create a greater sense of depth and loyalty to our epic musical journey and, who knows, a greater degree of longevity. The intro to this song has more in common with Stravinsky than Moroder, but it definitely makes a point that this was no ordinary album. Once again, this is the politics of teen-age relationships in a storytelling form of narrative, attempting to encapsulate the ambivalence and uncertainty of sexual identity at a very exciting and vulnerable period of development. The song's lyrics are also an effort to create a kind of 'film of the mind' within the constrictions of a pop song. I've always love storytelling songs – 'Wichita Lineman', 'Patches', 'Ruby', the magnificent 'W.O.L.D.' by Harry Chapin, and one of my all-time favourites, 'Reflections' by Diana Ross and the Supremes. The song is also about the big difference between perception of the opposite sex versus reality – a theme that is incredibly relevant in today's narcissistic, mobile-device-driven times. We tried a gentler vocal approach in the verses for a change, to show variation from the more stentorian approach (see 'Fascist Groove Thang'), and more backing vocal-led multitracked voice sound in the choruses. I'm not entirely sure what the varispeed low chant melody is all about, except that we found it hilarious as it reminded us of 'Song of the Volga Boatmen', a Russian folk tune. God knows what we were thinking, but that's the way it was at that point, nothing was out of the question. We even had a bizarre System 100 solo in the middle eight, which again was recorded at half speed to make it sound alien and cartoon-ish when played at normal speed. The rhythm track was played on our Dr Rhythm drum machine, which somehow we managed to sync to the rest of the track and our other synths – we were always experimenting with new and unusual techniques, not just synthetic, as sometimes the best option was tape manipulation.

'Let's All Make a Bomb'

Ian's basic rhythmic bubbling designed on the hardware sequencer of the System 100 is a thing of unique beauty – an almost Latin wah-wah flavour, enhanced by real whistles in the middle eight – and the polyrhythmic cross-patterns evoking an alien ethnicity. Ian Craig Marsh, take a bow, this is one of your finest moments. Lyrically, I honestly believe that this song is among our best and most memorable work. We were discussing the ludicrous new US policy of mutually assured destruction (with the appropriate acronym of MAD) and how crackers Reagan was, and how the US seemed intent on ending life on earth, when an idea occurred to me: if MAD is a rationally acceptable argument, maybe it should apply to smaller nations too? Or even, how about individuals? Hence – 'Let's All Make a Bomb', then we'll all be safer by MAD logic. There's yet another big chant/call to action in the chorus, 'Hey! There's no need to debate'. It's quite a revolutionary stance – 'let's celebrate and vaporise' – in essence, the whole song is railing against the powers that be while simultaneously subtly berating citizens for 'going with the flow' or being susceptible to rabble-rousing rhetoric: 'Ignore the sirens, let's have fun'. It all relates to the hedonistic attitudes of a lot of disco life. In fact, looking back on it now, I'm not really sure what we were specifically trying to say, but it's definitely one of my favourite songs on the album.

The Height of the Fighting (He-La-Hu)

Yet another attempt at innovation – this song is our Frankenstein version of marrying our love of soundtrack music in all its forms with, yes, you guessed it, more chants. It seems that I thought that it was the cure-all for the need for commercial success. We were partially right. This time we didn't even bother with real lyrics except for the title – 'Heat, War, Sweat, Law' – to say we were leaving the interpretation open was probably an understatement. In reality, we were trying to capture more of a mood of riotous, car-chase intensity but beyond that I can't recall any other stated objective, it just seemed like an interesting challenge. The backing track is genuinely electronically funky and weird, however, just how we liked it, and the sirens, etc., in the middle eight just added to the excitement. That and the gratuitous key change. The lyrics were inspired by 'War' by Edwin Starr and similar soul/R&B protest songs.

'Song with No Name'

We were keen not to come across as too poppy and lightweight, so in the service of balance we thought it would be interesting to create a darker, more psychologically disturbing story. Clearly this narrative is about someone losing their mind in a Hitchcockian tale with no sense of redemption. It's also about depression in general, and the lack of control one feels in those sorts of 'I'm losing my shit' situations. This song features my (fucking awesome) impression of Ennio Morricone's soundtrack harmonica in *Man with No Name*, hence the title. I've always been an obsessive fan of Morricone's work – as far as I'm concerned, he is a never-to-be-repeated genius and innovator, incorporating amazing orchestration and a gorgeous sense of melody and harmony with an obvious love of 'found sound'. Combine this with the impressionistic impersonation of real sounds using whatever instruments come to hand, and you have an inspiration for our recording techniques for the whole album and my career beyond.

We're Going to Live for a Very Long Time

I love the start of this track and the phased/flanged bass drone. The rhythm is inspired by the feel of Mike Leander's big drum sound for the Glitter productions. Of course, the lyrics are all about fundamentalist preachers and their insane certainty of an eternal life. Hence the almost childlike, playground na-na-nana-na, 'we're going to live forever, you're not, you're not' idea of yet another chant. As you can probably guess, none of us is religious. But the most fun was the idea of creating an endless chant at the end of the album by using a 'lock groove' technique – this is where the needle moves to a continuous physical loop near the centre of the vinyl record (but not too far, or automatic decks would lift the needle). This was quite a challenge for our mastering engineer, who was more than happy to be doing something creative for a change. After a few wasted acetates, finally a miracle happened, the lock groove was exactly the right length for the timing of the loop! Pure chance, but God loves a trier ... Incidentally, when we've performed this live in anniversary shows, it's proved to be one of the most popular songs.

That's the end of the vinyl album – but we were awkward bastards, so there were various singles, B-sides, odd tracks that were created at around the same time – here they are ...

'I'm Your Money'

Released only as a single (always loved that kind of thing since Roxy Music released 'Pyjamarama', and David Bowie's single 'John, I'm Only Dancing'), this was a straight-up, go-for-the-jugular attempt at a nakedly commercial, Giorgio Moroder-inspired single. It has a simplistic, catchy chorus, and the lyrics are deceptively clever – creating a meta-analogy between the world of love and finance, contrasting and comparing the two, with love emerging as a tradable commodity! Another example of Ian's incredible imagination and propensity for lateral thinking, he initiated the idea for these lyrics, which had us rolling in the aisles. It all started with the hilarious but downright rude implication of 'Chemical love bank within your grasp'. Looking back, it seems that the capacity for our lyrics to initiate laughter was a strong indication that we were on the right path. We also loved the multi-language approach as we thought this would appeal internationally, and this idea was inspired by Bowie's German version of 'Heroes', 'Helden'. We wanted different voices for the different nationalities, so we roped in my then wife Karen (who knew some Spanish), our mentor from Meatwhistle Chris Wilkinson, another great friend from Meatwhistle Nick Dawson (who threw himself method-style into the German character) and Liz Kardazinski, Polish girlfriend of a good friend of another Meatwhistle alumnus Howard Willey. Musically speaking, the groove was based on my love of the galloping rhythm of 'Happy Birthday' by Stevie Wonder, which we then achieved by somehow synchronising the System 100 with the Jupiter-4 – can't recall how we did it to be honest. Another stonking rhythm track by Ian and it shows our love of dub music – this is our first proper dub mix.

'Are Everything'

A chirpy reimagining of the great Buzzcocks song featuring acoustic guitar for the first time, played by yet another member of our Meatwhistle mafia, Dave Lockwood – apart from John Wilson, literally the only guitarist we knew, and he wasn't a professional. The unique sound of the ex-veterinary surgery's kitchen full of empty milk bottles created a shiny ambience around the heavily compressed, miked-up guitar, which was just perfect to make it sound untraditional enough for our tastes. Glenn hates performing this track, due to the byzantine complexity of the way the lyrics change and mutate throughout the song. 'I'll never get this bastard song right,' he would often inform us in rehearsals, and even if he did, when we eventually made him perform the track live, he would always make a point of saying to the audience, 'I'm never gonna do this ever again,' or even, 'Did I get it right? I've no idea.'

'Honeymoon in New York'

This bizarre but interesting rhythmic experiment emerged as a sketch/demo using a piece of technology the name of which has been lost in the mists of time. I'm pretty certain it was pattern-based (i.e. patterns linked together on an early computer system), and the reason I liked it so much was that it reminded me of the work of Japan, who we admired greatly. The device (whatever it was) also had an interesting palette of sounds, unlike any other rhythm machine at the time. The title is a reference to the fact that, although I had recently married Karen, Heaven 17 was taking off at such a rate of velocity and with such intense obsession that I could only promise her we would have an amazing and special honeymoon when things calmed down a little. That would be two years later – when we eventually spent our deferred honeymoon in New York. She must have thought I was taking the piss!

Track by Track ... *Music of Quality and Distinction Volume 1* by BEF (1982)

'Ball of Confusion' – Tina Turner

Ironically, this was the final vocal recorded on the album. James Brown originally agreed to perform the song, and the studio in Atlanta and James himself were booked in as a suitable climax to the recording sessions. The day before I was due to travel, James Brown's lawyers contacted our people to insist that James required 3 per cent on retail on *all* the tracks on the album, not just his own. A panicky meeting was quickly convened at Virgin Records. 'What are we going to do?' I moaned to Gemma Caulfield, our good friend and Virgin A&R co-ordinator. 'We can't possibly agree to those terms, or all the other artists will come running for more money and royalties.' You see, to convince all the artists that their relatively low fees didn't mean they were getting ripped off, we offered everyone the same terms – 3 per cent pro rata and £3000 advance recoupable against royalties, together with a 'most favoured nation' clause (this means no artists could get better terms than any other). So, if we'd agreed to James's terms, we would have had to give the same to all the other artists.

Gemma said, 'This is bloody typical, we've had no problems with the artists so far, this had to happen at the last song ...'

Gemma's desk was at reception, as she was the hub of pretty much all activity in the building at that time, and lots of people wandered past, often randomly chipping into conversations (I think this was a large reason for the success of Virgin in these early years). The financial director of Virgin Records, who happened to be walking past on the way to a meeting with Simon Draper, over-heard our conversation and casually threw in a comment which would change my career dramatically.

'Do you like Tina Turner? I'm just about to fly out to see her. She's a friend of a friend of mine.'

By coincidence, I'd just been to see Tina at the Venue in Victoria, London, where she was performing her famous 'Proud Mary' Las Vegas-style show, and she was incredible. I remember thinking, *How on earth has this woman not got a record deal?* Of course, I barely waited for his question to end ... 'I LOOOOOOVE Tina Turner, "River Deep Mountain High" is one of my top-three all-time records ... do you think she might be interested?' I said in almost a begging tone.

'Well, we can try ...'

Next thing we know, Glenn, Ian and I were booked on our first trip to Los Angeles to meet the legend herself. Tina could not have been kinder or more respectful if we'd been Phil Spector himself. She kindly agreed to take part on our album, and we felt like we'd won the pools. This felt like an even better result than JB himself! It's incredible what a fortuitous turn of fate that became.

As soon as we recorded the backing track, we were so thrilled, we felt we'd captured a highly unusual and respectful version of one of our favourite protest songs, helped by the superb guitar work of John McGeoch (Banshees, Magazine, etc.), Paul Jones's totally authentic harmonica wailing, and our first session with the brass section of Beggar & Co. (fresh from working with Spandau Ballet on 'Chant No. 1'). And of course, the cherry on the icing of the cake was Tina's flawless reading of the song. When she'd finished listening back to her perfect, one-take, no drop-in performance (with her new manager Roger Davies in attendance), she turned round to me and said, 'Thanks, Martyn, I'm happy with that – it was quite difficult to sing, it sounded like there were several different voices on the original.'

I looked at her, slack-jawed with amazement . . . 'Erm – that was the Temptations, there are four different voices.'

'Who are they?' she replied.

It was at this point that I realised that Tina had more or less lost interest in the world of soul and R&B, and that she now saw herself as a 'rock' artist. I put this down to part of the separation in all respects from Ike. All the tracks on the album were recorded and mixed at John Foxx's Garden Studio in Shoreditch, with Gareth Jones as house engineer and our engineer/assistant producer Nick Patrick. The sessions were a joy, I remember specifically a distinct feeling of shaking off the shackles of The Human League, and the impression of total freedom of musical direction. Things were going to be all right. It seemed everything we tried at that time paid off, and these periods don't happen too often – the stars (literally) were in alignment.

'The Secret Life of Arabia' – Billy Mackenzie

Billy, Billy, Billy – where do I start? What a character, what a voice . . .

When we were looking for artists to sing on the album, we were intent on finding unusual talents, and boy, oh boy, did we find one. We were at Ian's house a lot of the time around then, mainly because he had just acquired a brand-new piece of technology, a VHS video recorder. We were mesmerised by the possibilities of being able to record and watch anything at any time, and multiple times if desired, and to be able to pause images, and we used this to good effect on the cover photos of several of our early Human League singles. One of our favourite recordings was Billy performing with The Associates for the first time on *Top of the Pops*, singing 'Club Country' I think. We used to marvel at how bloody gorgeous he looked, and how much he resembled some kind of Hollywood star, and then there was the voice – part Bowie, part camp, part Scott Walker, part Klaus Nomi, with an unfeasibly wide range including a ridiculous falsetto and a strong lower tenor – all delivered with a gleaming confident smile and a defiantly mischievous twinkle. Fortunately, when we asked Virgin to help us contact Billy, they already were fans (I think they tried to sign him, but Billy being Billy, I think he went for the highest bidder instead), and quickly we met and he agreed to join our happy crew. We were so thrilled that we asked him to consider doing two songs – we already knew that a Bowie song would suit him, so I selected 'The Secret Life of Arabia' as a song that I believe should have been a much more popular track from the *Heroes* album. When he arrived at the studio, he said in his typical hyper-enthusiastic manner, 'Hi Martyn, I hope you like this, it might be a bit unusual.' We started the backing track, and before we could draw our breath, his first words emerged … 'The seeeeeeeeeeeecret liiii-ife of Arayyyyybeeeeeyaaaa' – it was like the clarion call of a long-forgotten alien banshee race … his voice combined so well with Glenn and me on backing vocals. To say that Billy made the song his own is an all-time understatement – he was fearlessly confident in his own ability, and his interpretation of this song will never be beaten in my humble opinion. It is a magnificent performance, and he sounds like no one else ever could. We were so lucky to have him in our lives. Friends of Beggar & Co., Breeze (rhythm guitar) and Tubbs (bass) became mainstays of our BEF studio band – all these musicians emerged from the London church/gospel British soul scene, from which bands like Heatwave and Light of the World had already had some chart success. Their brief was to make the track funky enough to dance to, but what we created was more manically insistent, almost demonic in its intensity.

'There's a Ghost in My House' – Paul Jones

Being a huge northern soul fan, I was determined to include one of my favourite writers on the album – R. Dean Taylor. He wrote 'Indiana Wants Me', a highly evocative biographical song about a fugitive criminal who killed a man for insulting his girlfriend. I was always intrigued by the title as I'm up for anything weird or meta-physical, and the allusion to the spirits of past relationships – it is a powerful metaphor that you can dance to. Paul Jones is a very talented and lovely guy and we have remained friends ever since.

'These Boots Are Made for Walking' – Paula Yates

I attended the New Music Seminar in New York in 1981, and Bob Geldof was travelling on the same flight to appear on the same panel. He happened to be sat next to me, which was fine and dandy, and we were getting on OK (although he can talk the back legs off a donkey) until he started 'advising' me about UK politics. 'Margaret Thatcher will be a great leader for your country, you need a strong leader,' he opined. I think you can probably imagine my response – I was particularly galled as he knew damn well that (We Don't Need This) Fascist Groove Thang had just been released. I started to argue with him, but the bullets just bounced off his bullshit armour. After a few minutes (which seemed like hours), I couldn't take it any more – the prospect of another five hours of this crap was not going to work for me, so I made a semi-polite excuse about being 'tired' or some such nonsense and quickly scuttled off to some spare seats a few rows away. To be fair to him, I'm not sure he cared whether or not I disagreed with him, he always loved the sound of his own voice. In any case, I'd already told him about the BEF album, and he immediately said, 'You should get Paula to sing on it.'

'Can she sing?' I enquired.

'Oh yes, of course.'

So, next thing I knew, Paula Yates came down to Virgin to our first meeting to discuss what we might do together. Glenn, Ian and I were nursing a hangover at ten in the morning: it was so bad that I had to lie down on the sofa in the meeting room. As we were having a chat, suffering with major headaches, Paula entered the room unannounced and proceeded to lie full length on top of me before whispering in my ear, 'Hello, Martyn.' This had a somewhat energising effect on me, as you can imagine, and Glenn and Ian were a little surprised to say the least, particularly as we'd never met before. Paula was quite a character, super-bright and coquettish, sexy and flirtatious, and not short of confidence. How could we resist?

We decided on 'These Boots Are Made for Walking' as an appropriate song, creating a kind of contemporary electro-funky backing track, and it struck me that she potentially could be an eighties version of Nancy Sinatra – a strong, sexy woman with a gentle hint of dominatrix mixed with Jane Birkin. A kind of ingénue femme fatale. Bob accompanied Paula to the studio, and attempted to commandeer proceedings, but I was having none of it, and he quickly got the message – I have to say that he had a good energy and was very enthusiastic and supporting of Paula, who was a bit nervous on her singing debut. She made the song her own, with her funny, squeaky voice and teasing delivery (Betty Boop may have been a role model), she could hold a tune, and there was no doubt that her interpretation was unique. Everybody loved Paula, it was impossible not to. Big shout out to Beggar & Co. for the brass arrangement. 'Are you ready boots? Start walking . . .'

'Suspicious Minds' – Gary Glitter and the Glitter Band

OK, let's get this elephant in the room out of the way . . . we had no idea about Gary Glitter's proclivities when we made this production. What we did know was that A) he was a total extrovert nutcase, and B) we loved his (and The Glitter Band's) early singles. Gary Glitter only had one setting, which was pedal to the metal and no brakes. I decided we should cover 'Suspicious Minds' by Elvis, and I also had a brainwave – could we get Gary Glitter and the Glitter Band to record this live? It transpired that all the records and hits they'd recorded were almost completely performed by Mike Leander, their producer – yes, every instrument, drums, guitars, everything except the voices. Our recording session was therefore a unique historical performance, Gary Glitter and the

Glitter Band on the same record at the same time. This never happened again, live or recorded.

Straight after the recording studio session (which they knocked out of the park), Gary and his long-suffering son (who was also his manager/minder) insisted on taking Ian, Glenn and me to his favourite Indian restaurant in Kensington. He was clearly in some form of altered state, even larger than his normal life – I suspected a combination of stimulants. We arrived in the cab and Mr Glitter led us down a flight of stairs to the restaurant in the basement, but disaster struck as he missed one of the steps and fell head over heels down the stairs ... Amazingly, despite several roly-poly rotations, he landed on his feet, astounding even himself. He accompanied the culmination of this gymnastic act with a very loud 'TA-DAAAA!' which startled the diners – however, as soon as they saw who it was, they simply carried on as if nothing had happened. It seems this sort of thing may have been a not-infrequent occurrence. He then said (again with no warning) that we should be introduced to the chef – but not in the public part of the restaurant. Instead, he barged into the kitchen and insisted that we followed, thereby breaking several local public health statutes. The chef didn't look surprised – *It's Mr Glitter again*, you could almost hear him think – but he took this bizarre drunken, boorish cabaret with good grace, not that he was given any option. We never kept in touch after that. He was clearly out of control, and I've always had a rule in my professional career: give people the benefit of the doubt, but no second chances for assholes. No exceptions. I should also point out that the guys in The Glitter Band were all very talented, lovely people, and on balance, my memories of these recordings focus on the prodigious energy and skill of all those long-suffering musicians involved.

'You Keep Me Hanging On' – Bernadette Nolan

In 1981, The Nolans were about as far from hip as it was possible to be. At that time their act was a mainstay act of Saturday-night light entertainment, a foursome of healthy, talented Irish girls, singing their wholesome hearts out on a succession of middle-of-the-road hits. One of the group, however, had an unusually versatile voice, and she was the de facto lead singer. I had a suspicion that Bernadette (Bernie) could blossom given a different context and, as usual wanting to surprise the public, we decided to give her a shot at a Supremes classic from my childhood listening to Radio Luxembourg – I felt it would suit her range and she agreed. Bernie was personable and professional, but in retrospect I feel I should have pushed her a little harder as the rendering was lacking in drama and oomph. But you have to bear in mind, I was still learning my trade at this point, and I didn't know what I didn't know, if you catch my drift. It's a nice but not exceptional performance – I'll own the responsibility for that. Can't win 'em all ...

'Wichita Lineman' – Glenn Gregory

There was always a hint of crooner in Glenn's voice. He was and still is a huge Bowie fan – as we all were – and in particular loved the hyper-melodramatic 'Wild is the Wind' (Bowie's cover is a tribute to Nina Simone's version), and I thought it would be cool and a bit cheeky to allow this facet of his talent free rein. I really had no idea whether or not he could pull it off, but the boy is a natural; the interpretation and nuance of the performance for someone so inexperienced are quite phenomenal. This was only the second ever vocal we had recorded with Glenn – it was almost his stealth audition piece. If he'd have struggled with this, then we might have had second thoughts, but we should never have worried. Musically, we wanted to create a lonely and evocative, fully electronic interpretation of one of Jimmy Webb's greatest ever songs, and I honestly believe we succeeded in recording a haunting evocation of the lonely lineman (had to look it up!) brooding over his lost love. I've always thought that the metaphorical genius of this song is the comparison of various electrical terms with emotional depth of feeling – pretty much nailing what we wanted to achieve with BEF, electronic music that could engage with the emotions. My favourite parts are the backing vocals before the outro, the drop down to the high string part and the soaked reverb, together with Glenn's wailing sax (or was it Ian?), recalling Bowie's partially successful efforts on some of his early songs. Oh, and the weird ending ...

'Anyone Who Had a Heart' – Sandie Shaw

Sandie Shaw is such a unique and iconic talent, we were so thrilled that she agreed to take part on the album, and her version of this song is particularly poignant considering she had a career-long rivalry with Cilla Black, who had one of her greatest hits with this song. I'm pretty certain that there was an element of 'I'll show her' involved in her agreeing to perform this magnum opus. My enduring memory of the day of recording was Sandie taking off her shoes (this was her trademark), and as I was discussing the approach we wanted to take with Ian and Nick Patrick, our engineer, I turned back to Sandie in the recording area behind the glass. All the lights were off. Where the hell had she gone? Had she had second thoughts? Maybe she'd done a runner? I looked at Nick, and then we heard, faintly picked up on the mike in the distance ... 'Nam Myōhō Renge Kyō ... Nam Myōhō Renge Kyō ... Nam Myōhō Renge Kyō.'

Sandie herself had turned the lights off, and was chanting, facing the wall five yards away from the mike ... We tended not to come across stuff like that in Sheffield, so it came as a bit of a surprise. I pressed the talkback button and gingerly asked, 'Are you OK, Sandie?' No response, then I realised she wasn't wearing her headphones so couldn't hear me. I said to Nick, 'Could you creep in politely and ask Sandie if she's ready, or we might be here all day?'

Nick slunk away, Sandie approached the microphone, the tape rolled, and she delivered a memorable and spine-tingling performance. Afterwards, I asked Sandie (for I was quite naive) the reason she picked that moment to chant. She replied, almost incredulously, 'I was chanting for success.'

I have remained really good friends with Sandie right up to the present day – she is a great character, full of spirit and elegance, with a mischievous sense of humour. The stories about her early career and TV appearances in the 1960s on shows like *Ready Steady Go!* and *Six-Five Special* were spellbinding, and her revealing insights into the Swinging Sixties and her contemporaries, in particular Dusty Springfield, were exciting and frankly eye-popping. What a privilege that she shares her knowledge ...

'Perfect Day' – Glenn Gregory

We were all huge Lou Reed fans, so much so that we held *Transformer* and *Berlin* in the highest regard, right up there with anything of Bowie's. There was something extremely mysterious and alluring about the half-sung, half-spoken nature of Lou's delivery in his New York drawl and the apparent incongruity of his sexual ambivalence. Eye make-up, open discussion of homosexual attraction, bisexuality, and the mythological nature of the New York scene, his friendship with Warhol, Bowie and seemingly every interesting club and rock freak in Manhattan – as exemplified by 'Walk on the Wild Side'. Even though I wasn't daunted by taking on classic songs, I just couldn't see a way of equalling or improving on the original of 'Walk on the Wild Side', so my thought process was this ... We all loved the album *Berlin*, but nearly all the songs were so dark and frankly depressing except for one, the beautiful atmospheric tone poem of 'Perfect Day'. It has an elegant apparent simplicity, which really encapsulates the yearning for an escape from gloom. It was only later that I realised that the song possibly alluded to heroin use (denied by Lou Reed himself), but I'd like to believe that the romantic message is what he intended. In any case, his description of a simple day out in Central Park transported me there, and still does. Now, of course, it has been 'over-covered', but at the time we regarded it as a forgotten masterpiece. Glenn's performance manages to stay clear of pastiche, with just a tiny hint of an American accent, and still I love the lighting the match and smoking intro. Our multitracked backing vocals were becoming more like our trademark by now, and I think they work really well here.

'It's Over' – Billy Mackenzie

Billy shows an astonishing range of delivery here, from tender and intimate on the opening verse, to almost whispering before the middle eight, to the full Scott Walker-esque hysteria hinted at before fully delivering in the electrifying outro. He effortlessly makes the song his own, important to an audience who may not have previously heard of Roy Orbison. He was always just a prodigious natural talent. The backing track features the most beautiful orchestral arrangement by John Wesley Barker, who was introduced to us by his friend Simon Draper. At the time he was arranger and performer for Lost Jockey, a systems music orchestral ensemble, and this appealed to us greatly. We went on to employ his very special talents to maximum effect on *The Luxury Gap* ('Temptation', 'Let Me Go', 'The Best Kept Secret', 'Come Live with Me') and *How Men Are* ('And That's No Lie'), and we remain firm friends to this day. There's something definitively album-ending about this recording, we simply couldn't have placed it anywhere else – I think it's the ba-ba-da-ba-dap resonant full stop which goes, 'Well, that was it, like it or lump it.' It sums up the attitude of the whole album.

Track by Track ... *The Luxury Gap* by Heaven 17 (1983)

'Crushed by the Wheels of Industry'

Greg Walsh, the brother of Peter Walsh, was keen to impress us with his encyclopaedic knowledge of recording techniques, so when we mentioned that we wanted to write a track about the decline of the steel industry and its effects on the spirit of a town like Sheffield, his imagination went into overdrive. We wanted to create a rhythm from industrial sounds – maybe existing documentary sounds – but he encouraged us to create our own. After several mad experiments, a loop was created from recordings of two concrete blocks hitting each other, the same blocks scraping against each other, and the metallic clang of a fire extinguisher being hit by a spanner. Glenn, Ian and I were very impressed by his ideas, which sat amazingly well with my skittering LinnDrum programming, the chants of 'Work Ha!' and the System 100 white-noise sequencers. 'Heatwave'-style vocal harmonies created a rich contrast with John Wilson's bass and guitar synth solos and my funky soul piano. The lyrics are a fine example of our dry wit, drenched in political sloganeering – 'there's a party going on that's going to change the way we live, but how do we know we've even been invited?' and the dual meaning of 'it's time for a party'. Is it futuristic soundtrack music, political sloganeering and analysis or just a pop song? Or all three? It's a bold opening track, a template for the album in style and meaning.

'Who'll Stop the Rain'

We had a penchant for trawling popular culture books for song title ideas, as part of our ripped-off Bowie/Burroughs cut-up technique. The title was stolen from a 1978 American neo-noir thriller starring Nick Nolte and Tuesday Weld. The reason it appealed to us was as an expression of a general feeling that things on the world stage were heading in the wrong direction (i.e. 'the rain'). A sort of *cri de coeur* for someone to save us all – similar in some ways to Bowie's 'Big Brother' from *Diamond Dogs*. The lyrics oscillate wildly between post-apocalyptic nightmare to faux-optimistic, almost ad-strapline banalities: 'It's a great day in the morning', for instance. Musically, funk is a big influence, once again featuring the hybrid between John Wilson's synth bass and our synth and LinnDrum programming, lovingly coated with John's sublime rhythm guitar playing and some playful vocal layering and speed manipulation (all influenced by the master of dark irony, Frank Zappa). There is a definite subconscious leaning towards fusion/ jazz on this track, a more worldly, grown-up approach which is aiming much more for the mass market – in a good way, we hoped.

'Let Me Go'

It's 5 a.m. I'm sleeping on the couch at Glenn's flat in Notting Hill, and we've been writing demos for *The Luxury Gap* for two weeks. I awaken haunted by a melody and chord sequence that has emerged fully formed from my dreams. This is a bit of a shock as it has never happened before. I quickly try to hum the melody into my dictation machine, and I feverishly attempt to deconstruct the chord sequence and record it on to my Portastudio. A bleary Glenn emerges as the sun rises to proclaim, 'What the fuck are you up to?'

'Have a listen to this – it came to me in a dream!'

'Don't be daft,' he sleepily mutters, but as he hears the haunting melody, he goes very quiet. 'This is really beautiful, Mart, what's the song about?'

I had no idea, but I told him it felt like sad, unrequited, poignant but unrepented love.

'But we don't write love songs!' he exclaimed.

'Well, there's a first time for everything.'

We knew the story had to have a twist, we never wanted to write anything banal or trite about love. By the time we'd finished the lyrics, we knew we'd written something truly to be proud of. A story of a life that hadn't worked out, but was full of significance and bittersweet memories. A shifting cloudscape of tonality and meaning, sometimes happy, sometimes sad. Is there still hope? Is there anger? Sadness? A fear of wasted lifetime and possibilities? It's all in there, together with John Wilson's sublime rhythm guitar playing, Glenn's magnificent vocals, Ian's beautiful System 100 tonalities, and even an opening thirteen-part, 128-voice vocal stack – a technique I later used on Tina Turner's 'Let's Stay Together' intro. The track is also one of the earliest pop records to feature

Roland's TB-303 Bassline synthesiser (later to become the iconic sound of a million acid-house records) – the bubbling characteristics and extreme resonant filtering made this instrument an immediate hit in our armoury.

Glenn, Ian and I are all in agreement: this is the most inspired and complete piece of work that we ever created, and it's an absolute joy to perform, frequently causing tears of joy, and often a choking inability to complete the occasional sentence. If you judge me as a songwriter on one song, please let it be this one.

'Key to the World'

Ah, the Phenix Horns ... how can you not love their unique sound? In my opinion, the greatest living horn section. They were in London working with Phil Collins on his new album, and Simon Draper suggested that we might be interested in using them. What a dream. They were demigods in the pop/rock/soul/R&B/jazz version of Valhalla to us and we felt that their very strong soul/jazz authenticity and talent would be a great flavour to incorporate into our new palette. We were determined to create a wall of sound as massive as the epic production of 'East River' by the Brecker Brothers, and having access to the Phenix Horns was our 'key to this world'. The powerful concoction of razor-sharp MC4 hardware programming, brass, bass, rhythm guitar and chutzpah was the sonic equivalent of a brass-driven sonic steamroller. The lyrics refer to consumer culture's obsession with the world of credit. This was something unbeknown to me, but Ian was getting heavily into debt at the time, which he would later regret. It was a cautionary tale about diminishing credit ratings and the extinguishing of personal identity. And we even managed to squeeze in a reference to 'the luxury gap' in the lyrics – more easter eggs and puzzle traps laid, all part of the meta-art project ...

'... but to the credit agencies, I'm Mr Obsolete – delete ...'

'Temptation'

Another epiphanic moment: as we were writing the demos, I realised that the Akai keyboard I was using had a function called 'auto-chord', which played one-finger chords of your choice. I was messing around with it, and I realised that I could easily create what appeared to be an endlessly climbing sequence of major chords that sounded both dynamic and almost sexually exciting. The technical term for this technique of Escher-like, illusory, constantly rising sonic staircase effect is called 'Shepard Tone'. Ours was more chord based, but nevertheless just as effective. So I thought, *What if this could be used compositionally to create the impression of endlessly rising sexual excitement, culminating in a final 'release' (i.e. orgasm)?* Another question – how could we write a lyric that didn't crudely give the game away, but implied the feeling in a stylish way? At this point, another idea occurred – one of my favourite songs by Prince was 'Controversy', where he recited the Lord's Prayer in a demonic/lascivious way which was deliciously naughty. Maybe we could use a line from the Lord's Prayer to make the theme obviously universal? Everybody knows these lyrics ... I've got it! How about 'Lead us not into temptation'? PERFECT! The lyrics pretty much wrote themselves from there, but there were a couple of missing arrangement ideas. The rhythm track in the pre-chorus and chorus is heavily influenced by the classic Motown backbeat, which is made even more effectively 'driving' in contrast to the half-time feel of the verses. I was always a fan of epic American Westerns, and in particular their soundtracks. Jerome Moross's sweeping orchestral frontierscape for the film *The*

Big Country perfectly embodies the spirit of exciting, life-affirming optimism that I was after for 'Temptation'. On the off-chance that 'if you don't ask you don't find out', I cheekily asked our good friend Gemma Caulfield (A&R co-ordinator) if we could book an orchestra. She said, ' Sure – how many players do you want?'

Gobsmacked, I quizzically blurted out, 'Err – thirty or forty? You know, about twenty strings plus harp, orchestral percussion, orchestral brass, woodwinds?'

'OK – when?' she continued.

'A week on Monday, if John Wesley Barker [our arranger] is available?'

'No problem,' Gemma replied.

I can confirm that this kind of conversation could *never* happen in today's world without jumping through endless hoops.

We recorded the brilliant orchestra (mainly members of the London Symphony Orchestra) in AIR Studio One at Oxford Circus the designated Monday – where they performed 'Temptation', 'Let Me Go', 'Come Live with Me' and 'The Best Kept Secret' all in one three-hour session – brilliance and professionalism of the highest order. A stone-cold guarantee of timelessness. We were living the dream, not too shabby for three poor working-class lads from Sheffield with no musical training . . .

Carol Kenyon, what a woman . . . Rusty Egan introduced us after failed auditions by some of our previous backing singers including Katie Kissoon and Lisa Strike – both great singers, but the wrong range and flavour. We needed someone with gospel/ soul stylings, with a mezzo-soprano voice but who could extemporise into higher registers, and most importantly, someone with a 'fuck you' attitude full of sexual potential. In other words, a diva.

Glenn said in an interview in 2016, 'We wanted to contrast my futuristic, humanoid-sounding vocal with a more emotional female one. While I was in the recording booth working on the line "I've never been closer / I've tried to understand", Martyn was urging me: "Push it harder – make it really strident." When Carol Kenyon came in and tried it we just went: "Yes!" Stratospheric is the only word for her style. Unfortunately, there was a bit of a disagreement over appearance money, so when it came to making the video we had to replace her with another girl, who happened to be a Page 3 model and couldn't sing a note. Everyone thought it was Carol, but it's not. Carol knocked it out of the park, and we will be forever grateful for her contribution to our most commercially successful recording.'

'Come Live with Me'

We knew that we needed a ballad on the album, and we'd programmed a lovely, languid, sequencer-driven instrumental that clearly fitted the bill. Once again, our assiduous collecting and research of film and book titles paid off – this time the title was borrowed from a 1941 MGM romantic comedy with James Stewart and Hedy Lamarr. Unbeknown to us, there was also a famous, more recent song of the same name by the brilliant Isaac Hayes on the album *Chocolate Chip* – shoulda known that … Anyway, we decided that it was a great title, but our usual caveats applied: the song can't be too bland and sentimental, and it has to have a twist. We were thinking that it would be good from an artistic conceit point of view if one of the characters was seventeen, then the mischievous Ian came up with the idea of a generation gap theme, maybe in the style of an edgy French noir romantic film (the French do this stuff better than anyone, in my opinion). So, we decided the male protagonist should be thirty-seven – it had a certain rhythmic beauty, thirty-seven and seventeen. Little did we know that as sensitivity to this subject became a hot topic in this decade, some fans would regard this fictitious relationship to be symbolically predatory. That was clearly never the intention but, to be fair, we wanted it to feel a little controversial. Some fans even complained about the arithmetical inaccuracy of seventeen being half of thirty-seven – good Lord, have people nothing better to do with their time? We've always loved storytelling in songs, and the way we constructed this lyric was as a three-act story, neatly packaged and delivered as our attempt at a perfect three-and-a-half-minute journey (à la Phil Spector). The combination of the beautiful orchestration and vocal arrangements, gorgeous guitar by Ray Russell, all overlaid with the excellence of the video we shot in Paris, in an authentic Parisian style, ensured the song was another top 5 smash hit.

'Lady Ice and Mr Hex'

Blending seamlessly with the outro of 'Come Live with Me', the musical arrangement is more redolent of one of our favourite bands, Weather Report (who knew?), and features the magnificent Simon Phillips on drums, Ray Russell on guitar and Nick Plytas on jazz piano.

I specifically remember Simon turning up to Townhouse Studios with the biggest kit I'd ever seen, including three kick drums, about ten toms and a sea of cymbals – definitely not our thing, but it shocked us so much we just let him get on with it. This was the start of our mission to hybridise programmed electronics with more traditional instruments, which caused us a great deal of excitement as no one else apart from the more forward-looking fusion bands (and artists like Stevie Wonder) were into this kind of thing. We felt truly musically free for the first time, and what's more it sounded unlike anyone else. Lyrically this is an allegorical song, anthropomorphising two characters, embodying cold-bloodedness (Lady Ice) and fate or bad luck (Mr Hex). Part of the appeal was definitely that they sounded like two comic-book villains – I have always loved American comic books, especially Marvel comics – and I'd go so far as to say that they were as big a cultural and philosophical influence as any traditional education I received during my teens and early twenties, especially the work of geniuses like Jack Kirby and Stan Lee.

'We Live So Fast'

As if to disavow our fans of any idea that, with all this jazz influence, we'd somehow turned our backs on our electronic pop roots, we created this Moroder-influenced juggernaut of skittering sequencers at a high tempo. A tribute to our breakneck lifestyle at the time, the lyrics refer to our migration to the big city (in this case London), and the dynamic effects both good and bad of that change. Leaving our families in Sheffield was both heartbreaking for them and exciting for us, and a song devoted to that special life event was a job worth doing. With Glenn in his neo-Bowie mode, it features both of us on backing vocals with soul-type chanting à la *Young Americans*. Ostensibly shallow, but really quite touching with a profound undercurrent, our loyal fans often quote this track as one of their favourites for personal reasons.

'The Best Kept Secret'

This song is almost like a musical theatre showstopper, featuring the same musical song structure as 'Let Me Go', but in an entirely different context. The true magnificence of John Wesley Barker's orchestral colours is deliberately blended seamlessly with Ian and my electronic abstract timbres, in an effort to hypnotically confuse the listener – is it real or electronic? I believe the 'magic special sauce' happens at the borderline between reality and imagination, and I have used this philosophy to inform my compositional and production techniques right up to the current day with my immersive soundscape company Illustrious. I like to call it 'sonic impressionism'. Lyrically, this returns to our global-political polemical roots – the reference in the chorus 'Who can remember just who is the leader?' is based on the rewriting of truth by Big Brother in Orwell's *Nineteen Eighty-Four*, and 'a soft-spoken showman, accepted, encouraged' was inspired by the election of Ronald Reagan. Of course, the message is that money (and capitalism) is the root of all evil. My favourite moment of magic occurs at three minutes eighteen seconds where the orchestration accentuates the lyric 'the power of choice is the power of reason, the power of voice is the key to the world' (more ironic self-reference). The final 'a certain smile conceals the highest card, beyond this place the rains are falling hard' is a chilling warning of the perils of succumbing to fascistic tendencies – ring any bells? Musically, the coda (inspired by Mahler's tenth symphony) is heartbreakingly beautiful, and when we perform this live, you can hear a pin drop . . .

A special word needs to be said for the 12-inch mixes we created for each of the single releases from this album. We always made an enormous effort to create unusual and eclectically different mixes, not just extended edits. The 'Let Me Go' 12-inch is frankly a masterpiece, definitely better than the cut down 7-inch version, elaborating on the elegance and poignancy of the original instrumental lead melody, so that the first half is all instrumental, and by the time the voices emerge, the backing track becomes stripped down and menacingly powerful. 'Who'll Stop the Rain' features Ray Russell on Roland guitar synth, effortless funking up the solid LinnDrum, weaving around a slowly building arrangement – all very influenced by Parliament/Funkadelic and Cameo. A lot of the chord sequences on this album were very influenced by artists like George Benson and Stevie Wonder. The 'Crushed by the Wheels of Industry' 12-inch is another funky dancefloor stripped-back stomper, revealing the majesty of John Wilson's synth and traditional bass playing, and the extended outro is a soulful funky dreamscape, with twinkling improvised jazz piano and backwards demonic vocals (à la Bowie). Finally, 'We Live So Fast' is a shame-less electronic dancefloor filler, full of youthful daring and excitement.

Track by Track ... *How Men Are* by Heaven 17 (1984)

'Five Minutes to Midnight'

By 1984, nuclear paranoia was at its peak. The Strategic Defense Initiative (SDI) was a proposed missile defence system intended to protect the United States from attack by nuclear weapons. The concept was first announced in 1983 by Reagan, who was a critic of the doctrine of mutually assured destruction (MAD), and he asked US scientists and engineers to develop a system that would render nuclear weapons obsolete. Various hare-brained schemes were researched and developed at great expense, including lasers and particle beam weapons. The overall catchphrase used to sell the concept to the general public was 'star wars'. Very scary, and utterly bonkers B-movie sci-fi stuff, actively encouraged by the US military–industrial complex. Our personal paranoia was probably not helped by the increasing intake of class-A substances, but these were genuinely frightening times, and we felt obligated to compose an impressionistic soundscape/song which would protest against this madness. We had already written a song about the ludicrous concept of mutually assured destruction ('Let's All Make a Bomb'), and this song seemed to be a logical sequel. It starts with a strange rhythmic breathing – almost sexually macho. I still love the contrast of weird programming, chanting, orchestra, melody and lyrics. 'Five Minutes to Midnight' refers to the 'nuclear destruction clock', portraying the risk as the number of minutes approaches 'midnight' (nuclear destruction) – the lower the number, the higher the risk. I also love the 'song as imaginary film soundtrack' methodology and inspiration. This eclectic construction changes mood constantly but still sounds coherent and surprising. Screams abound, tension is rampant in the sawing strings, Glenn interrupts the arrangement with the single word 'prayers', and the ending was designed to indicate an unfinished song due to nuclear annihilation. A chirpy little number.

'Sunset Now'

As a contrast to the violent annihilation of humankind on earth, 'Sunset Now' is a quirky and dynamic narrative pop song, ostensibly about a character called Blade (sounds like a futuristic gangster perhaps?). It's a metaphorical piece about wealth, sex, crime, excitement and American gangster-style optimism featuring the fantastic Afrodiziak backing singers Caron Wheeler (later lead singer with Soul II Soul), Claudia Fontaine and Naomi Thompson.

This was released as a single. Why? Good question.

'This Is Mine'

This song was conceived as an affectionate tribute to the prolif-eration of brass-driven R&B pop songs of the seventies that we all loved. We managed to persuade the greatest brass section on earth to perform with us – the incomparable Phenix Horns (the driving force behind Earth, Wind and Fire), with Don Myrick on saxophone, Louis 'Lui Lui' Satterfield on trombone, Rahmlee Michael Davis on trumpet, and Michael Harris on trumpet. Their arrangement, under our direction, was one of the greatest musical achievements of our career – it was as if we'd composed an updated Earth, Wind and Fire track. This song should have been a massive hit, but the reasons behind the lack of success are pain-fully described elsewhere in this book. The theme of the lyrics refers to the popular theme of many 1970s soul songs, particu-larly some of the best black protest songs, namely a call to action, a rallying cry for positivity and self-belief, a sense of leadership in the face of adversity, which was a stealth subliminal message in line with our strong socialist beliefs. Something I fear we are sadly lacking today . . .

'The Fuse'

> I wish I'd never heard the news
> (Never had a good day)
> Baby wants a pair of shoes
> (How'm I gonna repay?)
> A thousand fingers touch my heart
> I need so much
> Blue Force is tearing me apart

336

Another call-to-action song, attempting to foment revolution (in theory at least). On this album we moved away from literal meaning into impressionistic lyrical frameworks that could be populated with meaning by the observer. So, what exactly is 'Blue Force'? A general-ised conservative zeitgeist that was pervading the UK at the time (and is even worse now) is one interpretation – it really is meant as a meta-phorical device that can be interpreted in several ways. The Iceman refers to Conservative politicians (Blue Force) who pour words from the clouds, not caring about the consequences (ice is free).

> The iceman's back, he treats the crowds
> And ice is free
> Blue force is pouring from the clouds

The final twist is that there appears to be a potential alien (or deity?) intervention on the cards ... or maybe this lyric presages the forthcoming power of the internet?

> I heard a voice tonight
> Calling by satellite
> Thousands are right
> And some will light the fuse

'Shame Is on the Rocks'

This is a conceptually complex song featuring the brilliance of Ray Russell on guitar. The overall theme is that we are all suscep-tible to weakness, and that shame is the outcome should we weaken against the great forces at play. The title refers to shame itself as a concept being devalued as an attempt to manipulate the popula-tion. Heavy.

Shame is the one with power in his hand

There he waits, without a plan

But no one came, it's such a . . .

Shame is the same for you and you and you

There are no chosen few

Who will remain? It's such a . . .

The outro section is one of my favourite arrangements on any Heaven 17 album. It takes the form of a canon and is based around a leitmotiv inspired by Mick Ronson's guitar melody on the intro of 'All the Young Dudes', but this time making the key minor. It is also partly inspired by our love for 1970s prog-rock and in particular Peter Hammill's Van der Graaf Generator.

'The Skin I'm In'

More epic orchestration and a fantastic System 100 synthetic acoustic guitar performance by Nick Plytas. A beautifully nuanced vocal performance by Glenn emotively explores the idea of our innate sadness at the state of the world and fears for ourselves and humanity in general. A poignant warning regarding what may happen if we don't pay attention to all the issues discussed on the album. A plea for us to acknowledge our inner empathy.

'Flamedown'

A clarion call by the Phenix Horns announces a contrast to the languid elegance of the previous track. (See how important album sequencing is?) More iconic Earth, Wind and Fire-style muted flugelhorn and trumpet figures weave haunting melodic threads throughout the verses, contrasting with the dynamic strangeness of the choruses and pre-verse bebop jazz parts complete with Louis Armstrong-style 'yeahs'. Essentially this is a post-apocalyptic but semi-schmaltzy love song appropriating lounge-singer-type couplets, bringing to mind a *Diamond Dogs*-style twisted normality . . .

> You shall carry me
> Along the streets
> Awake and paralysed
> Take the slow lane
> We'll enjoy the view

'Reputation'

More faux-Americana . . . it seemed an obvious thing to utilise Nick Plytas and his jazz stylings, and the playful Afrodiziak parodying 'New York, New York'. Inspired by our trips to LA promoting *The Luxury Gap*, this song is an affectionate dig at the ever-changing status problems of people in the entertainment industry, particularly on the west coast. In a nutshell, you can go from hot to not in the twinkle of an eye, or the failure of an album or film. False friendships abound, and you can smell the quiet desperation of the hopeful career climber as their stock is falling . . .

> My clothes are too big for my body
> My body's too big for my mind
> I don't like humiliation
> I can change my clothes
> But I don't think I'll change my mind

'And That's No Lie'

Lyrically inspired by some of the great Motown heartbreak songs (primarily 'Heard It Through the Grapevine'), this is the longest and most completely fulfilling 'widescreen' recording we ever made. We regarded this song as our 'Surf's Up' – a rambling, immersive soundscape utilising all the forces at our disposal. The track took nearly two weeks to record and three days to mix – it was mixed in sections as there was no mix automation at the time, and synchronisation of the three twenty-four-track tape machines was a long-winded nightmare. We also had 60-foot-long tape loops winding around various machines in the control room at AIR Studios Two on Oxford Street. We were really pushing the frontiers of what was possible at the time. I have to say that our obsessive attention to detail and unwillingness to compromise meant that not only was this the most technically challenging recording, but also our best. The genius of John Wilson's bass playing elevates this track in so many ways, as it does on many other tracks on the album. There are so many outstanding elements to this recording, even though I say so myself – the bizarre and abstract vocal and synth intro, the delicate and nuanced rhythm guitar figures of Ray Russell, Glenn's effortless command of the lead vocal, acting as much as singing, Nick Plytas's fantastic piano solo section, Afrodiziak's chilling acapella at the end perfectly captured and recorded by Greg Walsh's magnificent sound engineering. And, to big myself up a little, the original idea of contrasting the drama of the soundscape approach with a twist on the power of love and attraction, verging on anger, flipping into tenderness and back again, was mine. The alternating macho declamations and painful realisation are both menacing and confusing. Isn't that what the break-up of a profound love affair feels like? The denouement is a chilling example of unexpectedly alternating the meaning of the lyric by having the girls sing the final refrains, leaving the listener disquieted ... who was not going to be beat? Or is this an example of inner monologues where both parties feel equally aggrieved? All these elements were endlessly discussed and considered. I am so proud of what we achieved here by reducing a complex emotional conflict to a dense, meaningful, elegant simplicity ...

Now that she has gone
I've got to shake the pain, act like a man
The sweetness that's inside
Will slowly die away
Who do you think you are? You're making a fool of me
Make no mistake, this is no fake, this is the end
Just shut your mouth, make room for someone new
So guess who's back, it's happy Jack, and that's no lie

We are now entering a strange phase of my Heaven 17 career, and I want to provide you with a little bit of context for the next two albums, not only by way of explanation, but also as a form of salutary warning for people involved in successful bands. Here are the factors at play at that time ...

- Heaven 17 money was coming in at last from our two successful albums.
- *Lots* of money was arriving from my production work, particularly Tina Turner.
- I had increased confidence in my judgement, verging on arrogance.
- Unlimited budgets for Heaven 17 meant less pressure to be creative.

- More money was available for recording session players – they became creative toys (partially replacing the time and effort we would spend on technology and programming).

- I was generous and had no sense of the value of money, therefore I spent a ludicrous amount on 'good living', fun, friends, eating out, clubbing, some drug and drink indulgence – basically full-time party time.

- Increased numbers of 'hangers-on' – I didn't realise this was happening at first, but I was always susceptible as I would often pay for my friends to join me at expensive restaurants; it wasn't unusual to have seven or eight people hanging out in our front room, just chilling – sometimes I barely knew some of them (friends of friends, etc.).

- I believed that the gravy train would never end (both creatively and financially)

In short, I got distracted, and 'lost my edge'. This is very easy to see now, but when I was inexperienced and living through it, the decisions I made seemed to make sense. My re-examination of these tracks in the cold light of day thirty-five years later is brutally honest. If a critic had done this, I'd be really upset, particularly re *Teddy Bear, Duke & Psycho*. In any case, it's an interesting exercise. Here we go …

Track by Track … *Pleasure One* by Heaven 17 (1986)

'Contenders'

The track starts with a fine example of the weirdness we could now achieve with my new Emulator II sampler keyboard: much,

much more interesting and flexible than our massively expensive Fairlight (which had now been relegated to the world's most expensive doorstop). The EII also had a brand new and huge sample library, for the first time on a CD-ROM via a magneto-optical drive (fancy, eh?) – this drive was world leading and cost £3000 but gave us access to a world of sounds not previously possible. Why spend so much? To sample these sounds ourselves would have taken months, so the cost was justified. Of course, this is all child's play compared to the vast, almost limitless sample libraries available now, but at the time this was the dog's bollocks. Backwards orchestras and compressed piano create a filmic intro-duction, calm and strange, with Glenn's now maturing baritone lulling the listener into a false sense of sci-fi calmness, overlaid with an almost preacher-like delivery. Who is he playing? In fact, he is the voice of the global elite – the 'powers that be' – that invisibly control world affairs. It was meant to presage a coming world order, which ironically appears to be coming to pass in the present day. More Nostradamus shit. The track transforms into a funky, Chic-inspired workout with the inimitable Carol Kenyon on backing vocals. My favourite part of the song is the middle-eight count-down, followed by an increase of funkiness and the words 'got the world on a string but it ain't got that swing'. We loved this tune, and there was an amazing video created in the US (under the terms of our new Arista deal, we were liable for half the budget of $300,000) – it featured most of the dancers from Michael Jackson's 'Thriller' video. The choreography is of the highest quality – I still love it.

'Trouble'

A more traditional electronic rock/pop track which again Arista loved and made a video for at the same time as Glenn (and his girlfriend-now-wife Lindsay) were in LA to shoot the 'Contenders' video. A cute melodic pop song with a cute video – not enough to impress the US market, but the song was a hit in Germany. My God, it even had a guitar solo . . .

'Somebody'

This is more like a 'normal' Heaven 17 song – the theme is about isolation. I really like this composition, particularly the chorus, the brass is awesome, the melodies are top class and the overall happy/ sad mood is very attractive. The vocal arrangements are cool too.

'If I Were You'

Ouch, not our best work, but the chorus is quite nice (although not good enough) – a bit facile in retrospect, I'm afraid.

'Low Society'

Back on familiar territory, funky bass, guitar, brass, girl backing vocals, a play on words of course – an efficient workout, but misses the mark in so many ways.

'Red'

This was written for the film *L'Unique* but was never used. Again, a comfortable and traditional piece of songwriting, but not

challenging, and frankly a little old-fashioned-sounding. It's interesting to consider that I felt that the use of samples was enough of
a contemporary flavour to balance the relatively boring instrumentation. I was wrong. I do, however, like the idea of the lyric: the
nebulous concept of an all-pervasive zeitgeist pulling us all into
conformity is kind of interesting . . .

'Look at Me'

A very odd, but strangely moving piece of music – however, we are
now straying into love-song territory, which is a world into which
we vowed at one time never to stray. This is another indication of
our drift into conformity in an effort to sell more records at the
behest of the pressure from the record companies, and a loss of
independence and confidence. Quite sad.

'Move Out'

Not very good, I'm afraid. The topline writing is unconvincing
and banal, and it just doesn't work at all. Oh dear, why couldn't we
see this at the time? It's quite horrible, a shadow of our former
daring songwriting.

'Free'

A muted intro leads into another languid funk workout – no edge
at all. The songwriting is 6/10 at best; it's easy to see now but just
shows how things can go wrong. How could we have justified six
minutes and thirty-two seconds of this? It's a relief when it ends.
Or am I being too harsh after the fact?

Track by Track ... *Teddy Bear, Duke and Psycho* by Heaven 17 (1988)

'Big Square People'

A bit more spirited than most of the funk workouts from *Pleasure One* – at least there's a kind of ironic lyrical approach and delivery, and the music's a bit more Cameo than The Meters. It's OK, but it really needs some sub-editing.

'Don't Stop for No One'

This starts well – and the string arrangement sounds brave and confident. The chorus is attractive and agreeable, but is that enough?

'Snake and Two People'

Featuring our friend Spike Denton as 'The Voice of God', this is an ironic take on the book of Genesis, but musically it's a fucking twelve-bar structure – how dull had we become?

'Can You Hear Me?'

A nice string arrangement, but it's a bit of mess. I like the chorus as it picks up for the outro. That's about it.

'Hot Blood'

An attempt at embodying some kind of sexual energy, this song at least has a different vibe, almost Hamilton Bohannon on the intro. Then it all goes wrong. Who were we then? Horrible.

'The Ballad of Go Go Brown'

Now this is more interesting (albeit still in a very conventional framework), but it sounds like a totally different band with Glenn as lead singer. Very odd – strangely this was a minor hit in Germany (which remained loyal to Heaven 17 when the rest of the world had lost interest).

'Dangerous'

A catchy chorus, but the rest is average at best. Nice middle eight though. Did we think we were American? Kids, don't do drugs . . .

'I Set You Free'

Another attempt at a love song, which misses the mark despite using all the usual tricks. Disappointing.

'Train of Love in Motion'

Starts like 'Station to Station' – this is catchy, in a chanty pop style, and was quite optimistically released as a single. Again this did OK in Germany, and it sounds more like a traditionally successful Heaven 17 song. Too much responsibility put on a simple band instrumentation framework to make average songwriting into something more attractive. Where is Heaven 17 as we know it? An outro featuring banjo? For fuck's sake. Speaking of responsibility . . .

'Responsibility'

I dreamt this song – well, the chorus anyway – and the string arrangement is lovely. What's more, the use of the typical Philly production hook of the Coral guitar-sitar is really effective. I still am very proud of this song and it really is a fine bit of pastiche work, but there's not much in the way of innovation. Which used to be our strong point.

Bonus tracks

'Work'

Not sure what this song is – appalling might be the word. At least there's a good Bowie impersonation and an interesting breakdown. But David Bowie it is not.

'Giving Up'

Nope. It hints at a vague reggae flavour but, nope, it means nothing to me. I had nothing to do with this. I hope.

'The Last Seven Days'

This showed a lot more promise. At least some beautiful chord progressions and an interesting lyrical approach. This should have been on the album, much better than most of it. Less 'try-hard', more relaxed but in a good way.

'The Foolish Thing to Do'

This was released as a standalone single with Jimmy Ruffin taking the lead, but Glenn takes the lead here. It is another Philly-flavoured arrangement which really works. There was a lovely video that we did for *The Tube*, which is still on YouTube. You could almost imagine Isaac Hayes or Barry White performing this song (yes, I know they weren't Philly, but you know what I mean). Glenn does a great job on this, but I still prefer Jimmy's version.

'Slow All Over'

A B-side that would have graced the album if we'd been braver – this definitely works as a piece of 'music for an imaginary film'. Great improvisational guitar work by Tim Cansfield. Six minutes forty-one seconds is a bit indulgent, though, I have to admit.

Some people liked the album – one reviewer (translated hilariously from German) kindly commented, 'I am pleasantly surprised! The disc lies well in the shaft. Here we experience Heaven 17 of mature age . . .' You are too kind.

Looking back, I'm not surprised that Virgin decided to drop us based on these two albums, however much it came as a shock at the time. We were still conscientious and determined, but believed probably a little too much in the quality of our songwriting and thought we were funkier than we actually were. The truth is that we'd lost our identity in an effort to become more commercial. The opposite had happened: we had chased success and it had run away from us. It's a tough lesson to learn . . .

Track by Track ... *Music of Quality and Distinction Volume 2* by BEF (1991)

My mission on this album was to nail the idea in people's minds once and for all that electronic music can be soulful. I suppose it's my USP as a producer, but for me this was the ultimate opportunity. Following the massive success of *Introducing the Hardline According to Terence Trent D'Arby*, I was going to try to get the crème de la crème of soul singers as guests on the album; I particularly wanted vocalists whose influence on me transcended their current sales potential. The idea was to give them the opportunity to interpret soul songs, songs which really meant something to them, in a way that they may never have had the chance to in their normal careers. I also wanted to give exposure to established soul artists who were no longer in the limelight but deserved to be. Tina and Chaka were not in that category, but their inclusion meant there would be guaranteed interest and exposure for the album.

Volume 2 was less experimental than Volume 1: with greater experience I was more focused and consistent, and the result was more mellow. I had no concerns that it would be no less exciting because of the work put into it and the quality of the work.

'Someday We'll All Be Free' – Chaka Khan

As Randy Hope-Taylor and I were programming the backing track for 'Someday We'll All Be Free', I intuitively felt that a female voice would give the interpretation an interesting spin. I had always wanted to work with Chaka Khan since her Rufus days, and I made the call, more in hope than expectation. Here was a woman who had won ten Grammys and sold around 70 million albums – it was quite a coup to get her on the album, especially as singer for the opening cut. Chaka had been hanging around the soul/jazz scene in London for a while, so I'm pretty sure she knew who I was, even though I'd never met her. She agreed, I sent her the rough backing track mix and she loved it. I explained that we were going to overlay a full live band in the studio as she was singing, to recreate the way spontaneity led to inspiration. I was hoping this would create the best of both worlds: the modernity of programmed beats and synths, combined with the human full-band element. I've always believed that great records need a significant percentage of randomness involved, as often fully programmed tracks can feel too robotic and sterile at a very deep level. The day arrived and we were all set up and rehearsed at Red Bus Studios, just off Edgware Road (which was my home studio for about seven years). From the same interview at the time . . .

[Red Bus is] not too hi tech – not all new chrome and muted blues and greys. I remember when Chaka came down she said the atmosphere reminded her of Atlantic in New York, or one of the old soul studios, where they're a little run-down. I think it's important for artists coming in from the cold, rather than feeling that they're in some kind of hit factory – you know, a lot of studios just have every gimmick under the sun – it's more important that the studio feels lived in.

Some of the musicians had already met and played with Chaka before, as she had a cute habit of turning up unannounced at various jazz venues and asking, no demanding, to sing with the band, no matter who they were. In the studio, Chaka arrived looking pretty tense but totally charming – she is a beautiful, talented person, but her troubles with drugs and alcohol around this time are well documented . . .

351

Thankfully her troubles are reportedly behind her, but I'm afraid she was in a bit of a state in 1992 when we recorded this album. This made for a very interesting and somewhat frustrating recording session. She entered the recording area, settled herself on a high stool, introduced herself to the musicians and we went for the first take ... It was, shall we say, irregular. Even though the song is a very well-known soul standard, originally written and performed by the late, great Donny Hathaway, and she had the lyrics written down on a music stand, she found it difficult to stick to the arrangement structure, let alone anything resembling the original melody. But there were flashes of the purest genius, and her voice was still as great as ever. So, I gave Chaka a few notes, and she seemed to understand that rather than do lines piecemeal (this tends to disrupt the creative flow and often frustrates the singer), I wanted to get a classic one-take performance from her, just like I'd achieved several times with Tina Turner.

In those days, you could get maybe three takes on a single reel of twenty-four-track tape, and each tape cost around £120, so while we weren't skimping, the sheer logistics of compiling bits of vocals from different takes and tapes were a highly time- and therefore money-consuming procedure. After takes two and three it was clear that, while Chaka was belting it out with gusto, no amount of guidance from me was being processed in the Khan mind. We ploughed on with take after take, but this was becoming subject to the law of diminishing returns. Every single take had elements of brilliance, but they were all substantially different. It was almost as though I'd set her a challenge never to repeat herself. Musicians are generally happy to play all day, especially with a legendary artist, but when we approached take fourteen, yes fourteen, I still didn't feel I had a possible combination of well-sung bits that could make an apparently flawless vocal. By this time Chaka was definitely not improving, and the musicians were getting mentally fatigued, so we had to abandon the session and hope for the best in the compilation process.

The comp took a day and a half (today's musicians have no idea how easy they have it), but after a massive effort of concentration by myself and my brilliant engineer Graham Bonnett, we proudly played back the finished, bounced vocal compilation, and it sounded like a flawless, passionate performance which did Chaka's reputation proud. I love this great version, and I must give special thanks to Randy Hope-Taylor, whose exceptional arrangement, military-style drum programming (like a call to action) and bass playing drive this arrangement along. Oh, and Tim Cansfield's funky guitar colours. Chaka's performance is chillingly dynamic and thrilling, ranging from sensitive and relaxed, to classic open-throated lack of inhibition, to exceptional ad-libbing and backing vocal harmonies.

Verse three makes me cry, what a climax ... she is a goddess. How this wasn't a hit is beyond me. Donny Hathaway would have been proud, and I know that Lalah (his daughter) was. Speaking of which ...

'Family Affair' – Lalah Hathaway

Lalah Hathaway was just twenty-three years old when she agreed to sing on our version of this iconic Sly and the Family Stone song. We knew she had the 'chops', but we had no idea just how much of her father's talent was living in her. Donny is probably tied at first place for me in terms of unique and brilliant male soul singers with Marvin Gaye, and this is a crowded field. Donny's elegance and flow, his technique and exceptional songwriting, but most of all his authenticity, make him one of the most revered artists by those 'in the know' in the pantheon of singer-songwriters who always touch your deepest soul. Lalah was, and still is, prodigious. Even though she was relatively inexperienced, when I challenged her to be creative with her interpretation, she confidently laid it out as though she was born to do it. When we came to the backing vocal ideas, her harmonies were highly innovative and close to atonal – the jazz force runs deep in this one. I would never have come up with the incandescent radiance of the vocal melody and timing improvisation (with harmony) on verse three, 'one child grows up to be ... [and then on the offbeat)] somebody who just loves to learn and' – it just explodes. Her coloratura is gorgeously heartfelt. I could listen to this all day.

We'd just finished working with Billy Preston, who was an absolute joy, and he was free to go but he spent the next couple of weeks hanging out in the studio, meeting incoming artists and laughing and joking with our house band – he clearly adored the environment, and, just as Chaka mentioned earlier, it must have felt a little like the good old days, just chilling and vibing. As we were coming up to recording the crucial Rhodes part on the backing track for 'Family Affair', I asked Billy if he'd honour us by playing it for us. 'Not only will I do it, but did you realise that I played the part on the original Sly version? They never gave me a credit.' *Fuck me*, I thought, *this is too good to be true, Billy Preston reprising his original performance?* I couldn't believe my luck. His magic is all over this recording, and to watch him perform it was one of the greatest moments of my recording career. What a talent. He worked with artists such as Little Richard, Sam Cooke, Ray Charles, the Everly Brothers and famously the Beatles, had his own solo hits, and co-wrote 'You Are So Beautiful'. All that and one of the greatest Afros on the planet. More from Billy later on the album ...

'Early in the Morning' – Richard Darbyshire

Tick-tock-tick-tock RINNNNGGGG!

The Gap Band were very popular in the kind of clubs that Glenn, Ian and I frequented, and this song is a mysterious and ominous blend of haunting guitar arpeggiation in a minor key and a massive Moog bass à la Funkadelic. There's something about the music that is hauntingly at odds with the lyrical content – it's almost poignantly sad against the macho attitude of the vocals, in this instance beautifully performed by Richard Darbyshire (a friend of mine from the Sheffield band Living in a Box) in a classic blue-eyed-soul style so popular in the late 1980s. I'm very fond of the break in the middle and the surprise accelerando, and what's more this track sounds incredible on a club sound system.

'Free' – Billy Mackenzie

Billy, Billy, Billy . . . my heart aches whenever I listen to his exceptional voice. What a tragic waste. Billy took his own life six years later as his battles with depression grew worse after his beloved mother passed away. We'd worked together on BEF *Volume 1*, and we'd become firm friends after I recorded several tracks for his album *Perhaps*, including the beautiful 'Those First Impressions'. Glenn was also a great friend and fellow dog lover – when Glenn and he agreed to meet at a launch party, Billy turned up and said, 'This is for you, Glenn.' Billy started to bring something out from under his overcoat.

'What is it?' Glenn was bemused.

'Well, Glenn, you mentioned you might one day like a whippet, and I breed them, so today's your lucky day!' He handed him a beautiful six-week-old whippet puppy. Glenn had been charmingly 'Billy'd'.

He was batshit crazy, but in the most lovable way. When I asked him to take part in BEF again, he was thrilled, and when I suggested the Deniece Williams classic 'Free', he loved the idea.

'How would you like me to sing it, Martyn?' he cooed in his lilting, eccentric delivery. 'It's quite high.'

'Don't be daft, Billy, I've never heard you complain about singing falsetto before.'

'Aye, OK, I'll have a go then . . .' Billy was never averse to 'having a go' – his entire career was simultaneously maddeningly close to major success and, on the other hand, always on the edge of falling apart.

Once again, the brilliant programming and arrangement by Randy gave a new and elegant life to the song, and Nick Plytas's sampled keyboard vibraphone improvisation in the middle eight is a thing of beauty. As soon as Billy started singing the intro on the first take, I knew we were on to something special. I had always felt that Billy sang with a great deal of natural soul, and that a song like this would flourish under his creativity. I was right. The sensitivity with which Billy delicately extricated the meaning of the song was completely electrifying. His improvisation in the intro enabled us to mystify the listener with what was his voice and what was synthesiser. Great Philly stylings from Tim Cansfield on electric guitar. Awe-inspiring vocal textures in Billy's lower range still raise the hairs on the back of my neck. I urge you to listen to this and defy you not to be moved. It makes me well up, and is particularly poignant as we later discovered his desire to be free led to his tragic demise. Rest in peace, Billy, we will never stop loving you.

'It's Alright Ma (I'm Only Bleeding)' – *Sananda Maitreya*

Sananda came up with this idea – I confess I'm really not a Bob Dylan fan. I respect Dylan's songwriting and his poetic talent, but I just can't get over his irritating vocal delivery. Sorry/not sorry. Anyway, this is an interesting song thematically if not musically, and Sananda wanted it to be as 'live band sounding' as possible (i.e. with virtually no synths or programming). So that was that – and in my humble opinion, all these decisions were badly considered. It's the one track on the album that we had major problems mixing, we just couldn't make it swing, and this was because, frankly, the sounds are a bit, well, white bread so there was little leeway to play with. No amount of added synth would have worked either, it would have just sounded incongruous. Not to mention that I usually had the best brass section in the business, but for this track we used some highly efficient but very 'white' sounding British musicians. All well played, with passion, but it still just doesn't work for me. The effort to make it sound authentically 1960s/70s soul was the wrong way to go – it sounds thin and unconvincingly old-fashioned, not in a good way. That's not saying that Sananda doesn't deliver, but ultimately I need to look in the time-travel mirror and give myself a good talking-to. Naughty Martyn, bad dog, go to your basket.

'I Want You' – *Tashan*

Tashan was a super-talented young soul singer from New York, real name Thomas Pearce. He got his big break when he performed and toured with Grandmaster Flash as a backing singer, as well as writing and producing for rappers Whodini. He also toured with the Zulu Nation. He was then signed by Russell Simmons at Def

Jam in 1985, and I produced several tracks with him for his album *Chasin' a Dream* at Red Bus Studios in London, some of which never made the final album. At one time, he was regarded as the natural successor to Alexander O'Neal (having a similar pop/soul voice), but O'Neal is still around now (despite his well-documented problems with cocaine addiction). He was undeniably a very talented singer-songwriter, and we got on like a house on fire, both of us from working-class backgrounds, both huge soul fans. I think he liked my blue-collar background, and respected my success coming from such unlikely beginnings. We both adored Marvin Gaye, and I felt he would do justice to one of my favourite songs of his, 'I Want You', surely one of the most sensual soul songs ever written, in this case by my namesake Leon Ware (no relation).

The live BEF band were completely in their comfort zone for this and created the most authentic and atmospheric version I could have wished for. The creative spin that I put on this was to fashion an extended intro based around a familiar soul trope – lovemaking and pillow talk. So I extracted the lyric 'come on babe' and made it into a hypnotic, harmonised chant of increasing intensity, extended over, if my memory serves me well, thirty-two bars. So I suppose you could call it foreplay? I remember all those epic Isaac Hayes cover versions, my favourites being the heroically epic sixteen-minute version of 'Joy' and the nearly nineteen-minute version of 'By The Time I Get to Phoenix' from the *Hot Buttered Soul* album. Our arrangement was a tribute to that era. Tashan included this recording on his album *For the Sake of Love* (I also produced four other tracks on the album including the title track).

'A Song for You' – Mavis Staples

I grew up with Mavis Staples and The Staples Singers, and the chance to work with her was too good to miss. Her husky voice is still instantly identifiable, and there's something in her body of work that taps directly into the gospel church – it's almost preacherly delivery, complete with the punctuation and emphasis of the ends of words. 'I am-uh, hear today-uh, to bring you the word-uh . . .' Gravel and truth. That's what Mavis means to me. When she came to the studio with her sister Yvonne, it became rapidly obvious that the pair were a force of nature. They were funny and honest, like some kind of vaudeville double-act that were never 'off'. If they were getting paid by the word, I would have been bankrupt. But I adored them, and I was a little surprised that Mavis seemed to be flirting with me! There was no doubt that the diminutive sisters were, shall we say, not backwards at coming forwards, but, although I was flattered, the age difference – seventeen years – was a bit too much for me. (Hang on, I hear you say, that's less than the age difference in 'Come Live with Me'. Fair point.)

I'm very proud of our programming on this track, and I think this is one of the most successful interpretations on the album. But jeez, it took us forever to get the non-programmed, real Steinway piano to work – the timing is so particular with the accelerandi and ritardandi that had to be just right or it sounded wrong. But Mavis created a reading of this song which would bring a tear to a glass eye, and I'm pretty sure Donny Hathaway himself would have approved of it. The song itself is a masterpiece, but Mavis's understanding of the themes takes this version to a different level. It speaks of love and loss, of life and experience, of joy and pain, and ultimately music as a form of redemption. None of this would have worked with a younger, less experienced artist. I am very, very proud of this. The success of this performance is made even more remarkable by the fact that we found out that Mavis was due for an operation to remove nodes on her vocal chords – years of empha-sising the grit in her voice had caused lesions which then scarred – so this recording was her last for a while. She later confessed it could have been the end of her career.

We attempted to record another cover version, one of her favourite songs, 'Trade Winds', originally released by The Three Degrees in 1972, but we only reached two-thirds of the way through the song before her voice completely collapsed. Fortunately, we decided to do 'Song for You' first, or else we'd have been scup-pered. The happy ending is that Mavis has had a great career since then as a highly successful solo artist. Grammys, multimillion-selling albums, and many other awards provide a powerful testament to her talent, perseverance and sheer hard graft, which epitomises many of the singers and artists of that generation – Tina Turner being a typical example of a late-career triumphant reimagining.

'Try a Little Tenderness' – Billy Preston

Another great survivor is Billy Preston, who has worked with a huge number of famous artists yet still managed to continually reinvent himself and have enormous success as a solo artist (despite not having the world's strongest voice). Billy's choice of song was based on my question, 'What was your favourite song as you were growing up?' His response was twofold – Otis Redding's 'Try a Little Tenderness' and The Beatles' 'In My Life'. Otis seems to be a constant inspiration for people who grew up with his music – he was a dynamic performer, as evidenced on his seminal album *Live in Europe* (Sananda would listen to this album in the dark in the studio control room before starting work most days, to study his spirit and technique). He was a great heart-throb, a true star. We recorded both songs, and we hired in a Hammond B3 for that authentic sound. Billy was an expert in the various techniques associated with this famous rock instrument. The most typical and unusual feature of the classic B3 is the Leslie rotating speaker, which gives a variable-speed chorus effect based on a motor activated from the keyboard. This creates a sense of animation and dynamism, which suits rock and soul in particular, but these organs were also popular in gospel churches. To be honest, while I was thrilled to be tapping into the authenticity of such a famous musician, I wasn't so bothered about these songs, primarily because I could see a way of effectively updating them easily. Looking back, they certainly didn't lend themselves to any form of synthetic approach, so I think maybe I got a little starstruck by agreeing to cover the two songs. Dammit, another schoolboy error . . .

'I Don't Know Why I Love You' – Green Gartside

Green Gartside is a genius, probably the only true genius I've ever worked with. I'd loved Scritti Politti since hearing their beautiful and soulful 'Faithless' on 12-inch from their luscious 1982 *Songs to Remember* album. But the real breakthrough album was *Cupid & Psyche 85*, featuring one of my top-ten favourite tracks, 'Absolute'. Green's voice is a thing of sublime delicacy, and he sings very quietly. This is not an affectation, it was exactly the same when we performed the song with him live. It was difficult to record, but well worth the effort. He was a little daunted by the challenge of singing a classic Stevie Wonder song, though he was always a little insecure, but his interpretation of this song is unique and heartfelt. No one else could have delivered this performance in anything like this style – there can be only one Green.

'A Change Is Gonna Come' – Tina Turner

Looking to repeat the phenomenal success of 'Let's Stay Together', Tina graciously agreed to participate on the album. By this time, she had become one of the most successful artists of the 1980s and had sold nearly seventy-five million records, so she certainly didn't need to help me out. But like all genuine people with a conscience, in the words of the greatest female soul singer who ever lived Aretha Franklin (another artist who turned me down), 'Don't forget the bridge that brought you over'. Tina had great respect for my role in the resurgence of her career and, as a Buddhist, probably believes in karma – she has good karma in spades. Once again, her performance was flawless – first take – and the recording and arrangement were an elegant thing of beauty, stylishly updating the original in my not-so-humble opinion. But unfortunately it was deemed too downbeat to be considered for single release, despite Tina's box-office appeal.

'Feel Like Makin' Love' – Ghida De Palma

Roberta Flack was heavily associated with Donny Hathaway, so the choice of this track felt like it made sense in the context of the Hathaway-heavy song lineup. I met Ghida De Palma when she approached me to produce a couple of songs for her debut album. Her Portuguese vocal style fascinated me, so I thought it would be cool to include a relatively unknown artist on the album as a counter-argument that this was only for 'oldies'. The smouldering performance stands up well to the more famous artists on the album (i.e. all of them).

Appendix 2:

My Personal Electronic Travelogue – 100 Electronic Music Influences 1945–92

Henry Blair	*Sparky's Magic Piano*
Louis and Bebe Barron	*Forbidden Planet*
Edgard Varèse	*Poème Électronique*
Raymond Scott	'Cindy Electronium'
Joe Meek and the Blue Men	'Magnetic Field'
The Tornadoes	'Telstar'
BBC Radiophonic Workshop	'Doctor Who'
Delia Derbyshire/Anthony Newley	'Moogies Bloogies'
Morton Subotnik	*Silver Apples of the Moon*
Diana Ross and the Supremes	'Reflections'
Walter Carlos	*Switched on Bach*
Terry Riley	*In C*
White Noise	'Love Without Sound'
Frank Zappa	'Peaches en Regalia'
King Crimson	'The Court of the Crimson King'
Alice Cooper	'Titanic Overture'
Moody Blues	'The Voyage'
Jean Jacques Perrey	'EVA'
Tonto's Expanding Head Band	'Jetsex'
Hot Butter	'Popcorn'
Curved Air	'Ultra-Vivaldi'
Chicory Tip	'Son of My Father'

Genesis	'Watcher of the Skies'
Hawkwind	'Silver Machine'
Van der Graaf Generator	'Plague of Lighthouse Keepers'
Roxy Music	'The Bob (Medley)'
Wendy Carlos	'Funeral March for Queen Mary'
Annette Peacock	'I'm the One'
Brian Eno	'Baby's on Fire'
Eno & Fripp	*(No Pussyfooting)*
Tangerine Dream	'Phaedra'
Todd Rundgren	'How About a Little Fanfare?'
Eno	'The True Wheel'
Can	'I Want More'
Stevie Wonder	'Pastime Paradise'
Devo	'Jocko Homo'
Flying Lizards	'Money'
M	'Pop Muzik'
Nag Nag Nag	'Cabaret Voltaire'
Talking Heads	'Once in a Lifetime
Peter Gabriel	'Intruder'
John Carpenter/Alan Howarth	*Escape from New York*
Landscape	'Einstein a Go-Go'
Blancmange	'Living on the Ceiling'
Freur	'Doot-Doot'
James Ingram	'Yah Mo B There'
Suicide	'Cheree'
Giorgio Moroder/Donna Summer	'Working the Midnight Shift'
Donna Summer	'I Feel Love'
Stevie Wonder	'Village Ghetto Land'
Iggy Pop	'Mass Production'
Cerrone	'Supernature'
Space	'Magic Fly'
Kraftwerk	'Trans-Europe Express'
David Bowie	'Warzawa'
Weather Report/Joe Zawinul	'River People'
Scott Walker	'Nite Flights'

Funkadelic	'One Nation Under a Groove'
The Normal	'Warm Leatherette'
Sylvester	'You Make Me Feel (Mighty Real)'
The Residents	'Constantinople'
King Tubby	'Murderous Dub'
Yellow Magic Orchestra	'Behind the Mask'
Sparks	'The Number One Song in Heaven'
Tubeway Army	'Are Friends Electric'
Telex	'Moskow Diskow'
John Foxx	'Underpass'
Ultravox	'Vienna'
Visage	'Fade to Grey'
Simple Minds	'I Travel'
Philip Glass	'Rubric'
Yarbrough & Peoples	'Don't Stop the Music'
Soft Cell	'Tainted Love'
Japan	'Ghosts'
Vangelis	'Tears in Rain' (*Blade Runner*)
Laurie Anderson	'O Superman'
Thomas Dolby	'Windpower'
George Clinton	'Atomic Dog' (Original Extended Version)
Herbie Hancock	'Rockit'
Prince	'Purple Music'
Yazoo	'Situation'
The Associates	'Party Fears Two'
William Onyeabor	'Good Name'
Ryuichi Sakamoto	'Forbidden Colours'
New Order	'Blue Monday'
Tomita	'Prélude à L'Après Midi d'une Faune'
Cabaret Voltaire	'Sensoria' 12-inch
Cameo	'She's Strange'

Pet Shop Boys	'West End Girls'.
Bronski Beat	'Smalltown Boy'
Scritti Politti	'Absolute'
Fad Gadget	'Collapsing New People'
Maze/Frankie Beverly	'Twilight'
Art Of Noise	'Moments in Love'
Propaganda	'p:Machinery'
Kate Bush	'Running Up that Hill'
Erasure	'A Little Respect'
Rufus and Chaka Khan	'Ain't Nobody'
Marc Almond	'Caged'
Lil Louis	'French Kiss'

Credits

Thanks to ... Landsley Ware, Elena Ware, Gabriel Ware, Paul Bower, Paul Hollins, Pete Walsh, Greg Walsh, John Wesley Barker, Tim Cansfield, Nick Plytas, Sarah Jane Morris, Sandie Shaw, Bob Last, Ian Craig Marsh, Richard Manwaring, David Buckley, Viv Owen, Paul Wilkinson, Sumo, Glenn Gregory, Ian Reddington, Nick and Nicky.